Lecture Notes in Economics and Mathematical Systems

Managing Editors: M. Beckmann and W. Krelle

240

Contributions to Operations Research

Proceedings of the Conference on Operations Research
Held in Oberwolfach, West Germany
February 26 – March 3, 1984

Edited by K. Neumann and D. Pallaschke

Springer-Verlag
Berlin Heidelberg New York Tokyo

Managing Editors

Prof. Dr. M. Beckmann
Brown University
Providence, RI 02912, USA

Prof. Dr. W. Krelle
Institut für Gesellschafts- und Wirtschaftswissenschaften
der Universität Bonn
Adenauerallee 24–42, D-5300 Bonn, FRG

Editors

Prof. Dr. Klaus Neumann
Institut für Wirtschaftstheorie und Operations Research
Universität Karlsruhe
Postfach 6380, D-7500 Karlsruhe 1, FRG

Prof. Dr. Diethard Pallaschke
Institut für Statistik und Mathematische Wirtschaftstheorie
Universität Karlsruhe
Postfach 6380, D-7500 Karlsruhe 1, FRG

ISBN-13: 978-3-540-15205-7 e-ISBN-13: 978-3-642-46534-5
DOI: 10.1007/978-3-642-46534-5

Softcover reprint of the hardcover 1st edition 1985

2142/3140-543210

P R E F A C E

This volume presents lectures, hold at the conference on Operations Research, which took place from February 26 - March 3, 1984 in Oberwolfach, Germany.

About 50 participants from 7 countries took the opportunity to present and discuss their results in their fields of research: Mathematical Programming, Game Theory, Graph Theory, Queueing Theory, Network Theory, Control Theory, Special Stochastic Problems in Operations Research and Applications of Operations Research in Economy.

In this way the organizers, K. Neumann (Karlsruhe) and D. Pallaschke (Karlsruhe), could state with great satisfaction that the result of this conference was an efficient platform of the exchange of new ideas in the above mentioned fields. Therefore the aim of strengthening the mutual understanding of the different fields of research had been reached.

We owe special thanks to the director of the institute, Prof. Dr. Barner, but also to all the participants of the conference. And we also appreciate the excellent cooperation of Springer Verlag.

Also we particularly appreciate the efforts Mrs. C. Forler, made in helping to publish this volume and Mr. P. Recht, made in helping to organize the conference.

K. Neumann D. Pallaschke

TABLE OF CONTENTS

On using the linear programming relaxation of assignment type mixed integer problems

by Jo van Nunen*, Jacq Benders** and Adrie Beulens*

* Graduate School of Management, Delft

** Eindhoven University of Technology, department of mathematics and computing science.

Abstract

In this paper we combine some results that are published elsewhere. We prove that tight upperbounds can be given for the number of non-unique assignments that remain after solving the linear programming relaxation of some types of assignment problems.
For the generalized assignment problem and time table problems we will give these bounds explicitly.
Moreover, we will give bounds for the required capacity to ensure easy solutions.

Keywords: mixed integer problems, assignment problems, time tables, linear programming.

1. Introduction

In recent papers [1], [2], and [10] , we showed that many practical assignment type problems can be solved almost completely by using the linear programming relaxation of the problem. Tight bounds for the number of non-unique assignments were given. The remaining not uniquely determined assignments could be handled by using a heuristic.

We extensively described an application in the area of distribution of beer in [1]. Moreover we mentioned some applications in the area of LP-gas distribution, catalogue space planning [7], and assignment problems [3]. In this paper we will combine some of these results. We will discuss a time table problem as well as the generalized assignment problem. Moreover we will describe how dynamic bounds on the requested overcapacity can be given which enable the classification of easy solvable problems. Section 2 is devoted to the generalized assignment problem. In section 3 we discuss certain types of time table problems while the final section is used to make some concluding remarks and describe some extensions.

2. The generalized assignment problem

In this section we treat the generalized assignment problem (GAP) in order to introduce some of the basic ideas about solving assignment type mixed integer problems by means of the linear programming relaxation of the problem. For a more detailed description we refer to [3].

Suppose n jobs have to be assigned to m machines with restricted capacity. Each job has to be assigned to at most one machine, but machines can handle several jobs, as long as the capacity is not violated. Let b_i be the capacity of machine i, and let a_{ij} be the required capacity if job j is performed on machine i. Moreover let c_{ij} be the cost of executing job j on machine i. Finally let x_{ij} be the 0-1 variable which equals 1 if job j is assigned to machine i and 0 if not. Now the GAP can be formulated as follows:

$$\text{minimize} \quad \sum_{i,j} c_{ij}\, x_{ij} \qquad (1)$$

subject to

$$\sum_j a_{ij}\, x_{ij} \leq b_i \qquad i = 1, 2, .., m \qquad (2)$$

$$\sum_i x_{ij} = 1 \qquad j = 1, 2, .., n \quad (3)$$

$$x_{ij} \in \{0,1\} \qquad i = 1, 2, .., m \quad (4)$$
$$j = 1, 2, .., n$$

The linear programming relaxation of this problem is obtained if condition (4) is replaced by $x_{ij} \geq 0$. It is well known that the original problem is NP-hard see e.g. [8]. Several heuristic algorithms are developed to "solve" that problem we refer to e.g. [6],[9],[11]. We will show that in many practical situations the L.P. relaxation produces a good starting solution for such a heuristic.

Theorem 1

The number of non-unique assignments in the linear programming relaxation of the generalized assignment problem is less than or equal to the number of fully occupied machines.

Proof

Let us consider any basic feasible solution of the relaxed problem. This solution will in general have a number of non-integer assignments. Let the number of nonzero slack activities with respect to the capacity restrictions (2) be m_1. So, the number of fully occupied machines can be given by $m_2 = m-m_1$. Now, let n_1 be the number of non-splitted jobs, and let us denote by λ the average number of machines to which a splitted job is assigned. So we have that $\lambda \geq 2$. If we denote the number of splitted jobs $n-n_1$ by n_2, then the number of nonzero activities equals.

$$n_1 + \lambda\, n_2 + m_1 = n + (\lambda - 1)n_2 + m_1$$

On the otherhand the number of constraints in the relaxed problem and thus the maximum of nonzero variables is n + m. Consequently

$$n + (\lambda-1)n_2 + m_1 \leq n + m$$

this means that

$$n_2 \leq \frac{m_2}{\lambda - 1} \leq m_2$$

since $\lambda \geq 2$ □

Since the number of machines is in general small compared with the number of jobs, this relaxed solution often yields a good starting point for a heuristic which assignes the remaining splitted jobs. In the practical problems we solved the heuristics led to solutions that were within .1% of the solution of the linear programming relaxation and thus within .1% of the optimal integer solution. For a rough description of a heuristic see [10]. We also considered some problems which were of the typical scheduling type, this means that the available overcapacity was so small that in fact the problems seemed to be more or less of a combinatorial type. For these problems it was necessary to construct more sophisticated heuristics. In the following we will describe a (dynamic) condition on the required overcapacity which was used in the heuristics.
If the condition is satisfied it is easy to find feasible solutions to the integer problem, starting from the solution of the linear programming relaxation.

To illustrate the relevant ideas we consider a simplified version of the generalized assignment problem for which $a_{ij} = a_j$ for all machines i. If for the overcapacity oc of all the machines, which is equal to $oc = \sum_i b_i - \sum_j a_j$, it holds that

$$oc \geq (m-1)\, a_1 \qquad (6)$$

then it is easy to find a feasible integer solution. We supposed here that the jobs are ordered according to there requested capacity, so a_1 is the biggest job, a_2 the second biggest and so on. Clearly conditions (6) enables the construction of a feasible solution since in the L.P. relaxation at most (m-1) jobs are splitted. They all have a capacity less than or equal to a_1. It is easily seen that these (m-1) jobs can be assigned since the overcapacity is sufficient.
Often so much overcapacity will not be available. However, if the overcapacity equals

$$oc \geq (m-1)\, a^*$$

with a* the largest splitted job that remains after the linear programming relaxation solution of the problem then it is also easy to find a feasible integer assignment. This means that if only small jobs remain to be assigned, it is easy to find a solution. Such a solution occurs sometimes in practice since for the big jobs it might be clear on which machine they have to be performed. On the other-hand if the cost structure is not such that the big jobs are directly assigned it will often happen that the big jobs are splitted in the relaxed solutions because of their size. In that case a heuristic can be developed, see [10], which incorporates in each iteration step a mixed integer option of the computer package that is used to assign a small number of big jobs. The assigned big jobs are fixed and the solution procedure is continued with the remaining jobs. For a detailed description see [10] .

3. Time table problems

As we mentioned before the idea that was illustrated in the previous section can be used in many more complicated practical situations. We first used it in a decision support system for location allocation problems within a brewery, see [1], [2].

In this section we will show that similar results hold for time table problems. Let us therefore consider a time table scheduling problem as it occurred for planning of secondary schools in the Netherlands where a solution for a so called clustering problem is required.

There are s students each of who choose in advance a package of p courses out of a set of c possible courses. The problem is to make clusters of courses that are given at the same time. Each course that is chosen by a student must be assigned to one of the clusters. Of course each student should not be scheduled twice in the same cluster. Moreover the classroom capacity m of the r available classrooms can not be exeeded.

Let x_{ijk} be the assignment variable which is equal to 1 if student i who has chosen course j is assigned to cluster k for this course, and o otherwise, only the relevant i,j combinations are introduced.

z_{jk} is an assignment variable which is equal to 1 if course j is assigned to cluster k, and o otherwise.

l_{ij} is equal to one if student i has chosen course j, and is o otherwise, so l_{ij} are input data.

The above problem can now be formulated as: find a feasible solution for the following pure integer programming problem

$$\sum_{k=1}^{K} x_{ijk} = l_{ij} \qquad \begin{array}{l} i = 1, \ldots, s \\ j = 1, \ldots, c \end{array} \qquad (7)$$

$$\sum_{j=1}^{c} x_{ijk} + x_{ik} = 1 \qquad \begin{array}{l} i = 1, \ldots, s \\ k = 1, \ldots, K \end{array} \qquad (8)$$

$$\sum_{i=1}^{s} x_{ijk} - m\, z_{jk} \leq 0 \qquad \begin{array}{l} j = 1, \ldots, c \\ k = 1, \ldots, K \end{array} \qquad (9)$$

$$\sum_{j=1}^{c} z_{jk} \leq r \qquad k = 1, \ldots, K \quad (10)$$

$$x_{ijk} \in \{0,1\} \quad (11)$$

$$z_{jk} \in \{0,1\} \quad (12)$$

A detailed study will appear in a separate paper [4] , here we restrict ourselves to the case that the clusters are known beforehand. Hence the variabels z_{jk} have already been assigned a value of 0 or 1, and satisfy the conditions (10). The above problem is clearly of the following type.

$$\text{maximize} \quad p^t x = q^t y \quad (13)$$

$$Ax + By = b \quad (14)$$

$$Dy \mathrel{\overset{=}{+}} e \quad (15)$$

$$x \geq 0 \quad (16)$$

$$y_i \in \{0,1\} \quad (17)$$

Where, y should be interpreted as a multiple choice type variable

$$\sum_{j=1}^{n} y_{ij} = 1 \qquad i = 1, \ldots, m$$

$$\sum_{i=1}^{m} y_{ij} + y_{oj} = 1 \qquad j = 1, \ldots, n$$

Now, the correspondence with the classroom scheduling problem will be clear if A is the negative unit matrix corresponding to the slack variable in the classroom capacity restriction (9). For the above problem we can show (see [5]) that for any basic feasible solution ($\bar{x},\bar{y}$) of the relaxed problem, the number of indices i that are assigned to indices j does not exceed the number of restrictions involved in (14) minus the number of non zero x-components.

In terms of the classroom scheduling problem this means that the total number of courses that are not uniquely assigned to clusters does not exceed the number of fully occupied classrooms.

4. Conclusions and comments

We gave two examples of mixed integer problems which in practical situations can be solved adequately by using the linear programming relaxation. We also indicated a condition on the requested overcapacity to call a problem easy. In several practical situations it appeared that it was rather easy to find practically acceptable solutions. For the classroom scheduling problem acceptable solutions were obtained just by adding at most one student to a cluster. For a brewery problem as described in [2] , such practical solutions were obtained by a simple round off of fractions, which meant practically that minor changes occurred in the throughput time of beer.

In a multi-period brewery problem with inventory control similar results could be achieved. The lesson that can be drawn from this study is that in many practical situations one can prove beforehand that only a relatively small number of non-unique assignments will remain after solving the linear programming relaxation of the problem. Moreover, this solution proves to be a good starting point for a heuristic. While the quality of the solution can be judged by comparing it with the L.P. solution which is lowerbound for the optimal integer solution.

References

[1] Benders, J.F. and J.A.E.E. van Nunen, "A linear programming based decision support system for location and allocation problems", Informatie 23, 1981, p.p. 693-703 (in Dutch)

[2] Benders, J.F. and J.A.E.E. van Nunen, "A decision support system for location and allocation problems within a brewery", Operations research proceedings, 1981, Springer Verlag Berlin, 1982, p.p. 96-105

[3] Benders, J.F. and J.A.E.E. van Nunen, "A property of assignment type mixed integer linear programming problems", Operations research letters 2, 1983, p.p. 47-52

[4] Benders, J.F., "A linear programming approach to the clustering problem in class-room scheduling" Memorandum COSOR, Eindhoven University of Technology, in preparation

[5] Benders J.F. and J.A.E.E. van Nunen, "Decomposition properties of assignment type mixed integer problems", Working paper Graduate School of Management, Delft, in preparation

[6] Fisher, M., R. Jaikumar and L van Wassenhoven, "Adjustment method for the generalized assignment problem", Tims/ORSA joint national meeting, Washington D.C., may 1980

[7] Johnson, J.M., A.A. Zoltners and P. Sinba, "An allocation model for catalogue space planning", Management Sci. 25, 1979, p.p. 117-129

[8] Lenstra, J.K., "Sequencing by enumerative methods", Mathematical centre Track 69, Mathematical centre, Amsterdam

[9] Martello, S. and P. Toth, "An alogrithm for the generalized assignment problem", Operational research, 1981

[10] Van Nunen, J., J. Benders and A. Beulens, "On solving assignment type mixed integer linear programming problems within decision support systems", Working paper Graduate School of Management, Delft, september 1983

[11] Ross, G.T. and R.H. Soland, "A branch and bound algorithm for the generalized assignment problem", Mathematical programming 8, 1975, p.p. 91-103

CONTRIBUTIONS TO DUALITY THEORY OF CERTAIN NONCONVEX OPTIMIZATION PROBLEMS

R. Deumlich, PH Halle, 4020 Halle, DDR
K.-H. Elster, TH Ilmenau, 6300 Ilmenau, DDR

1. Introduction

In the last years a considerable effort was made to treat nonconvex optimization problems. Quite naturally, one direction of research consists in generalizations of the Lagrange concept and numerous papers were published concerning this subject. Besides such investigations, since a couple of years a wide class of nonconvex optimization problems has been considered by DEUMLICH and ELSTER using the concept of generalized conjugate functions. Starting from geometrical properties of the classical FENCHEL's conjugates, the notion of Φ-conjugate functions was introduced by these authors (cf. /1/, /2/, /4/). The polar theory in projective spaces plays a key role with respect to the geometrical background of Φ-conjugate functions. As in all generalizations of the FENCHEL's conjugates before, the crucial question is for Φ-conjugates, too, of which way dual problems can be formulated and convenient duality theorems can be proved. It turns out that the theory of Φ-conjugate functions performs a remarkable contribution to the treatment of nonconvex optimization problems. Contributions to the finite dimensional case are given in /2/, /3/, /4/, /15/, /16/.

It is possible to extend results to the infinite dimensional case which was done in /5/, /12/, /13/, /14/, /17/. Especially Lagrange duality is considered in /14/, /18/.

It is possible to establish well-known optimality conditions concerning convex optimization problems and fractional programming problems as special cases of the developed theory.

Recently, some new results about Φ-conjugation could be obtained, and that

(i) an extension of the concept of Φ-conjugation to product spaces due to unify the approach to Φ-dual sets, Φ-conjugate sets and Φ-conjugate functions,

(ii) the introduction and application of a generalized notion of stability including the possibility to omit convexity assumptions in duality theorems,

(iii) duality theorems for families of dual optimization problems,

(iv) applications in mathematical economics.

Results were published by part in /6/, /7/, /8/, /9/, /10/, /11/.

In the present paper a review is given on some new results concerning especially (i) and (iii).

2. Some Basic Results on Φ-conjugation

2.1. Generalized Epigraphs of Sets and the Hypersurface Φ

Let V and V^* be a real linear space and the algebraical dual space of V, respectively. Moreover, let $F \subset V$ be an arbitrary subset of V and let $(\hat{t},\hat{v}) \in R \times V$ such that $(\hat{t},\hat{x}) \neq (0,0)$.

To the set F two other sets can be associated which we call the generalized epigraphs of F according

$$\left.\begin{aligned} M_j(\hat{P},F) &:= \{\bar{x} \in V \mid \bar{x} = (1-\mu\hat{t})x + \mu\hat{x},\ \mu \in I_j,\ x \in F\}, \\ I_j &:= \{\mu \in R \mid 1-\mu\hat{t} > 0,\ (-1)^j\mu \leq 0\}, \\ j &= 1,2. \end{aligned}\right\} \quad (2.1)$$

Note that $M_j(\hat{P},F)$, $j = 1,2$, is the reunion of the subset of the straight lines passing through $\hat{P}$.

In the projective extended space $\mathcal{J}(R \times V)$ a geometrical interpretation of the sets $M_j(\hat{P},F)$, $j = 1,2$, can be given with respect to the point $\hat{P} \in \Pi(R \times V)$, where $\hat{P}$ is determined by the pair $(\hat{t},\hat{x})$. It is well-known that the line

$$\{(t,x) \in R \times V \mid (t,x) = \lambda(\hat{t},\hat{x}),\ \lambda \in R\}$$

can be considered as the point $\hat{P}$ of the projective space $\Pi(R \times V)$ and we denote this point $\hat{P}$ by $((\hat{t},\hat{x}))$, (cf. /1/, /4/).

If we assume (without loss of generality)

$$\hat{t} \leqq 0,$$

then in the case $\hat{t} \neq 0$ the set $M_2(\hat{P},F)$ always contains the point $\frac{\hat{x}}{\hat{t}}$.

To obtain a unified approach to Φ-conjugate sets, Φ-dual sets and Φ-conjugate functions we assume V to be a product space of the linear spaces V_1 and V_2 according to $V = V_1 \times V_2$. In the following we use the notation $x := (z,v) \in V$.

Remark: In former papers we considered the special case $V_2 = R$.

The hypersurface of second order

$$\Phi := \{(z,v) \in V_1 \times V_2 \mid \langle(1,z,v),\ A(1,z,v)\rangle = 0\} \quad (2.2)$$

which is substantial for all considerations, is determined by the linear mapping $A: R \times V \longrightarrow R \times V^*$ according to

$$A: \begin{array}{l} t' = a_0 t + \langle a,z\rangle + \langle c,v\rangle \\ z' = at + B_1 z + E^* v \\ v' = ct + Ez + B_2 v \end{array} \qquad (t,z,v) \in R \times V_1 \times V_2, \quad (2.3)$$

where

$$a_0 \in R,\ a \in V_1^*,\ c \in V_2^*$$

and

$B_1: V_1 \rightarrow V_1^*$, $B_2: V_2 \rightarrow V_2^*$ symmetrical linear mappings,

$E: V_1 \longrightarrow V_2^*$ a linear mapping.

2.2. Φ-dual and Φ-conjugate Sets

By the mapping (2.3) we introduce certain sets according to the following definitions.

Definition 2.1: Let $F \subset V$. Then the set

$$\overset{*}{F}{}^{\Phi} := \{x^* \in V \mid \inf_{x \in F} \langle(1,x),\ A(1,x^*)\rangle \geqq 0\}$$

is called the upper Φ-dual set of F and the set

$$\overset{*}{F}_{\Phi} := \{x^* \in V \mid \sup_{x \in F} \langle(1,x),\ A(1,x^*)\rangle \leqq 0\}$$

is called the lower Φ-dual set of F.

Remarks: 1. Φ-dual sets are generalizations of dual sets introduced by Ruys and Weddepohl /19/ in the framework of abstract economics. In the special case

$$V = R^n = R^k \times R^m$$

$$a_0 = -1,\ a = 0,\ c = 0,\ B_1 = I_k,\ B_2 = I_m,\ E = 0.\ ^{*)}$$

Ruys and Weddepohl used the upper dual set F_+^* and the lower dual set F_-^*. If Φ is especially a hypersphere then it holds

$$F_+^* = \overset{*}{F}{}^{\Phi},\quad F_-^* = \overset{*}{F}_{\Phi}.$$

2. In Theorem 2.1 we shall use bidual sets of F according to

$$\overset{*}{F}{}^{\Phi\Phi} := (\overset{*}{F}{}^{\Phi})^{\overset{*}{\Phi}},\quad \overset{*}{F}_{\Phi\Phi} := (\overset{*}{F}_{\Phi})_{\overset{*}{\Phi}}.$$

Definition 2.2: Let $F \subset V$. Then the set

$$F^{\Phi} := \{x^* \in V \mid \inf_{x \in F} \langle(1,x),\ A(1,x^*)\rangle = 0\}$$

is called the upper Φ-conjugate set of F and the set

$$F_{\Phi} := \{x^* \in V \mid \sup_{x \in F} \langle(1,x),\ A(1,x^*)\rangle = 0\}$$

---

*) In the finite dimensional case we denote the linear mappings B_1, B_2, E and the corresponding matrices (with respect to the canonical bases) by the same letters.

is called the lower Φ-conjugate set of F.

Obviously is

$$F^{\Phi} \subseteq \overset{*}{F}{}^{\Phi}, \quad F_{\Phi} \subseteq \overset{*}{F}_{\Phi} \tag{2.4}$$

and (in the case $\hat{t} < 0$)

$$\frac{\hat{x}}{\hat{t}} \in \overset{*}{F}_{\Phi},$$

if $(\hat{t}, \hat{x}) = A^{-1}(1,0)$.

Fig. 1 gives an illustration of (lower) Φ-dual sets and Φ-conjugate sets.

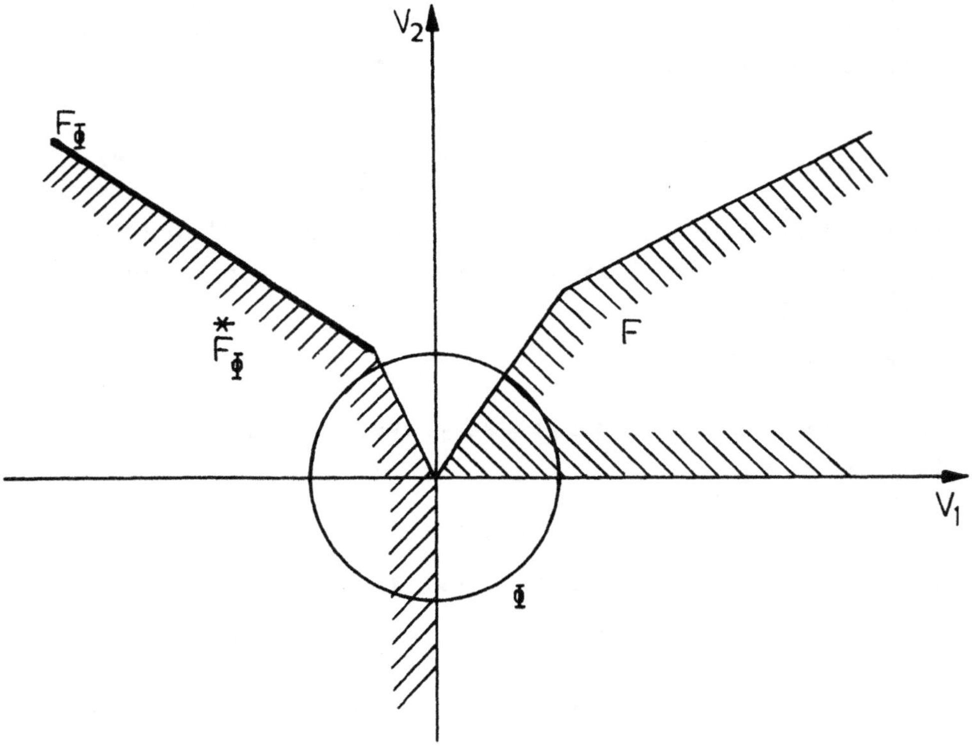

Fig. 1

Correspondingly fig. 2 shows, for another Φ, the (upper) Φ-dual set and Φ-conjugate set.

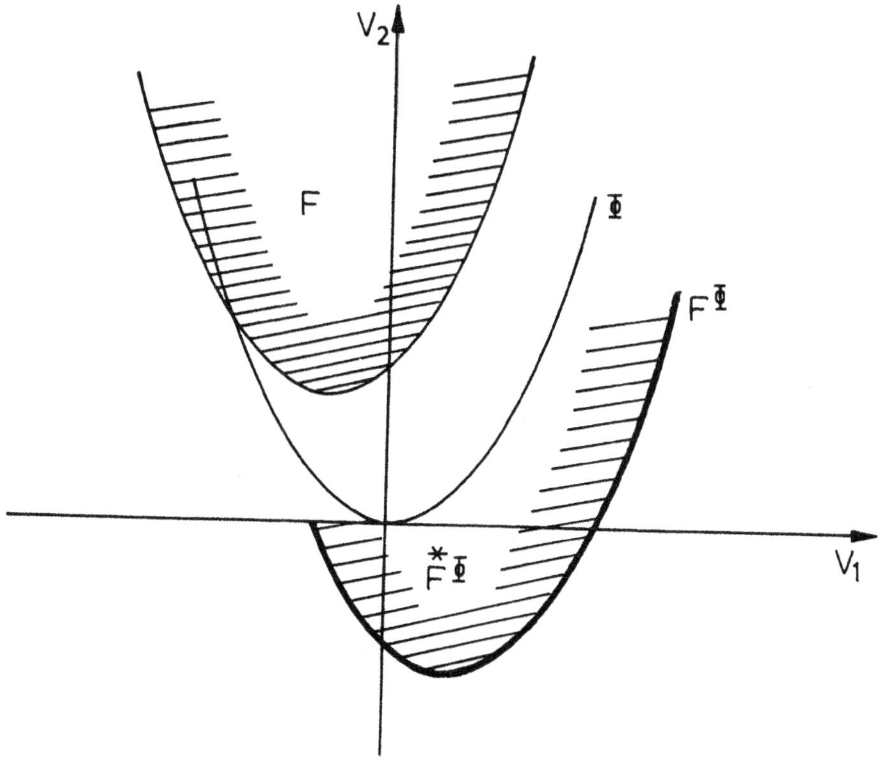

Fig. 2

From the definition of Φ-conjugate sets and of Φ-dual sets it follows immediately that Φ-conjugate sets are always subsets of the boundary of the corresponding Φ-dual sets. We introduce Φ-dual sets on the one hand to describe all propositions in a unified approach without any exceptions (this is a formal reason) and on the other hand to use Φ-dual sets with advantage for treating certain problems in mathematical economics.

As we showed in several of the mentioned papers the use of Φ-conjugate sets is full justified by their applications in nonconvex optimization. Moreover, there are close connections between Φ-conjugate sets and Φ-conjugate functions. The latter we used to establish dual optimization problems in a convenient manner.

If we consider the special case

$$V = R^k \times R^m = R^n$$

then the set F^{Φ} (resp. F_{Φ}) is the hypersurface enveloped by the polar hyperplanes

$$H^*(x) := \{ x^* \in V \mid \langle (1,x), A(1,x^*) \rangle = 0 \}, \quad x \in F; \qquad x \neq \frac{\hat{x}}{\hat{t}} \text{ if } \hat{t} \neq 0, \tag{2.5}$$

of x with respect to Φ.

In the following we always assume

(C1) $F^{\Phi} \neq \emptyset$, $F_{\Phi} \neq \emptyset$,

(C2) the cernel $N[A]$ of the linear mapping A contains only the origin.

(C3) A is chosen in such a way that $(\hat{t},\hat{z},\hat{v}) := A^{-1}(1,0,0)$ and $\hat{t} \leqq 0$.

By (C1) the following inequalities hold:

$$(a_0 + \langle a,z \rangle + \langle c,v \rangle) + \langle a + B_1 z + E^* v, z^* \rangle + \langle c + Ez + B_2 v, v^* \rangle \geqq 0 \quad \forall (z,v) \in F, \ \forall (z^*,v^*) \in \overset{*}{F}{}^{\Phi}, \tag{2.6a}$$

$$(a_0 + \langle a,z \rangle + \langle c,v \rangle) + \langle a + B_1 z + E^* v, z^* \rangle + \langle c + Ez + B_2 v, v^* \rangle \leqq 0 \quad \forall (z,v) \in F, \ \forall (z^*,v^*) \in \overset{*}{F}_{\Phi} . \tag{2.6b}$$

By (2.4) these inequalities hold also for F^{Φ} and F_{Φ}, respectively.

In the following we need the notions of uniqueness and convexity of a set with respect to the point $\hat{P}$. In a topological space the Φ-dual sets are intersections of closed halfspaces. So we introduce the closeness of a set with

respect to $\hat{P}$.
There exist numerous interesting properties of Φ-conjugate sets including possibilities of their representation (cf. /1/, /4/, /7/, /8/).
In particular such properties are of importance which are connected with the two-fold Φ-conjugation. Using the abbreviations

$$F^{\Phi\Phi} := (F^{\Phi})^{\Phi}, \quad F_{\Phi\Phi} := (F_{\Phi})_{\Phi}$$

we derive some corresponding results.

Definition 2.3: A set $F \subset V$ is called unique with respect to $\hat{P}$, if

$$g(x) \cap F = \{x\} \ \forall x \in F, \text{ where}$$
$$g(x) := \{\bar{x} \in V \mid \bar{x} = (1 - \mu\hat{t})x + \mu\hat{x}, \ \mu \in R\}.$$

Definition 2.4: A set $F \subset V$ is called convex with respect to $\hat{P}$, if

(i) F is unique with respect to $\hat{P}$,

(ii) $M_j(\hat{P},F)$ is convex for at least one $j \in \{1,2\}$.

Definition 2.5: Let V be a locally convex Hausdorff space, let $F \subset V$ be unique with respect to $\hat{P}(\hat{t} \leqq 0)$.
Then the set

$$\overline{\text{cl}}F := \{\bar{x} \in V \mid \bar{x} = (1-\bar{\mu}_1(x)\hat{t})x + \bar{\mu}_1(x)\hat{x}, \ x \in \text{cl}M_1(\hat{P},F)\},$$

with

$$\bar{\mu}_1(x) := \sup\{\mu \in R \mid (1 - \mu\hat{t})x + \mu\hat{x} \in \text{cl}M_1(\hat{P},F)\}, \quad x \in \text{cl}M_1(\hat{P},F),$$

is called the upper closure of F with respect to $\hat{P}$, and the set

$$\underline{\text{cl}}F := \{\bar{x} \in V \mid \bar{x} = (1-\underline{\mu}_1(x)\hat{t})x + \underline{\mu}_1(x)\hat{x}, \ x \in \text{cl}M_2(\hat{P},F)\},$$

with

$$\underline{\mu}_1(x) := \inf\{\mu \in R \mid (1 - \mu\hat{t})x + \mu\hat{x} \in \text{cl}M_2(\hat{P},F)\}, \quad x \in \text{cl}M_2(\hat{P},F),$$

is called the lower closure of F with respect to $\hat{P}$.

We have the following propositions.

Theorem 2.1: Let V be a locally convex Hausdorff space and let $F \subset V$.

(i) If $M_1(\hat{P},F)$ is convex and $\frac{\hat{x}}{\hat{t}} \notin \mathrm{cl} M_1(\hat{P},F)$ in the case $\hat{t} < 0$, then

(1) $(\mathrm{cl}\ M_1(\hat{P},F))^{*\Phi} = F^{*\Phi}$,

(2) $F^{*\Phi\Phi} = \mathrm{cl}\ M_1(\hat{P},F)$,

(3) $F^{*\Phi\Phi} = F \Leftrightarrow F = \mathrm{cl}\ M_1(\hat{P},F)$.

(ii) If $M_2(\hat{P},F)$ is convex and $\frac{\hat{x}}{\hat{t}} \notin \mathrm{cl}\ M_2(\hat{P},F)$ in the case $\hat{t} < 0$, then

(1) $(\mathrm{cl}\ M_2(\hat{P},F))^{*}_{\Phi} = F^{*}_{\Phi}$,

(2) $F^{*}_{\Phi\Phi} = \mathrm{cl}\ M_2(\hat{P},F)$,

(3) $F^{*}_{\Phi\Phi} = F \Leftrightarrow F = \mathrm{cl}\ M_2(\hat{P},F)$.

Proof: We prove (i); the proof of (ii) is similar.
Proof of (i) (1):

1. Let $x_0^* \in (\mathrm{cl}\ M_1(\hat{P},F))^{*\Phi}$. Then $\inf\limits_{x \in \mathrm{cl}\ M_1(\hat{P},F)} h(x, x_0^*) \geq 0$,

where $h(x,x^*) := \langle (1,x), A(1,x^*) \rangle$, and thus

$$h(x,x_0^*) \geq 0 \quad \forall\, x \in F. \tag{2.7}$$

Hence $x_0^* \in F^{*\Phi}$ and therefore

$$(\mathrm{cl}\ M_1(\hat{P},F))^{*\Phi} \subseteq F^{*\Phi}. \tag{2.8}$$

2. Let $x_0^* \in F^{*\Phi}$. Then (2.7) is valid. Let

$$\bar{x} := (1 - \mu\hat{t})x_0 + \mu\hat{x},\ x_0 \in F,\ 1 - \mu\hat{t} > 0,\ \mu \geq 0,$$

then $\bar{x} \in M_1(\hat{P},F)$. Hence

$$x_0 = \frac{1}{1-\mu\hat{t}}\,\bar{x} - \frac{\mu}{1-\mu\hat{t}}\,\hat{x} \in F$$

and therefore

$$h(x_o, x_o^*) = h\left(\frac{1}{1-\mu\hat{t}}\,\bar{x} - \frac{\mu}{1-\mu\hat{t}}\,\hat{x},\ x_o^*\right)$$

$$= \left(a_o + \left\langle a, \frac{1}{1-\mu\hat{t}}\,\bar{x} - \frac{\mu}{1-\mu\hat{t}}\,\hat{x}\right\rangle\right) + \left\langle a + B\left(\frac{1}{1-\mu\hat{t}}\,\bar{x} - \frac{\mu}{1-\mu\hat{t}}\,\hat{x}\right), x_o^*\right\rangle$$

$$= \left(a_o - \frac{\mu}{1-\mu\hat{t}}(\langle a,\hat{x}\rangle + \langle B\hat{x}, x_o^*\rangle) + \frac{1}{1-\mu\hat{t}}(\langle a,\bar{x}\rangle + \langle B\bar{x}, x_o^*\rangle)\right) + \langle a, x_o^*\rangle$$

$$= \frac{1}{1-\mu\hat{t}}\Big[(1-\mu\hat{t})a_o - \mu\langle a,\hat{x}\rangle - \mu\langle B\hat{x}, x_o^*\rangle + \langle a,\bar{x}\rangle + \langle B\bar{x}, x_o^*\rangle + (1-\mu\hat{t})\langle a, x_o^*\rangle\Big]$$

$$= \frac{1}{1-\mu\hat{t}}\Big[a_o - \mu(a_o\hat{t} + \langle a,\hat{x}\rangle + \langle a\hat{t} + B\hat{x}, x_o^*\rangle) + \langle a + Bx_o^*, \bar{x}\rangle + \langle a, x_o^*\rangle\Big]$$

$$= \frac{1}{1-\mu\hat{t}}\Big[-\mu + (a_o + \langle a, x_o^*\rangle) + \langle a + Bx_o^*, \bar{x}\rangle\Big].$$

By (2.7) we obtain

$$a_o + \langle a, x_o^*\rangle + \langle a + Bx_o^*, \bar{x}\rangle \geqq \mu \geqq 0 \quad \forall\, \bar{x} \in M_1(\hat{P}, F)$$

and thus

$$h(\bar{x}, x_o^*) \geqq 0 \quad \forall\, \bar{x} \in M_1(\hat{P}, F).$$

Obviously then we have also

$$h(\bar{x}, x_o^*) \geqq 0 \ \forall\, \bar{x} \in \mathrm{cl}\ M_1(\hat{P}, F),$$

that is

$$x_o^* \in (\mathrm{cl}\ M_1(\hat{P}, F))^{*\Phi}. \tag{2.9}$$

From (2.8) and (2.9) we conclude the equation (i) (1).

Proof of (i)(2).

1. Let $x_0 \in \mathrm{cl}\, M_1(\hat{P}, F)$. Then $h(x_0,x^*) \geqq 0 \;\forall x^* \in \overset{*}{F}{}^{\Phi}$ and thus $\inf\limits_{x^* \in \overset{*}{F}{}^{\Phi}} h(x_0,x^*) \geqq 0$, that is $x_0 \in \overset{*}{F}{}^{\Phi\Phi}$.
   We obtain therefore $\mathrm{cl}\, M_1(\hat{P}, F) \subseteq \overset{*}{F}{}^{\Phi\Phi}$.

2. Now let $x_0 \in \overset{*}{F}{}^{\Phi\Phi}$. Then $h(x_0,x^*) \geqq 0 \;\forall x^* \in \overset{*}{F}{}^{\Phi}$.

To prove $x_0 \in \mathrm{cl}\, M_1(\hat{P}, F)$ indirectly we assume $x_0 \notin \mathrm{cl} M_1(\hat{P},F)$. Then the closed sets $\{x_0\}$ and $\mathrm{cl}\, M_1(\hat{P}, F)$ can be separated strictly by a hyperplane

$$H := \{y \mid \langle m,y\rangle + \beta = 0,\; m \in V^*\}.$$

In the following we distinguish the cases $\hat{t} < 0$ and $\hat{t} = 0$.

Case 1: $\hat{t} < 0$.

Case 1.1: $\frac{\hat{x}}{\hat{t}} \in H$. Then there exists an $x_0^* \in V$ such that H can be given as

$$h(y, x_0^*) - (a_0 + \langle a,y\rangle) = \langle a + By,\; x_0^*\rangle = 0$$

and it holds

$$\langle a + By,\; x_0^*\rangle > 0 \;\; \forall y \in \mathrm{cl}\, M_1(\hat{P}, F),$$
$$\langle a + Bx_0,\; x_0^*\rangle < 0.$$

Since $\frac{\hat{x}}{\hat{t}} \notin \mathrm{cl}\, M_1(\hat{P}, F)$ there is a hyperplane H_1, which separates strictly $\{\frac{\hat{x}}{\hat{t}}\}$ and $\mathrm{cl}\, M_1(\hat{P}, F)$. Then there exists an $x_1^* \in V$ such that H_1 can be represented according to $h(y,x_1^*) = 0$,

setting $(1,x_1^*) = A^{-1} \dfrac{(\beta_1,\; m_1)}{\langle m_1,\hat{x}\rangle + \beta_1 \hat{t}}$, and

hence $h(y,x_1^*) > 0 \;\; \forall y \in \mathrm{cl}\, M_1(\hat{P}, F)$,

$$h\left(\frac{\hat{x}}{\hat{t}},\; x_1^*\right) = \frac{1}{\hat{t}} < 0.$$

Let us consider the following set of hyperplanes
($\lambda \geqq 0$ is a parameter)

$$\lambda\left[h(y,x_0^*) - (a_0 + \langle a,y\rangle)\right] + h(y,x_1^*) = 0 .$$

Then

$$\lambda \langle a + By,\ x_0^*\rangle + h(y,x_1^*) = 0$$

or

$$h(y,x_1^* + \lambda x_0^*) = 0.$$

Obviously is

$$h(y,x_1^* + \lambda x_0^*) \geqq 0 \quad \forall\, y \in \mathrm{cl}M_1(\hat{P},F),\ \forall\ \lambda \geqq 0.$$

Since

$$h(x_0,x_0^*) - (a_0 + \langle a,x_0\rangle) = \langle a + Bx_0,x_0^*\rangle < 0$$

we can choose $\lambda = \lambda_0$ so large that

$$h(x_0,x_1^* + \lambda_0 x_0^*) < 0 \tag{2.10}$$

and

$$h(y,x_1^* + \lambda_0 x_0^*) \geqq 0 \quad \forall\, y \in \mathrm{cl}M_1(\hat{P},F).$$

Obviously is $x_1^* + \lambda_0 x_0^* \in \overset{*}{F}{}^{\Phi}$ because of

$$\inf_{y \in F} h(y,\ x_1^* + \lambda_0 x_0^*) \geqq 0.$$

This contradicts to (2.10). Hence we conclude $x_0 \in \mathrm{cl}M_1(\hat{P}_1,F)$ and therefore $\overset{*}{F}{}^{\Phi\Phi} \subseteq \mathrm{cl}\ M_1(\hat{P},F)$. Regarding the first part of the proof we obtain $\overset{*}{F}{}^{\Phi\Phi} = \mathrm{cl}\ M_1(\hat{P},\ F)$.

Case 1.2: $\frac{\hat{x}}{t} \notin H$. Then there exists an $x_0^* \in V$ such that H can be represented by

$$h(y,\ x_0^*) = 0\ ,$$

setting

$$(1, x_o^*) = A^{-1} \frac{(\beta, m)}{\langle m, \hat{x}\rangle + \beta \hat{t}} .$$

We have

$$h\left(\frac{\hat{x}}{\hat{t}}, x_o^*\right) = \frac{1}{\hat{t}} < 0,$$

$$h(y, x_o^*) > 0 \quad \forall \ y \in \mathrm{cl}\ M_1(\hat{P}, F) , \qquad (2.11)$$

Now let $h(x_o, x_o^*) < 0$. Then from (2.11) we conclude

$$\inf_{y \in F} h(y, x_o^*) \geqq 0$$

and thus $x_o^* \in \overset{*}{F}{}^{\Phi}$. By $x_o \in \overset{*}{F}{}^{\Phi\Phi}$ we obtain $h(x_o, x_o^*) \geqq 0$ which contradicts to the assumption. Thus we obtain for this case $x_o \in \mathrm{cl}\ M_1(\hat{P}, F)$.

If in the opposite case $h(x_o, x_o^*) > 0$, then we have

$$h(y, x_o^*) < 0 \quad \forall \ y \in \mathrm{cl}\ M_1(\hat{P}, F)$$

and

$$\inf_{y \in F} h(y, x_o^*) < 0,$$

that is $x_o^* \in \overset{*}{F}{}^{\Phi}$. There exists a hyperplane $H' \parallel H$ such that $\frac{\hat{x}}{\hat{t}} \in H'$, which separates (properly) $\{x_o\}$ and $M_1(\hat{P}, F)$. In the opposite case we would have $H \cap \mathrm{cl}\ M_1(\hat{P}, F) \neq \emptyset$ in contradiction to the strict separation of $\{x_o\}$ and $\mathrm{cl}\ M_1(\hat{P}, F)$ by the hyperplane H. The further proof is according to the case 1.1.

So in the case 1.2 we always obtain $x_o \in \mathrm{cl}\ M_1(\hat{P}, F)$ and hence $\overset{*}{F}{}^{\Phi\Phi} \subseteq \mathrm{cl}\ M_1(\hat{P}, F)$. Regarding the first part of the proof we obtain $\overset{*}{F}{}^{\Phi\Phi} = \mathrm{cl}\ M_1(\hat{P}, F)$.

Case 2: $\hat{t} = 0$.

Case 2.1: $\langle m, \hat{x}\rangle + \beta \hat{t} = \langle m, \hat{x}\rangle = 0$.

Then there is an $x_o^* \in V$ such that H is given as

$$\langle a + By, x_o^*\rangle = 0$$

and we have

$$\langle a + By, x_o^* \rangle > 0 \quad \forall\, y \in \mathrm{cl}\, M_1(\hat{P}, F),$$

$$\langle a + Bx_o, x_o^* \rangle < 0.$$

Since F is a proper subset of V, we have $\mathrm{cl}\, M_1(\hat{P},F) \neq V$. Hence there exists a hyperplane $H_1 = \{y \mid h(y,x_1^*) = 0, x_1^* \in V\}$ such that $h(y,x_1^*) \geqq 0 \ \forall\, y \in \mathrm{cl}\, M_1(\hat{P}, F)$. The further proof is as in the case 1.1.

Case 2.2: $\langle m, \hat{x}\rangle + \beta\hat{t} = \langle m,\hat{x}\rangle \neq 0$,

Then H can be represented according to

$h(y,x_o^*) = (a_o + \langle a,y\rangle) + \langle a + By, x_o^*\rangle = 0, \ x_o^* \in V.$

Obviously is

$$(a_o\hat{t} + \langle a,\hat{x}\rangle) + \langle a\hat{t} + B\hat{x}, x_o^*\rangle = 1 > 0,$$

$$h(y, x_o^*) \geqq 0 \quad \forall\, y \in \mathrm{cl}\, M_1(\hat{P}, F).$$

The further proof is as in the case 1.2.

Proof of (i)(3):

If $F = \mathrm{cl}\, M_1(\hat{P}, F)$ then by (i)(2) we have immediately $F^{*\Phi\Phi} = F$.

If $F^{*\Phi\Phi} = F$ then by (i)(2) we obtain $F^{*\Phi\Phi} = \mathrm{cl} M_1(\hat{P},F) = F$. □

If $F \subset V$ is convex with respect to $\hat{P}$ ($\hat{t} \leqq 0$) then we obtain analogously results concerning Φ-conjugate sets (/1/, /4/).

The propositions (i)(2) and (ii)(2) in Theorem 2.1 are generalizations of former results of Rockafellar, where he proved that a closed convex function f is the pointwise supremum of certain affine functions. With respect to Φ-conjugate sets in a finite dimensional space a corresponding theorem is published in /4/.

Theorem 2.2: Let V be a locally convex Hausdorff space and let $F \subset V$ be convex with respect to $\hat{P}$ ($\hat{t} \leqq 0$).

(i) If $M_1(\hat{P}, F)$ is convex and $\frac{\hat{x}}{\hat{t}} \in \overline{cl}\, F$ in the case $\hat{t} < 0$, then

(1) $(\overline{cl}\, F)^{\Phi} = F^{\Phi}$,

(2) $F^{\Phi\Phi} = \overline{cl}\, F$,

(3) $F^{\Phi\Phi} = F \Longleftrightarrow F = \overline{cl}\, F$.

(ii) If $M_2(\hat{P}, F)$ is convex and $\frac{\hat{x}}{\hat{t}} \in \underline{cl}\, F$ in the case $\hat{t} < 0$, then

(1) $(\underline{cl}\, F)_{\Phi} = F_{\Phi}$,

(2) $F_{\Phi\Phi} = \underline{cl}\, F$,

(3) $F_{\Phi\Phi} = F \Longleftrightarrow F = \underline{cl}\, F$.

The proof of Theorem 2.2, which is given in the finite dimensional case in /1/, can be extended to the infinite dimensional case considered here.

With respect to applications in mathematical economics (and as an interesting question for itself, too) we discuss sufficient conditions for

$$\left.\begin{aligned} M_1(\hat{P}, F) &= M_1(\hat{P}, F^{\Phi\Phi}), \\ M_2(\hat{P}, F) &= M_2(\hat{P}, F_{\Phi\Phi}). \end{aligned}\right\} \tag{2.12}$$

We emphasize that the closeness of F with respect to $\hat{P}$ is not necessary for the validity of the equations (2.12). Even the uniqueness of F with respect to $\hat{P}$ must not be required.

Example 2.1: Let

$$F := \left\{x = (z,v) \in R^2 \mid z \in [3,5),\ v = [3,5) \cup \{(5,3),(3,5)\}\right\},$$
$$\Phi := \left\{(z,v) \in R^2 \mid z^2 + v^2 = \varrho^2,\ \varrho > 0\right\}.$$

Then

$$F^{\Phi} = \left\{(z,v) \in R^2 \mid v = f(z)\right\},$$

where

$$f(z) = \begin{cases} -\frac{5}{3} z + \frac{4}{3} & \text{if } z \in (-\infty, 0), \\ -z + \frac{4}{3} & \text{if } z \in [0, \frac{4}{3}], \\ -\frac{3}{5} z + \frac{4}{5} & \text{if } z \in (\frac{4}{3}, \infty) \end{cases}$$

and

$$F^{\Phi\Phi} = \{(z,v) \in R^2 \mid z = 3,\ v \in [3,5]\} \cup \{(z,v) \in R^2 \mid v = 3,\ z \in [3,5]\}.$$

Hence with $(\hat{t},\hat{z},\hat{v}) = (-\frac{1}{\varrho^2}, 0,0)$ we obtain

$$M_1(\hat{P}, F) = M_1(\hat{P}, F^{\Phi\Phi}).$$

If we choose $F_1 := M_1(\hat{P}, F)$, then $\overset{*}{F}_1{}^{\Phi} = F_1{}^{\Phi}$ and

$$F_1 = M_1(\hat{P}, F_1) = M_1(\hat{P}, F_1^{\Phi\Phi}). \tag{2.13}$$

Sets possessing properties (2.12) are of special interest for the following considerations.

Now let us introduce the notions of an aureole set and a star set with respect to $\hat{P}$. Such sets are generalizations of the corresponding dual sets used in /19/ which follow from Definition 2.6 in the case $\hat{P} = ((1,0,0))$.

Definition 2.6: Let $F \subset V$.

a) F is called aureole set with respect to $\hat{P}$, if $F = M_1(\hat{P}, F)$.

b) F is called star set with respect to $\hat{P}$, if $F = M_2(\hat{P}, F)$.

Aureole sets and star sets with respect to $\hat{P}$ can be characterized by the following

Theorem 2.3: Let V be a locally convex Hausdorff space and let $F \subset V$ be a closed convex set.

(i) F an aureole set with respect to $\hat{P}$, $\frac{\hat{x}}{\hat{t}} \notin \operatorname{cl} F$ if $\hat{t} < 0$ $\iff$ $F = \overset{*}{F}{}^{\Phi\Phi}$.

(ii) F a star set with respect to $\hat{P}$ $\iff$ $F = \overset{*}{F}{}_{\Phi\Phi}$.

Proof: We prove (i).

1. Let F be an aureole set with respect to $\hat{P}$. Then we have according Definition 2.6 the relation $F = M_1(\hat{P}, F)$, where in the case $\hat{t} < 0$ holds $\frac{\hat{x}}{\hat{t}} \notin \operatorname{cl} M_1(\hat{P}, F) = M_1(\hat{P}, F)$. By Theorem 2.1 follows $\overset{*}{F}{}^{\Phi\Phi} = \operatorname{cl} M_1(\hat{P}, F) = F$.

2. Now let $F = \overset{*}{F}{}^{\Phi\Phi}$. Then by Theorem 2.1 we conclude $F = \overset{*}{F}{}^{\Phi\Phi} = \operatorname{cl} M_1(\hat{P}, F)$. The set $M_1(\hat{P}, F)$ is closed since F is a closed set by assumption. Hence $F = \operatorname{cl} M_1(\hat{P}, F) = M_1(\hat{P}, F)$, that means F is an aureole set.

The proof for (ii) is similar. □

From Theorem 2.3 we conclude in the special case

$$V = R^n, \ \hat{P} = ((1,0,0)), \ \overset{*}{F}{}^{\Phi} = F_+^*, \ \overset{*}{F}{}_{\Phi} = F_-^*$$

the following result (cf. /19/).

Theorem 2.4: Let $F \subset R^n$ be a closed convex set.

(i) F an aureole set, $0 \notin F$ $\iff$ $F = (F_+^*)_+^*$.

(ii) F a star set $\iff$ $F = (F_-^*)_-^*$.

2.3. Φ-conjugate Functions

Now let us consider the case $V_2 = R$. Then with respect to the mapping A we have

$$B_2 := b \in R, \ E =: e \in V_1^*. \tag{2.14}$$

Furthermore let the set $F \subset V = V_1 \times R$ be the graph of a function $f\colon D(f) \longrightarrow R$, $D(f) \subseteq V_1$, such that

$$D(f) = V^o(f) := \{y \in D(f) \mid c + \langle e,y\rangle + bf(y) > 0\}. \tag{2.15}$$

From the inequalities (2.6a) and (2.6b) we conclude the inequalities

$$v^* \geqq k(z,\ f(z),\ z^*) \quad \forall\, z \in D(f),\ \forall\, (z^*,\ v^*) \in F^{\Phi}, \tag{2.16a}$$

$$v^* \leqq k(z,\ f(z),\ z^*) \quad \forall\, z \in D(f),\ \forall\, (z^*,\ v^*) \in F_{\Phi}, \tag{2.16b}$$

where

$$k(z,f(z),z^*) := \frac{-(a_o+\langle a,z\rangle+cf(z)) - \langle a+B_1z+ef(z),z^*\rangle}{c + \langle e,z\rangle + bf(z)} . \tag{2.17}$$

Regarding to these inequalities we introduce Φ-conjugate functions of a function f according to

Definition 2.7: Let f: $D(f) \longrightarrow R$, $D(f) = V^o(f) \subset V_1$. Then the function

$$f^{\Phi}(z^*) := \sup_{z\in D(f)} k(z,f(z),z^*),\ z^* \in D(f^{\Phi}),$$

$$D(f^{\Phi}) := \{z^* \in V_1 \mid \sup_{z\in D(f)} k(z,f(z),z^*) < \infty\},$$

is called the upper Φ-conjugate function of f and the function

$$f_{\Phi}(z^*) := \inf_{z\in D(f)} k(z,f(z),z^*),\ z^* \in D(f_{\Phi}),$$

$$D(f_{\Phi}) := \{z^* \in V_1 \mid \inf_{z\in D(f)} k(z,f(z),z^*) > -\infty\},$$

is called the lower Φ-conjugate function of f.

From Definition 2.7 and Definition 2.2 we obtain a close connection between Φ-conjugate sets and the graphs of Φ-conjugate functions. This was considered in the finite dimensional case $V_1 = R^n$ in /1/.

Properties of Φ-conjugate functions are given in /1/, /3/, /4/ (finite dimensional case) and in /5/, /12/, /17/, /18/ (infinite dimensional case).

Here we mention some of these properties.

The linear mapping A (cf. (2.3) and (C1) - (C3)) is given here as

$$A: \quad \begin{aligned} t' &= a_0 t + \langle a,z\rangle + cv \\ z' &= at + B_1 z + ev \qquad (t,z,v) \in R\times V_1\times R, \\ v' &= ct + \langle e,z\rangle + bv \end{aligned} \tag{2.18}$$

where

$$a_0, b, c \in R,\ a,\ e \in V_1^*,\ (c,e,b) \neq (0,0,0),$$

$$B_1 : V_1 \longrightarrow V_1^* \text{ a symmetrical linear mapping.}$$

Another linear mapping $\tilde{B}: R\times V_1\times R \longrightarrow V_1^*$ will be considered given by

$$\tilde{B}(t,z,v) = at + B_1 z + ev,\ (t,z,v) \in R\times V_1\times R. \tag{2.19}$$

Moreover, we use the hyperplane

$$H_0 := \{(z,v) \in V_1 \times R \mid\ c + \langle e,z\rangle + bv = 0\}. \tag{2.20}$$

Theorem 2.5 (/3/, /12/): Let $f: D(f) \longrightarrow R$, $V^0(f) = D(f) \subseteq V_1$, A a linear mapping according (2.18) and $b \geqq 0$.
Then

(i) f^{Φ} ist convex,
f_{Φ} is concave,

(ii) $$(c + \langle e,z\rangle + bf(z))f^{\Phi}(z^*) + (c + \langle e,z^*\rangle)f(z) \geqq -(a_0 + \langle a,z\rangle) - \langle a + B_1 z, z^*\rangle \quad \forall (z,z^*) \in D(f)\times D(f^{\Phi}),$$

(iii) $$(c + \langle e,z\rangle + bf(z))f_{\Phi}(z^*) + (c + \langle e,z^*\rangle)f(z) \leqq -(a_0 + \langle a,z\rangle) - \langle a + B_1 z, z^*\rangle \quad \forall (z,z^*) \in D(f)\times D(f_{\Phi}),$$

(iv) $D(f^{\Phi}) = V^{o}(f^{\Phi}) \neq \emptyset \Longrightarrow$

$$f^{\Phi\Phi}(z) \leqq f(z) \ \forall z \in D(f),$$

(v) $V^{o}(f_{\Phi}) \neq \emptyset \Longrightarrow$

$$f_{\Phi\Phi}(z) \geqq f(z) \ \forall z \in D(f).$$

Theorem 2.6 (/3/, /12/): Let $f\colon D(f) \longrightarrow R$, $V^{o}(f) = D(f) \subseteq V_1$, A a linear mapping according (2.18) and $\hat{t} < 0$.

Then

(i) $\frac{\hat{z}}{\hat{t}} \in D(f_{\Phi})$,

(ii) $f_{\Phi}(\frac{\hat{z}}{\hat{t}}) \geqq \frac{\hat{v}}{\hat{t}}$,

(iii) $b \geqq 0 \Rightarrow (\frac{\hat{z}}{\hat{t}}, f_{\Phi}(\frac{\hat{z}}{\hat{t}})) \in V^{o} \cup H_{o}$.

Theorem 2.7 (/12/): Let V_1 be a topological linear space, let $\tilde{B}(R\times V_1\times R) = V_1'$, where V_1' is the topological dual space of V_1, let $f\colon D(f) \longrightarrow R$, $V^{o}(f) = D(f) \subseteq V_1$.

Then

(i) f^{Φ} is lower semicontinuous,

(ii) f_{Φ} is upper semicontinuous.

Theorem 2.8 (/12/): Let V_1 be a topological linear space, let $\tilde{B}(R\times V_1\times R) = V_1'$, where V_1' is the topological dual space of V_1, let $f\colon D(f) \longrightarrow R$, $V^{o}(f) = D(f) \subseteq V_1$ and $b \geqq 0, \hat{t} < 0$. If $\mathfrak{U}$ is a filter of neighbourhoods of $z_o \in \overline{D(f)}$ and

$$\underline{f}(z_o) := \sup_{U\in\mathfrak{U}} \ \inf_{z\in U\cap D(f)} f(z), \text{ then}$$

$$\text{(i)} \quad \left.\begin{array}{l} \frac{\hat{z}}{\hat{t}} \in \overline{D(f)} \\ \underline{f}(\frac{\hat{z}}{\hat{t}}) > \frac{\hat{v}}{\hat{t}} \end{array}\right\} \Rightarrow V^{o}(f^{\Phi}) = D(f^{\Phi}),$$

$$\text{(ii)}\quad \left.\begin{array}{l} D(f) \text{ convex} \\ \text{int } D(f) \neq \emptyset \\ V^o(f^\Phi) = D(f^\Phi) \end{array}\right\} \Longrightarrow \left\{\begin{array}{l} \frac{\hat z}{\hat t} \in \overline{D(f)}, \\ \underline{f}(\frac{\hat z}{\hat t}) > \frac{\hat v}{\hat t} \,. \end{array}\right.$$

A nonvertical hyperplane $H \subset V_1 \times R$ has a representation

$$H := \left\{(z,v) \in V_1 \times R \;\middle|\; v = \langle m,z\rangle + \beta,\ m \in V_1^*,\ \beta \in R\right\}. \quad (2.21)$$

H is called a supporting hyperplane of a set $M \subseteq V_1 \times R$ if H satisfies the conditions

(1) $v - \langle m,z\rangle - \beta \geqq 0 \quad \forall\ (z,v) \in M$,

(2) $\exists (z_o, v_o) \in M: \quad v_o - \langle m, z_o\rangle - \beta = 0.$

Theorem 2.9 (/3/, /12/): Let V_1 be a topological linear space, let $\tilde{B}(R \times V_1 \times R) \supseteq V_1'$, where V_1' is the topological dual space of V_1, let $f\colon D(f) \longrightarrow R$, $V^o(f) = D(f) \subseteq V_1$ and $b \geqq 0$.

(i) If $V^o(f^\Phi) = D(f^\Phi)$, $\text{int}(\text{epi } f) \neq \emptyset$, H according to (2.21) is a supporting hyperplane of epi f at $(z_o, f(z_o))$, $\hat v - \langle m, \hat z\rangle - \beta \hat t > 0$, then

$$f^{\Phi\Phi}(z_o) = f(z_o).$$

(ii) If $V^o(f_\Phi) \neq \emptyset$, $\text{int}(\text{hypo } f) \neq \emptyset$, H according to (2.21) is a supporting hyperplane of hypo f at $(z_o, f(z_o))$, $\hat v - \langle m, \hat z\rangle - \beta \hat t > 0$, then

$$f_{\Phi\Phi}(z_o) = f(z_o).$$

(iii) If $z_o \in D(f)$, H a hyperplane according to (2.21), then the following propositions are equivalent:

(1) H is a supporting hyperplane of epi f at $(z_o, f(z_o))$, where $\hat v - \langle m, \hat z\rangle - \beta \hat t > 0$.

(2) There exists a $z_o^* \in D(f^\Phi)$, $(z_o^*, f^\Phi(z_o^*)) \in V^o$, such that in Theorem 2.5 (ii) equality holds for $z = z_o$, $z^* = z_o^*$.

(iv) If $z_o \in D(f)$, H a hyperplane according to (2.21), then the following propositions are equivalent:

(1) H is a supporting hyperplane of hypo f at $(z_o, f(z_o))$, where $\hat{v} - \langle m, \hat{z} \rangle - \beta \hat{t} > 0$.

(2) There exists a $z_o^* \in D(f_\Phi)$, $(z_o^*, f_\Phi(z_o^*)) \in V^o$, such that in Theorem 2.5 (iii) equality holds for $z = z_o$, $z^* = z_o^*$.

3. Duality Theorems

Using Φ-conjugate functions we introduce dual nonconvex optimization problems.

Let $f\colon D(f) \longrightarrow R$, $D(f) \subseteq V_1$, $g\colon D(g) \longrightarrow R$, $D(g) \subseteq V_1$,
$D(f^\Phi) = V^o(f^\Phi)$, $D(g) = V^o(g)$.

For abbreviation we set

$$D(f,g) := D(f) \cap D(g), \quad D(f^\Phi, g_\Phi) := D(f^\Phi) \cap D(g_\Phi).$$

In the following we always assume

$$D(f,g) \neq \emptyset, \quad D(f^\Phi, g_\Phi) \neq \emptyset.$$

In the case $b \neq 0$ we consider the dual optimization problems

$$P_1\colon \ p_1(z) := \frac{c + \langle e,z \rangle + bf(z)}{c + \langle e,z \rangle + bg(z)} \longrightarrow \inf, \ z \in D(f,g),$$

$$D_1\colon \ d_1(z^*) := \frac{c + \langle e,z^* \rangle + bg_\Phi(z^*)}{c + \langle e,z^* \rangle + bf^\Phi(z^*)} \longrightarrow \sup, \ z^* \in D(f^\Phi, g_\Phi),$$

in the case $b = 0$ we consider the dual optimization problems

$$P_2\colon \ p_2(z) := \frac{f(z) - g(z)}{c + \langle e,z \rangle} \longrightarrow \inf, \ z \in D(f, g),$$

$$D_2\colon \ d_2(z^*) := \frac{g_\Phi(z^*) - f^\Phi(z^*)}{c + \langle e,z^* \rangle} \longrightarrow \sup, \ z^* \in D(f^\Phi, g_\Phi).$$

Without further assumptions we have the following weak duality theorem.

Theorem 3.1 (/3/, /12/): Let $D(f,g) \neq \emptyset$, $D(f^{\Phi}, g_{\Phi}) \neq \emptyset$, $D(f^{\Phi}) = V^{o}(f^{\Phi})$, $D(g) = V^{o}(g)$ and $b \geqq 0$. Then

$$\inf_{z \in D(f,g)} p_j(z) \geqq \sup_{z^* \in D(f^{\Phi}, g_{\Phi})} d_j(z^*), \quad j = 1, 2.$$

Immediately from Theorem 3.1 we conclude

Theorem 3.2: Let the assumptions of Theorem 3.1 be satisfied.

(i) If there is a $z_o \in D(f,g)$ such that

$$p_j(z_o) = \sup_{z^* \in D(f^{\Phi}, g_{\Phi})} d_j(z^*), \quad j = 1, 2,$$

then z_o is a solution of P_j, $j = 1, 2$.

(ii) If there is a $z_o^* \in D(f^{\Phi}, g_{\Phi})$ such that

$$\inf_{z \in D(f,g)} p_j(z) = d_j(z_o^*), \quad j = 1, 2,$$

then z_o^* is a solution of D_j, $j = 1, 2$.

Now we give strong duality theorems. We introduce the following condition.

(T') $\begin{cases} \text{Let } V = V_1 \times R, \text{ where } V_1 \text{ is a topological linear space,} \\ A \text{ a symmetrical linear mapping according (2.18),} \\ \tilde{B}(R \times V_1 \times R) = V_1', \text{ where } V_1' \text{ is the topological dual} \\ \text{space of } V_1 . \end{cases}$

Theorem 3.3: Let (T') be satisfied, let f and $-g$ be convex functions, let $D(f) = V^{o}(f)$, $D(g) = V^{o}(g)$, $D(f^{\Phi}) = V^{o}(f^{\Phi})$ and $b > 0$.

If

(i) $\operatorname{int}(\operatorname{epi} f) \neq \emptyset$, $\operatorname{int} D(f) \cap D(g) \neq \emptyset$,

(ii) $\hat{t} < 0$, (iii) $\frac{\hat{z}}{\hat{t}} \in \overline{D(g)}$, (iv) $\overline{\lim}_{z \to \frac{\hat{z}}{\hat{t}}} g(z) > \frac{\hat{v}}{\hat{t}}$,

(v) $\exists r > 0, \forall z \in D(f,g): c + \langle e,z\rangle + bf(z) \geqq br > 0$,

then there exists a $z_o^* \in D(f^\Phi, g_\Phi)$ such that

$$\inf_{z\in D(f,g)} p_1(z) = \max_{z^*\in D(f^\Phi, g_\Phi)} d_1(z^*) = d_1(z_o^*).$$

Remark: Instead of (i) we can require

(i') $\operatorname{int}(\text{hypo } g) \neq \emptyset$, $D(f) \cap \operatorname{int} D(g) \neq \emptyset$.

Theorem 3.4: Let (T') be satisfied, let f and $-g$ be convex functions, let $D(f) = V^o(f)$, $D(g) = V^o(g)$, $D(f^\Phi) = V^o(f^\Phi)$ and $b = 0$.

If

(i) $\operatorname{int}(\text{epi } f) \neq \emptyset$, $\operatorname{int} D(f,g) \neq \emptyset$, *)

(ii) $\hat{t} < 0$, (iii) $\{z \in V_1 \mid \hat{t}z = \hat{z}\} \cap \overline{D(g)} \neq \emptyset$,

(iv) $\overline{\lim}_{z \to \frac{\hat{z}}{\hat{t}}} g(z) > \frac{\hat{v}}{\hat{t}}$,

(v) $\inf_{z\in D(f,g)} p_2(z) > -\infty$,

then there exists a $z_o^* \in D(f^\Phi, g_\Phi)$ such that

$$\inf_{z\in D(f,g)} p_2(z) = \max_{z^*\in D(f^\Phi, g_\Phi)} d_2(z^*) = d_2(z_o^*).$$

The proofs of Theorem 3.3 and Theorem 3.4 are given in /12/.

---

*) Cf. the remark following Theorem 3.3.

4. Duality for Families of Optimization Problems

Let $V = V_1 \times V_2$ and $F \subset V_1 \times V_2$.
If we choose $(p, -q) \in \overset{*}{F}_{\Phi}$ then we obtain by the inequality (2.6b)

$$(a_0 + \langle a,z\rangle + \langle c,v\rangle) + \langle a + B_1 z + E^* v, p\rangle \leqq \langle c + Ez + B_2 v, q\rangle \qquad (4.1a)$$
$$\forall (z,v) \in F,\ \forall (p,-q) \in \overset{*}{F}_{\Phi}.$$

Correspondingly we obtain for $(p, -q) \in \overset{*}{F}{}^{\Phi}$ from (2.6a)

$$(a_0 + \langle a,z\rangle + \langle c,v\rangle) + \langle a + B_1 z + E^* v, p\rangle \geqq \langle c + Ez + B_2 v, q\rangle \qquad (4.1b)$$
$$\forall (z,v) \in F,\ \forall (p,-q) \in \overset{*}{F}{}^{\Phi}.$$

In the following we consider only the special case characterized by $E = 0$ (then $E^* = 0$). We obtain the two inequalities

$$(a_0 + \langle a,z\rangle) + \langle a + B_1 z, p\rangle \leqq \langle c + B_2 v, q\rangle - \langle c,v\rangle \qquad (4.2a)$$
$$\forall (z,v) \in F,\ \forall (p,-q) \in \overset{*}{F}_{\Phi},$$

$$(a_0 + \langle a,z\rangle) + \langle a + B_1 z, p\rangle \geqq \langle c + B_2 v, q\rangle - \langle c,v\rangle \qquad (4.2b)$$
$$\forall (z,v) \in F,\ \forall (p,-q) \in \overset{*}{F}{}^{\Phi},$$

which leads to two pairs of families of optimization problems.

Let $z_0 \in P_{V_1}(F)$, $-q_0 \in P_{V_2}(\overset{*}{F}_{\Phi})$, where $P_{V_1}(F)$ is the projection of F onto V_1 and $P_{V_2}(\overset{*}{F}_{\Phi})$ is the projection of $\overset{*}{F}_{\Phi}$ onto V_2.

Because of (4.2a) we have a weak duality theorem with respect to the following families of optimization problems.

$$P_1^{-q_0}:\ \langle c + B_2 v, q_0\rangle - \langle c, v\rangle \longrightarrow \inf,$$
$$v \in \{v' \in P_{V_2}(F) \mid (z_0, v') \in F\} =: P_{V_2}^{z_0}(F),$$

$D_1^{z_o}$: $(a_o + \langle a,z_o\rangle) + \langle a + B_1 z_o, p\rangle \longrightarrow \sup,$

$$p \in \{p' \in P_{V_1}(\overset{*}{F}_\Phi) \mid (p', -q_o) \in \overset{*}{F}_\Phi\} =: P_{V_1}^{-q_o}(\overset{*}{F}_\Phi).$$

The two parameters of these families are $-q_o \in P_{V_2}(\overset{*}{F}_\Phi)$ and $z_o \in P_{V_1}(F)$, respectively.

The following strict duality theorem can be proved.

Theorem 4.1: Let $F \subset V_1 \times V_2$, $F \neq \emptyset$, $F_\Phi \neq \emptyset$, $F_{\Phi\Phi} \neq \emptyset$ and $(z_o, v_o) \in F_{\Phi\Phi}$, $(p_o, -q_o) \in \overset{*}{F}_\Phi$.

If

$$\langle(1,z_o,v_o), A(1,p_o,-q_o)\rangle = 0 \tag{4.3}$$

then

(i) p_o is a solution of $D_1^{z_o}$,

(ii)
$$\max_{p\in P_{V_1}^{-q_o}(\overset{*}{F}_\Phi)} \left[(a_o + \langle a,z_o\rangle) + \langle a+B_1 z_o, p\rangle\right] = \inf_{v\in P_{V_2}^{z_o}(F)} \left[\langle c+B_2 v, q_o\rangle - \langle c,v\rangle\right]. \tag{4.4}$$

Proof. Since (4.3) we have

$$a_o+\langle a,z_o\rangle + \langle a+B_1 z_o, p_o\rangle = \langle c+B_2 v_o, q_o\rangle - \langle c,v_o\rangle.$$

By the definition of $\overset{*}{F}_\Phi$ the inequality holds

$$a_o+\langle a,z_o\rangle + \langle a+B_1 z_o, p\rangle \leqq \langle c+B_2 v, q_o\rangle - \langle c,v\rangle$$

$$\forall p \in P_{V_1}^{-q_o}(\overset{*}{F}_\Phi), \quad \forall v \in P_{V_2}^{z_o}(F).$$

Hence (i) and (ii) follow immediately. □

As a geometrical interpretation of (4.3) and (4.4) we consider the hyperplane

$$H^*(z_o,v_o) := \left\{(z^*,v^*) \in V_1 \times V_2 \;|\; \langle (1,z_o,v_o), A(1,z^*,v^*)\rangle = 0 \right\} \tag{4.5}$$

to be a supporting hyperplane to $\overset{*}{F}_{\Phi}$ at $(p_o,-q_o)$. Hence we can replace (4.3) by this condition.

In fig. 3 we give an illustration to the problem (cf. fig. 1).

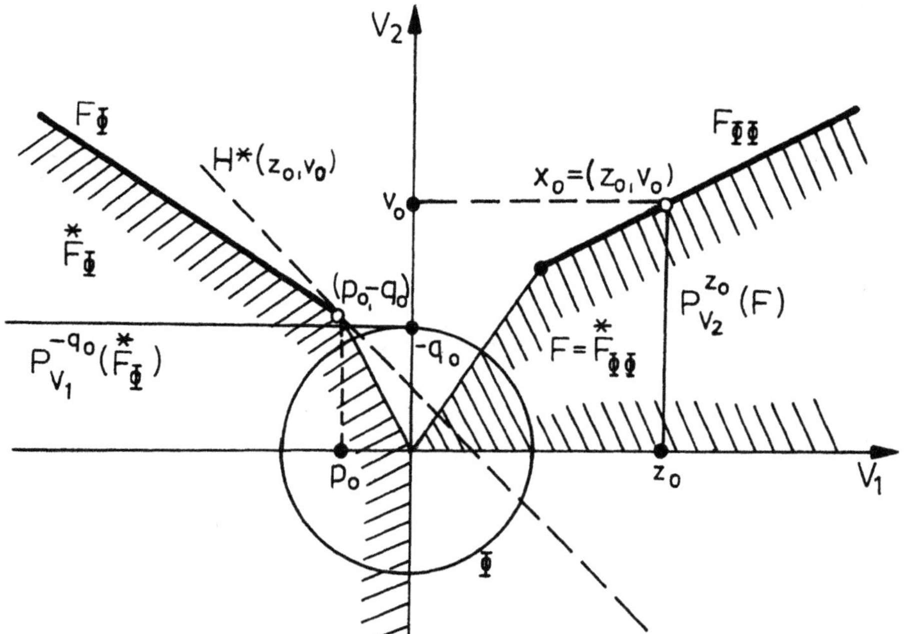

Fig. 3

If we choose $(p,\ -q) \in \overset{*}{F}\Phi$ we obtain the inequality (4.2b) and introduce correspondingly the families of optimization problems

$$P_2^{-q_o}:\ \langle c + B_2 v,\ q_o\rangle - \langle c,v\rangle \longrightarrow \sup,$$
$$v \in P_{V_2}^{z_o}(F),$$

$$D_2^{z_o}: \ (a_o + \langle a, z_o \rangle) + \langle a + B_1 z_o, p \rangle \longrightarrow \inf,$$

$$p \in P_{V_1}^{-q_o}(\overset{*}{F}{}^{\Phi}) := \{ p' \in P_{V_1}(\overset{*}{F}{}^{\Phi}) \mid (p', -q_o) \in \overset{*}{F}{}^{\Phi} \},$$

where the parameters of the families are $-q_o \in P_{V_2}(\overset{*}{F}{}^{\Phi})$ and $z_o \in P_{V_1}(F)$, respectively.

Analogously to Theorem 4.1 we have the following strict duality theorem.

Theorem 4.2: Let $F \subset V_1 \times V_2$, $F \neq \emptyset$, $F_{\Phi} \neq \emptyset$, $F_{\Phi\Phi} \neq \emptyset$ and $(z_o, v_o) \in F^{\Phi\Phi}$, $(p_o, -q_o) \in \overset{*}{F}{}^{\Phi}$.

If (4.3) is satisfied then

(i) p_o is a solution of $D_2^{z_o}$,

(ii)
$$\min_{p \in P_{V_1}^{-q_o}(\overset{*}{F}{}^{\Phi})} [\, (a_o + \langle a, z_o \rangle) + \langle a + B_1 z_o, p \rangle \,] = \sup_{v \in P_{V_2}^{z_o}(F)} [\, \langle c + B_2 v, q_o \rangle - \langle c, v \rangle \,] . \tag{4.6}$$

The proof is similar to that of Theorem 4.1.

A geometrical interpretation of (4.3) and (4.6) can also be given. The hyperplane (4.5) is a supporting hyperplane to $\overset{*}{F}{}^{\Phi}$ at $(p_o, -q_o)$ and therefore we can replace (4.3) by this geometrical condition.

Fig. 4 illustrates the situation (cf. fig. 2).

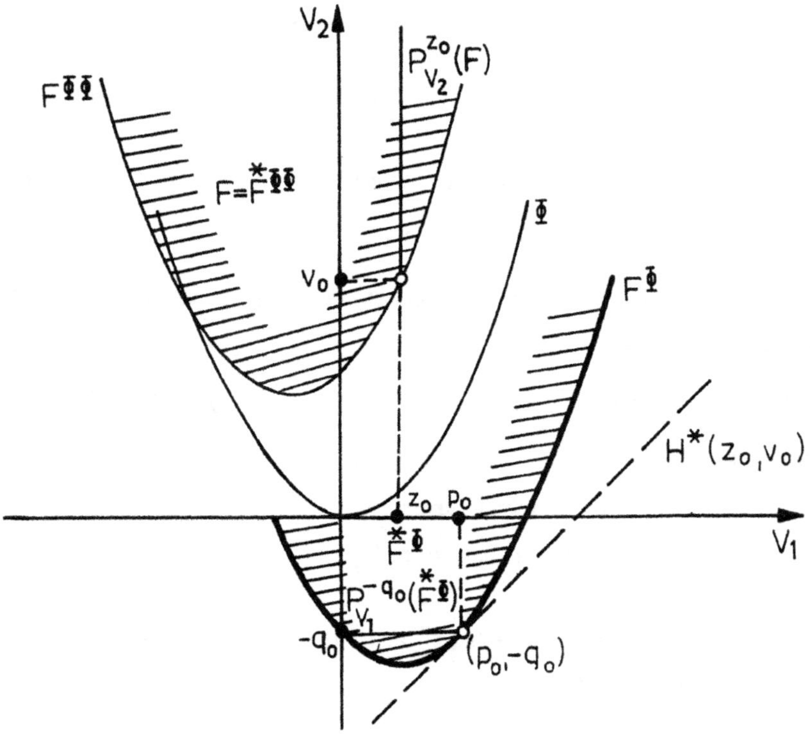

Fig. 4

5. References

/1/ Deumlich, R.; K.-H. Elster: Generalized conjugate functions. Math. Operationsforsch. u. Statist., Ser. optimization, 8 (1977), 2, 151 - 179.

/2/ Deumlich, R.; K.-H. Elster: Duality theorems and nonconvex optimization problems. Math. Operationsforsch. u. Statist., Ser. optimization, 9 (1978), 3, 335 - 347.

/3/ Deumlich, R.; K.-H. Elster: Duality theorems and optimality conditions for nonconvex optimization problems. Math. Operationsforsch. u. Statist., Ser. optimization, 11 (1980), 2, 181 - 219.

/4/ Deumlich, R.; K.-H. Elster: On the theory of conjugate functions. In: Studies on Mathematical Programming. Akadémiai Kiadó, Budapest 1980, 19 - 45.

/5/ Deumlich, R.; K.-H. Elster: Recent results on Φ-conjugation and nonconvex optimization. In: G. Feichtinger and P. Kall (eds.), Operations Research in Progress. D. Reidel Publ. Comp. 1982, 27 - 40.

/6/ Deumlich, R.; K.-H. Elster: Theorie nichtkonvexer Optimierungsprobleme: Stabilität und Dualität. 27. Internat. Wiss. Koll. d. TH Ilmenau 1982, Heft 5, 25 - 28.

/7/ Deumlich, R.; K.-H. Elster: On a class of nonconvex optimization problems. In: Hammer, G.; Pallaschke, D. (eds.): Selected Topics in Op. Res. and Mathematical Economics, Proceedings Karlsruhe 1983. Lecture Notes in Economics and Mathem. Systems, Vol. 226, Springer Verlag, Berlin, Heidelberg, New York, Tokyo 1984, 13-29.

/8/ Deumlich, R.; K.-H. Elster: Some results on nonconvex optimization. Proc. of Conf. Mathemat. Methods in Economics, Sofia (Bulgarien) 1983, to appear.

/9/ Deumlich, R.; K.-H. Elster: Teorija dvojstvennosti v nelinejnoj optimizatii i ee priloženie k economičeskim problemam. Internat. Microsymposium III-'82: Mathematical Methods of Modeling in Economics. EÚ ČSAV Prague 1983, 276 - 289.

/10/ Deumlich, R.; K.-H. Elster: Neuere Beiträge zu Theorie und Anwendungen der Φ-Konjugation. Internat. Tagung "Mathemat. Optimierung - Theorie und Anwendungen" Eisenach (DDR) 1983, Abstracts, 22 - 25.

/11/ Deumlich, R.; K.-H. Elster: On perturbations of certain nonconvex optimization problems, to appear.

/12/ Deumlich, R.; K.-H. Elster: Φ-conjugation and nonconvex optimization. A survey (Part I). Math. Operationsforsch. u. Statist., Ser. optimization 14 (1983), 1, 125 - 149.

/13/ Deumlich, R.; K.-H. Elster: Φ-conjugation and nonconvex optimization. A survey (Part II). To appear in Mathem. Operationsforsch. u. Statist., Ser. optimization 15 (1984).

/14/ Deumlich, R.; K.-H. Elster: Φ-conjugation and nonconvex optimization. A survey (Part III). To appear in Mathemat. Operationsforsch. u. Statist., Ser. optimization.

/15/ Deumlich, R.; K.-H. Elster; R. Nehse: Generalizations of conjugate functions. In: Prékopa, A. (ed.): Survey of Mathematical Programming (Proceedings of 9th Internat. Mathem. Programming Symposium, Budapest 1976). Akadémiai Kiadó, Budapest 1979, Vol. 1, 193 - 204.

/16/ Elster, K.-H.: On the theory of nonconvex optimization problems. In: W. Oettli and F. Steffens (eds.): Proceedings III. Symp. on Oper. Res., Mannheim (BRD) 1978; Operations Research Verfahren, Vol. 31, 173-184.

/17/ Elster, K.-H.; R. Deumlich: On duality concepts for nonconvex optimization problems. In: R. Burkard (ed.): Proceedings V. Symp. on Oper. Research, Köln (BRD) 1980; 81 - 84.

/18/ Elster, K.-H.; R. Deumlich: Lagrange duality for nonvex optimization problems. In: Proceedings of 6. Sympos. über Oper. Research, Augsburg (BRD) 1981; Methods of Operations Research, Vol. 43, 53 - 61.

/19/ Ruys, P. H. M.; H. N. Weddepohl: Economic theory and duality. In: J. Kriens (ed.): Convex Analysis and Mathematical Economics. Lecture Notes in Economics and Mathem. Systems, Vol. 168, 1979, 1 - 72.

MULTISTATE RELIABILITY PROBLEMS FOR GSP-DIGRAPHS

W. Gaul[1], J. Hartung[2]

Summary:

Assume that the arcs of the underlying graph can take m + 1 states of reliability from complete failure (state 0) to perfect functioning (state m) where m is a non-negative integer.

For m = 1 an extensive literature about reliability problems on graphs is available, for m > 1 this paper gives bounds for the distribution function (and for the expectation, variance, etc. if necessary) of an intuitively appealing reliability measure of the graph in terms of properly chosen subgraphs based on a suitable two vertex connectivity notation.

A successive determination of lower and upper bounding distribution functions (and of bounds of the moments, if necessary) of the reliability measure is possible allowing improvements due to the choice of proper subgraph systems.

1. Introduction

There exists an extensive literature about reliability problems on graphs if the reliability-behaviour of the elements of the underlying graph is described in terms of only the two states failure (state 0) and functioning (state 1), see e.g. GILBERT (1959), LEE (1955), MOORE/ SHANNON (1956) for early references, WILKOV (1972) for an early survey and FRANK/GAUL (1982), GAUL (1983) for more recent work.

Since the late seventies more and more researchers stress the fact that the two-state description of reliability-behaviour phenomena is an oversimplification of real world situations and use multistate reliability systems the elements of which can take m + 1 states of reliability from complete failure (state 0) to perfect functioning

1) Institut für Entscheidungstheorie und Unternehmensforschung, Universität Karlsruhe (TH)

2) Lehrstuhl für Statistik mit Anwendungen in den Ingenieurwissenschaften, Universität Dortmund

(state m) where m is a non-negative integer, see e.g. BARLOW/WU (1978), EL-NEWEIHI/PROSCHAN/SETHURAMAN (1978), EL-NEWEIHI/PROSCHAN (1980), GRIFFITH (1980), FARDIS/CORNELL (1981) (and ROSS (1979) for the still more general case when reliability states are described by arbitrary non-negative numbers).

The m-state reliability approach is used in this paper assuming that the underlying reliability system is or can be described by a gsp (generalized series-parallel)-digraph which is a finite, acyclic, weakly connected, directed graph the vertex-basis (vertex-contra-basis) of which consists of a single vertex, see e.g. HARARY/ NORMAN / CARTWRIGHT (1965) for needed graphtheoretical notations. This type of graph is useful for reliability considerations, it generalizes the description of two terminal series-parallel systems whose elements can be represented by the arcs of corresponding gsp-digraphs, see e.g. LEE (1955) for an early paper and GAUL (1983), SATYANARAYANA/ PRABHAKAR (1978) for more recent contributions in which gsp-digraphs play an important role.

In the next section necessary notation is given, and it is shown how an intuitively appealing reliability measure based on two vertex connectivity considerations in digraphs can be handled. As the distribution function of this reliability measure is difficult to obtain section 3 shows how bounding distribution functions can be determined and how improvements of the bounding distribution functions can be yielded depending on the choice of proper subgraph systems. Bounds for the expectation and the variance of the reliability measure are described in section 4.

2. Two vertex connectivity reliability measure

Let

(1) $D = (V,X,f)$

be a finite, acyclic, weakly connected directed graph with vertex-set V, arc-set X and incidence-mapping $f = (f^1,f^2)$ with $f^i: X \to V$, $i=1,2$ ($f^1(x)$, $f^2(x)$ gives the starting-, end-vertex of $x \in X$). For abbreviation, mostly, only D is written for such a graph and $V(D)$, $X(D)$ (and $f(D)$, if needed) for its vertex-, arc-set (and incidence-mapping).

Omitting the incidence-mapping for D', D'' the subgraph-notation

$$D' \subset D'' \text{ iff } V(D') \subset V(D''),\ X(D') \subset X(D'')$$

and the union-intersection-notation

$$D' \underset{\cap}{\cup} D'' \text{ iff } V(D' \underset{\cap}{\cup} D'') = V(D') \underset{\cap}{\cup} V(D''),\ X(D' \underset{\cap}{\cup} D'') = X(D') \underset{\cap}{\cup} X(D'')$$

is used.

(2) $Y = (Y_x \mid x \in X(D))$

gives a vector of discrete random variables Y_x defined on some probability space $(\Omega, \mathfrak{T}, Pr)$ with values from $\{0,1,\ldots,m\}$ interpreted as reliability-states of $x \in X(D)$ (state 0 corresponds to complete failure, state m to perfect functioning). If one selects two vertices $t, r \in V(D)$ in such a way that for the subgraph

(3) D_{tr} with $t, r \in V(D_{tr})$

t resp. r, solely, is the vertex-basis resp. -contrabasis of D_{tr}, the following reliability measure is of interest

(4) $$\Phi_{D_{tr}}(Y) = \max_{P_{tr} \in P(D_{tr})} \min_{x \in X(P_{tr})} \{proj_x(Y)\}$$

where P_{tr} is a subgraph of D_{tr} described by the following sequence of vertices and arcs,

$$t = i_o,\ x \in \{x \mid f(D_{tr})(x) = (i_o, i_1)\},\ i_1, \ldots, i_{p-1},$$

$$x \in \{x \mid f(D_{tr})(x) = (i_{p-1}, i_p)\},\ i_p = r,$$

called path from t to r in D_{tr}. $P(D_{tr})$ denotes the set of these paths. In BARLOW/WU (1978) properties of an expression like (4) are described in terms of coherent structure theory, and, although GRIFFITH (1980) shows that multistate reliability models with structure function according to (4) establish only a subclass of the weakly coherent multistate reliability systems (which also contain the EL-NEWEIHI/PROSCHAN/ SETHURAMAN (1978) multistate coherent systems as special cases), for graphtheoretical reliability considerations an expression of the form (4) is well-suited for describing the reliability-behaviour of a graph with unreliable arcs.

Use the abbreviation gsp-digraph for a finite, acyclic, directed graph with single-element vertex-basis and single-element vertex-contrabasis, assume that the starting graph (1) is already a gsp-digraph, i.e.

$D = D_{ab}$ for specified basis- and contrabasis-vertices $a,b \varepsilon V(D_{ab})$,

and notice, that for a large gsp-digraph D_{ab} the determination of the distribution function

$$(5) \quad F_{D_{ab}}(\tau) = Pr(\Phi_{D_{ab}}(Y) \leq \tau) \quad , \quad \tau \in \mathbb{R},$$

can be difficult. Therefore possibilities for computing bounding distribution functions for (5) should be of interest and are described in the following.

The approach uses properties yielded in GAUL (1978) for project digraphs (which are gsp-digraphs having no parallel arcs) which, however, can be carried over to gsp-digraphs. In this context the following notations are useful:
For the sequential determination of the reliability bounds an ordering of the vertex-set $V(D_{ab})$ is needed according to a bijective mapping $l:V(D_{ab}) \to \{0,1,...,n\}, n=|V(D_{ab})|-1$, with

$$x \varepsilon X(D_{ab}) \Longrightarrow l(f^1(D_{ab})(x)) < l(f^2(D_{ab})(x))$$

$$l(a) = 0, \; l(b) = n.$$

Now, if for two vertices $t, r \varepsilon V(D_{ab})$ a gsp-subdigraph D_{tr} exists, use the notation $\tilde{D}_{tr}$ for the maximal gsp-subdigraph and notice that the paths P_{tr} are minimal gsp-subdigraphs with respect to $t,r \varepsilon V(D_{ab})$. Select a system of gsp-subdigraphs of the form

$$\delta_v = \{D_{iv} | D_{iv} \text{ is gsp-subdigraph, } i < v\}, \; v \varepsilon V(D_{ab}), \; v \geq 1,$$

in which all gsp-subdigraphs have the common vertex-contrabasis v, and denote by $B(\delta_v) = \{i | i \varepsilon V(D_{ab}), D_{iv} \varepsilon \delta_v\}$ the vertex-basis of δ_v.

Call δ_v proper (with respect to $\tilde{D}_{ov}$) if

$$(6) \quad \forall D^1_{i_1 v}, D^2_{i_2 v} \varepsilon \delta_v: D^1_{i_1 v} \cap D^2_{i_2 v} = \begin{cases} (\{i,v\},\emptyset) & , \; i_1 = i_2 = i \\ (\{v\},\emptyset) & , \; \text{otherwise} \end{cases}$$

$$(7) \quad \forall P_{ov} \subset D_{ab} \; \exists D_{iv} \varepsilon \delta_v :$$

$$P_{ov} = (P_{ov})_i \cup (P_{ov})^i \text{ with} \begin{cases} (P_{ov})_i \cap \delta_v \subset (B(\delta_v),\emptyset) \\ (P_{ov})^i \varepsilon P(D_{iv}) \end{cases}$$

where for a path $P_{tr} \subset D_{ab}$ the subpath of P_{tr} from t to i resp. from i to r, $i \in V(P_{tr})$, is denoted by $(P_{tr})_i$ resp. $(P_{tr})^i$. The usefulness of proper gsp-subdigraph systems is shown in

1 Theorem:

If $\delta_v = \{D_{iv}\}$ is a proper gsp-subdigraph system then

$$\Phi_{\tilde{D}_{ov}} = \max_{D_{iv} \varepsilon \delta_v} \min \{\Phi_{\tilde{D}_{oi}}, \Phi_{D_{iv}}\}$$

Proof:

Pointwise, for $\omega \in \Omega$, and for $k \in \{0,1,\dots,m\}$ one gets

$$\Phi_{\tilde{D}_{ov}}(Y(\omega)) = k \underset{(4)}{\Longrightarrow} \exists\, P^*_{ov} \in P(\tilde{D}_{ov}) \text{ with } \Phi_{P^*_{ov}}(Y(\omega)) = k$$

$$\underset{(7)}{\Longrightarrow} \exists\, D_{i^*v} \in \delta_v \text{ with } P^*_{ov} = (P^*_{ov})_{i^*} \cup (P^*_{ov})^{i^*} \text{ and } (P^*_{ov})^{i^*} \varepsilon P(D_{i^*v}),$$

but

$$\Phi_{(P^*_{ov})_{i^*}}(Y(\omega)) \geq k \underset{(4)}{\Longrightarrow} \Phi_{\tilde{D}_{oi^*}}(Y(\omega)) \geq k,$$

$$\Phi_{(P^*_{ov})^{i^*}}(Y(\omega)) \geq k \underset{(4)}{\Longrightarrow} \Phi_{D_{i^*v}}(Y(\omega)) \geq k,$$

thus, $\Phi_{\tilde{D}_{ov}}(Y(\omega)) \leq \max_{D_{iv} \varepsilon \delta_v} \{\min\{\Phi_{\tilde{D}_{oi}}(Y(\omega)), \Phi_{D_{iv}}(Y(\omega))\}\}$,

on the other hand,

$$\max_{D_{iv} \varepsilon \delta_v} \{\min\{\Phi_{\tilde{D}_{oi}}(Y(\omega)), \Phi_{D_{iv}}(Y(\omega))\}\} = k \Longrightarrow \exists\, D_{i^{**}v} \varepsilon \delta_v \text{ and } \tilde{D}_{oi^{**}}$$

with $\Phi_{\tilde{D}_{oi^{**}}}(Y(\omega)) \geq k \underset{(4)}{\Longrightarrow} \exists\, P_{oi^{**}} \varepsilon P(\tilde{D}_{oi^{**}})$ with $\Phi_{P_{oi^{**}}}(Y(\omega)) \geq k$,

$$\Phi_{D_{i^{**}v}}(Y(\omega)) \geq k \underset{(4)}{\Longrightarrow} \exists\, P_{i^{**}v} \varepsilon P(D_{i^{**}v}) \text{ with } \Phi_{P_{i^{**}v}}(Y(\omega)) \geq k,$$

but $P^{**}_{ov} = P_{oi^{**}} \cup P_{i^{**}v} \in P(\tilde{D}_{ov})$,

thus, $\Phi_{\tilde{D}_{ov}}(Y(\omega)) \geq \max_{D_{iv} \varepsilon \delta_v} \{\min\{\Phi_{\tilde{D}_{oi}}(Y(\omega)), \Phi_{D_{iv}}(Y(\omega))\}\}$.

3. Bounding distributions functions

The advantage of theorem 1 is that the determination of the reliability-behaviour of large gsp-subdigraphs $\tilde{D}_{ov}$ can be facilitated when the reliability-behaviour of certain gsp-subdigraphs $\tilde{D}_{oi}$, $i \in B(\delta_v)$, $D_{iv} \in \delta_v$, of $\tilde{D}_{ov}$ is known (For v=n=1(b) one gets the reliability measure of the underlying gsp-digraph D_{ab}.). This idea will also be used for the determination of bounding distributions.

For the stochastic dependence-structure of Y association is assumed, see BARLOW/PROSCHAN (1978), ESARY/PROSCHAN/WALKUP (1965), JOGDEO (1977), aditionally, independence for $(Y_x | x \in X_1)$, $(Y_x | x \in X_2)$ for appropriate chosen partitions X_1, X_2 of X(D) is needed.

Association is basic for reliability problems and the knowledge of some of its properties is useful for later reference. Call a random vector $Y = (Y_1, \ldots Y_\ell)$ or the set of random variables $\{Y_1, \ldots, Y_\ell\}$ associated if for every pair of functions $g_1, g_2 : \mathbb{R}^\ell \to \mathbb{R}$ which are non-decreasing in each argument and for which $Eg_1(Y)$, $Eg_2(Y)$, $Eg_1(Y)g_2(Y)$ exist

$$\operatorname{cov}(g_1(Y), g_2(Y)) \geq 0$$

holds.

Needed properties of association are:

(A.1) Independent random variables are associated.

(A.2) Non-decreasing (in each argument) functions of associated random variables are associated.

(A.3) The union of independent sets of associated random variables is associated.

(A.4) Any subset of associated random variables is associated.

(A.5) If Y is associated, so is - Y.

(A.6) If Y is associated then

$$\left.\begin{aligned} \Pr(Y \leq c) &\geq \prod_{j=1}^{q} \Pr(Y_i \leq c_i,\ i \in I_j) \\ \Pr(Y \geq c) &\geq \prod_{j=1}^{q} \Pr(Y_i \geq c_i,\ i \in I_j) \end{aligned}\right. \quad , \ c \in \mathbb{R}^\ell \ ,$$

where I_j are subsets of $I = \{1, \ldots, \ell\}$ the union of which is I.

Now, let $\delta_v = \{D_{iv}\}$ be a proper gsp-subdigraph system. Assume that for $i \in B(\delta_v)$

$$S_{\tilde{D}_{oi}} \quad , \quad S^{\tilde{D}_{oi}}$$

are given lower, upper bounding distribution functions for $F_{\tilde{D}_{oi}}$, i.e.

$$S_{\tilde{D}_{oi}}(\tau) \le F_{\tilde{D}_{oi}}(\tau) \le S^{\tilde{D}_{oi}}(\tau) \quad , \quad \tau \in \mathbb{R} ,$$

then for

(8) $$S_{\delta_v}(\tau) = \prod_{D_{iv} \in \delta_v} (1 - \overline{S}_{\tilde{D}_{oi}}(\tau)\, \overline{F}_{D_{iv}}(\tau)) \quad , \quad \tau \in \mathbb{R} ,$$

(9) $$S^{\delta_v}(\tau) = 1 - \max_{D_{iv} \in \delta_v} \{\overline{S}^{\tilde{D}_{oi}}(\tau)\, \overline{F}_{D_{iv}}(\tau)\} \quad , \quad \tau \in \mathbb{R} ,$$

with $\overline{F} = 1 - F$ for a distribution function F, one has

2 <u>Theorem</u>:

If $\delta_v = \{D_{iv}\}$ is a proper gsp-subdigraph system, if Y is associated then

(a) S_{δ_v} is lower bounding distribution function for $F_{\tilde{D}_{ov}}$

if $(Y_x | x \in X(\delta_v))$, $(Y_x | x \in \overline{X(\delta_v)})$ are independent,

(b) S^{δ_v} is upper bounding distributions function for $F_{\tilde{D}_{ov}}$

<u>Proof:</u>

(a) $$\begin{aligned} F_{\tilde{D}_{ov}}(\tau) &= \Pr(\max_{D_{iv} \in \delta_v} \{\min\{\Phi_{\tilde{D}_{oi}}, \Phi_{D_{iv}}\}\} \le \tau) \\ &\ge \prod_{D_{iv} \in \delta_v} \Pr(\min\{\Phi_{\tilde{D}_{oi}}, \Phi_{D_{iv}}\} \le \tau) \\ &= \prod_{D_{iv} \in \delta_v} (1 - \Pr(\Phi_{\tilde{D}_{oi}} > \tau,\ \Phi_{D_{iv}} > \tau)) \\ &= \prod_{D_{iv} \in \delta_v} (1 - \overline{F}_{\tilde{D}_{oi}}(\tau)\, \overline{F}_{D_{iv}}(\tau)) \\ &\ge \prod_{D_{iv} \in \delta_v} (1 - \overline{S}_{\tilde{D}_{oi}}(\tau)\, \overline{F}_{D_{iv}}(\tau)) = S_{\delta_v}(\tau), \quad \tau \in \mathbb{R} , \end{aligned}$$

where the first equality follows from theorem 1, the first inequality from properties (A.2), (A.3), (A.4), (A.6) of association, the second equality from elementary probability calculus, the third equality from the independence assumption, the last inequality from the bounding distribution property of $S_{\tilde{D}_{oi}}$. That S_{δ_v} is a distribution function is seen by checking that for the finite product expression continuity from the right and limes behaviour of the distribution functions $S_{\tilde{D}_{oi}}$, $i \in B(\delta_v)$, $F_{D_{iv}}$, $D_{iv} \in \delta_v$, is maintained.

(b) Because of

(10) $$\{\omega \mid \Phi_{\tilde{D}_{ov}}(Y(\omega)) \le \tau\} \subset \{\omega \mid \min\{\Phi_{\tilde{D}_{oi}}(Y(\omega)), \Phi_{D_{iv}}(Y(\omega))\} \le \tau\}$$

for arbitrary $D_{iv} \in \delta_v$, $\tau \in \mathbb{R}$,

one gets

$$F_{\tilde{D}_{ov}}(\tau) \le \min_{D_{iv}\in\delta_v} \{Pr(\min\{\Phi_{\tilde{D}_{oi}}, \Phi_{D_{iv}}\} \le \tau)\}$$

$$= \min_{D_{iv}\in\delta_v} \{1 - Pr(\Phi_{\tilde{D}_{oi}} > \tau, \Phi_{D_{iv}} > \tau)\}$$

$$\le 1 - \max_{D_{iv}\in\delta_v} \{\overline{F}_{\tilde{D}_{oi}}(\tau)\, \overline{F}_{D_{iv}}(\tau)\}$$

$$\le 1 - \max_{D_{iv}\in\delta_v} \{\overline{S}^{\tilde{D}_{oi}}(\tau)\, \overline{F}_{D_{iv}}(\tau)\}$$

$$= S^{\delta_v}(\tau), \quad \tau \in \mathbb{R},$$

where the first inequality follows from (10), the second inequality from properties (A.2), (A.4), (A.6) of association, the last inequality from the bounding distribution property of $S^{\tilde{D}_{oi}}$. That S^{δ_v} is a distribution function is seen by checking that for the finite maximum expression continuity from the right and limes behaviour of the distribution functions $S^{\tilde{D}_{oi}}$, $i \in B(\delta_v)$, $F_{D_{iv}}$, $D_{iv} \in \delta_v$, is maintained.

The usefulness of the bounding distribution functions (8), (9) depend on the choice of the proper gsp-subdigraph system $\delta_v = \{D_{iv}\}$ and the given bounding distribution functions $S_{\tilde{D}_{oi}}$, $S^{\tilde{D}_{oi}}$, $i \in B(\delta_v)$. Thus, the question is of interest whether a change from one proper gsp-subdigraph system to another yields improvements.

One can prove, see GAUL (1978):

If $\left\{\begin{array}{l}\delta_v = \{D_{iv}\} \\ \\ \delta'_v = \{D'_{jv}\}\end{array}\right.$ are proper gsp-subdigraph systems with $\delta_v \supset \delta'_v$ then

(11) there exists a proper gsp-subdigraph system $\delta''_v = \{D''_{qv}\}$ with

$$X(\delta''_v) = X(\delta_v),$$

$$\forall D'_{jv} \varepsilon \delta'_v \;\exists\; D''_{qv} \varepsilon \delta''_v: \quad D'_{jv} \subset D''_{qv}.$$

Using the abbreviation $\delta'_v \Subset \delta''_v$ for proper gsp-subdigraph systems fullfilling (11) the next theorem formulates sufficient conditions for the case when a change from δ'_v to δ''_v allows improvements. For its proof one needs the following

<u>Lemma:</u>

For $0 \leq \alpha \leq 1,\ 0 \leq \gamma_i \leq 1,\ i=1,\dots,\ell,$ it follows

$$\alpha(1 - \prod_{i=1}^{\ell} (1 - \gamma_i)) \leq 1 - \prod_{i=1}^{\ell} (1 - \alpha\gamma_i).$$

<u>Proof:</u>

An easy induction argument shows:
For $\ell = 1$ equality holds. Assuming that the lemma is true for arbitrary ℓ one gets

$$\alpha(1 - \prod_{i=1}^{\ell+1} (1 - \gamma_i)) = \alpha((1 - \gamma_{\ell+1})(1 - \prod_{i=1}^{\ell}(1 - \gamma_i)) + \gamma_{\ell+1})$$

$$\leq (1 - \alpha\gamma_{\ell+1})\ \alpha\ (1 - \prod_{i=1}^{\ell} (1 - \gamma_i)) + \alpha\gamma_{\ell+1}$$

$$\leq (1 - \alpha\gamma_{\ell+1})\ (1 - \prod_{i=1}^{\ell} (1 - \alpha\gamma_i)) + \alpha\gamma_{\ell+1} = 1 - \prod_{i=1}^{\ell+1}(1 - \alpha\gamma_i).$$

3 <u>Theorem:</u>

If $\left\{\begin{array}{l}\delta'_v = \{D'_{jv}\} \\ \delta''_v = \{D''_{qv}\}\end{array}\right.$ are proper gsp-subdigraph systems with $\delta'_v \Subset \delta''_v$,

if Y is associated then

(a) $S_{\delta'_v}(\tau) \le S_{\delta''_v}(\tau)$, $\tau \in \mathbb{R}$,

if $\bar{S}_{\tilde{D}_{oj}}(\tau) \ge \bar{S}_{\tilde{D}_{oq}}(\tau)\, \bar{F}_{\tilde{D}_{qj}}(\tau)$, $\tau \in \mathbb{R}$, for $\begin{cases} q \in B(\delta''_v) \\ j \in B(\delta'_v) \cap D''_{qv} \end{cases}$,

and, additionally, $(Y_x|x \in X(\delta'_v)), (Y_x|x \in X^*), (Y_x|x \in \overline{X(\delta''_v)})$ are independent where X^* is chosen s.t. $X^* \cup X(\delta'_v) = X(\delta''_v), X^* \cap X(\delta'_v) = \emptyset$,

(b) $S^{\delta'_v}(\tau) \ge S^{\delta''_v}(\tau)$, $\tau \in \mathbb{R}$,

if $\bar{S}^{\tilde{D}_{oj}}(\tau) \le \bar{S}^{\tilde{D}_{oq}}(\tau)\, \bar{F}_{\tilde{D}_{qj}}(\tau)$, $\tau \in \mathbb{R}$, for $\begin{cases} q \in B(\delta''_v) \\ j \in B(\delta'_v) \cap D''_{qv} \end{cases}$.

<u>Proof:</u>

Notice first that for arbitrary chosen $D''_{qv} \in \delta''_v$ it follows

$\delta'_v \cap D''_{qv}$ is a proper gsp-subdigraph system <u>(with respect to D''_{qv})</u>

thus,

$$\Phi_{D''_{qv}} = \max_{D'_{jv} \in \delta'_v \cap D''_{qv}} \{\min\{\Phi_{\tilde{D}_{qj}}, \Phi_{D'_{jv}}\}\}$$

by similar considerations as used in theorem 1 and

$$(12) \qquad F_{D''_{qv}}(\tau) \ge \prod_{D'_{jv} \in \delta'_v \cap D''_{qv}} (1 - \bar{F}_{\tilde{D}_{qj}}(\tau)\, \bar{F}_{D'_{jv}}(\tau)), \qquad \tau \in \mathbb{R},$$

by similar considerations as used in theorem 2(a) therefore

$$\begin{aligned} S_{\delta''_v}(\tau) &= \prod_{D''_{qv} \in \delta''_v} (1 - \bar{S}_{\tilde{D}_{oq}}(\tau)\, \bar{F}_{D''_{qv}}(\tau)) \\ &\ge \prod_{D''_{qv} \in \delta''_v} (1 - \bar{S}_{\tilde{D}_{oq}}(\tau)\, [1 - \prod_{D'_{jv} \in \delta'_v \cap D''_{qv}} (1 - \bar{F}_{\tilde{D}_{qj}}(\tau)\, \bar{F}_{D'_{jv}}(\tau))]) \\ &\ge \prod_{D''_{qv} \in \delta''_v} (\prod_{D'_{jv} \in \delta'_v \cap D''_{qv}} (1 - \bar{S}_{\tilde{D}_{oq}}(\tau)\, \bar{F}_{\tilde{D}_{qj}}(\tau)\, \bar{F}_{D'_{jv}}(\tau))) \\ &\ge \prod_{D'_{jv} \in \delta'_v} (1 - \bar{S}_{\tilde{D}_{oj}}(\tau) \bar{F}_{D'_{jv}}(\tau)) = S_{\delta'_v}(\tau), \qquad \tau \in \mathbb{R}, \end{aligned}$$

where the first inequality follows from (12), the second inequality from the lemma, the third inequality from the assumption. Thus, part (a) is proved.

The proof of part (b) is similar and omitted.

Theorems 1, 2 and 3 allow to suggest the following

Procedure:

Step v:
Choose $v \in V(D_{ab})$, $l(a) = 0 \leq v \leq n = l(b)$ (remember the ordering of the vertices), and a proper gsp-subdigraph system $\delta_v = \{D_{iv}\}$ for the vertex-basis vertices $i \in B(\delta_v)$ of which lower and upper bounding distribution functions $S_{\tilde{D}_{oi}}, S^{\tilde{D}_{oi}}$ for $F_{\tilde{D}_{oi}}$ are known (e.g. begin with $S_{\tilde{D}_{oo}}(\tau) \equiv S^{\tilde{D}_{oo}}(\tau) \equiv 1$).

Determine S_{δ_v}, S^{δ_v}.

Use these bounding distribution functions to increase v in a suitable way until $v = n = l(b)$ is reached.

4. Bounds for expectation and variance

If the determination of distribution functions or bounding distribution functions is still too difficult some moments or bounds of moments of the underlying random variables can be computed. In the special case m = 1 all needed information is yielded from the expectation $E\Phi_{\tilde{D}_{ov}}, v \in V(D_{ab})$. For the here described generalization notice that if Z is a discrete random variable with integer values from $\{0,1,\ldots,m\}$ and distribution function $F_Z(\tau)$ then

$$EZ = m - \sum_{\tau=0}^{m-1} F_Z(\tau)$$

$$EZ^2 = m - \sum_{\tau=0}^{m-1} (2\tau+1)\, F_Z(\tau)$$

holds.

Therefore, from

$$E_\ell(\Phi_{\tilde{D}_{ov}}, S^{\delta_v}) = m - \sum_{\tau=0}^{m-1} S^{\delta_v}(\tau)$$

$$E^u(\Phi_{\tilde{D}_{ov}}, S_{\delta_v}) = m - \sum_{\tau=0}^{m-1} S_{\delta_v}(\tau)$$

$$V_\ell(\Phi_{\tilde{D}_{ov}}, S^{\delta_v}) = m - \sum_{\tau=0}^{m-1} (2\tau+1)\, S^{\delta_v}(\tau)$$

$$V^u(\Phi_{\tilde{D}_{ov}}, S_{\delta_v}) = m - \sum_{\tau=0}^{m-1} (2\tau+1)\, S_{\delta_v}(\tau)$$

and

$$var_\ell(\Phi_{\tilde{D}_{ov}}, S_{\delta_v}, S^{\delta_v}) = V_\ell(\Phi_{\tilde{D}_{ov}}, S^{\delta_v}) - (E^u(\Phi_{\tilde{D}_{ov}}, S_{\delta_v}))^2$$

$$var^u(\Phi_{\tilde{D}_{ov}}, S_{\delta_v}, S^{\delta_v}) = V^u(\Phi_{\tilde{D}_{ov}}, S_{\delta_v}) - (E_\ell(\Phi_{\tilde{D}_{ov}}, S^{\delta_v}))^2$$

one gets

$$E_\ell(\Phi_{\tilde{D}_{ov}}, S^{\delta_v}) \leq E\, \Phi_{\tilde{D}_{ov}} \leq E^u(\Phi_{\tilde{D}_{ov}}, S_{\delta_v})$$

$$var_\ell(\Phi_{\tilde{D}_{ov}}, S_{\delta_v}, S^{\delta_v}) \leq var\, \Phi_{\tilde{D}_{ov}} \leq var^u(\Phi_{\tilde{D}_{ov}}, S_{\delta_v}, S^{\delta_v})$$

if the conditions of theorem 2 hold, additionally

$$E_\ell(\Phi_{\tilde{D}_{ov}}, S^{\delta'_v}) \leq E_\ell(\Phi_{\tilde{D}_{ov}}, S^{\delta''_v})$$

$$E^u(\Phi_{\tilde{D}_{ov}}, S_{\delta'_v}) \geq E^u(\Phi_{\tilde{D}_{ov}}, S_{\delta''_v})$$

and

$$var_\ell(\Phi_{\tilde{D}_{ov}}, S_{\delta'_v}, S^{\delta'_v}) \leq var_\ell(\Phi_{\tilde{D}_{ov}}, S_{\delta''_v}, S^{\delta''_v})$$

$$var^u(\Phi_{\tilde{D}_{ov}}, S_{\delta'_v}, S^{\delta'_v}) \geq var^u(\Phi_{D_{ov}}, S_{\delta''_v}, S^{\delta''_v})$$

if the conditions of theorem 3 hold.

5. Conclusion

Choosing $\delta_v = \tilde{D}_{ov}$ the described approach contains the possibility for an exact determination of $F_{\tilde{D}_{ov}}$ (and of the moments of $\Phi_{\tilde{D}_{ov}}$), $v \epsilon V(D_{ab})$. For large systems, however, computations of this kind can become difficult, thus a sequential determination of bounding distributions functions (and of bounds for the moments of $\Phi_{\tilde{D}_{ov}}$) according to a decomposition in terms of a proper gsp-subdigraph systems is of interest. Depending on the choice of the proper gsp-subdigraph systems improvements are possible.

References

(1) BARLOW, R.E./F. PROSCHAN (1978): Statistische Theorie der Zuverlässigkeit, Verlag H. Deutsch.

(2) BARLOW, R.E./A.S. WU (1978): Coherent Systems with Multi-State Components, Math. Operat. Res. 3, 275 - 281.

(3) EL-NEWEIHI, E./F. PROSCHAN (1980): Multistate Reliability Models: A Survey, in KRISHNAIAH, P.R. (Ed.): Multivariate Analysis-V, North-Holland Publishing Company, 523 - 541.

(4) EL-NEWEIHI, E./F. PROSCHAN/J. SETHURAMAN (1978): Multistate Coherent Systems, J. Appl. Prob. 15, 675 - 688.

(5) ESARY, J.D./F. PROSCHAN/D.W. WALKUP (1967): Association of Random Variables, with Applications, Ann. Math. Statist. 38, 1466 - 1474.

(6) FARDIS, M.N./C.A. CORNELL (1981): Analysis of Coherent Multistate Systems, IEEE Transactions on Reliability, R-30, 117 - 122.

(7) FRANK, O./W. GAUL (1982): On Reliability in Stochastic Graphs, Networks 12, 119 - 126.

(8) GAEDE, K.W. (1977): Zuverlässigkeit: Mathematische Modelle, Verlag C. Hanser.

(9) GAUL, W. (1978): Some Structural Properties of Project Digraphs, J. Comb., Inf. & Syst. Sc. 3, 217 - 222.

(10) GAUL, W. (1983): Reliability-Estimation in Stochastic Graphs with Time-Associated Arc-Set Reliability Performance Processes, Diskussionspapier Nr. 56, Institut für Entscheidungstheorie und Unternehmensforschung, Universität Karlsruhe (TH).

(11) GILBERT, E.N. (1959): Random Graphs, Ann. Math. Statist. 30, 1141 - 1144.

(12) GRIFFITH, W.S. (1980): Multistate Reliability Models, J. Appl. Prob. 17, 735 - 744.

(13) HARARY, F./F.Z. NORMAN/D. CARTWRIGHT (1965): Structural Models: An Introduction to the Theory of Directed Graphs, Wiley.

(14) HARTUNG, J./B.ELPELT/K.H. KLÖSENER (1982): Statistik: Lehr- und Handbuch der angewandten Statistik, Kap. XIII, Oldenbourg Verlag.

(15) JOGDEO, K. (1977): Association and Probability Inequalities, Ann. Statist. 5, 495 - 504.

(16) LEE, C.Y. (1955): Analysis of Switching Networks, Bell System Techn. J. 34, 1287 - 1315.

(17) MOORE, E.F./C.E. SHANNON (1956): Reliable Circuits Using Less Reliable Relays, J. of the Franklin Institute 262, 191 - 208 and 281 - 297.

(18) ROSS, S. (1979): Mulitvalued State Component Systems, Ann. Prob. 7, 379 - 383.

(19) SATYANARAYANA, A./A. PRABHAKAR (1978): New Topological Formula and Rapid Algorithm for Reliability Analysis of Complex Networks, IEEE Transactions on Reliability, R-27, 82 - 100.

(20) WILKOV, R.S. (1972): Analysis and Design of Reliable Computer Networks, IEEE Transactions on Communications 20, 660 - 678.

IMPROVED BOUNDS FOR THE S_n/n PROBLEM

D. Kadelka
Institut für Mathematische Statistik der Universität Karlsruhe
Englerstraße, D-7500 Karlsruhe 1

and

N. Schmitz
Institut für Mathematische Statistik der Universität Münster
Einsteinstraße 62, D-4400 Münster

1. Introduction

A famous problem of optimal stopping is the "S_n/n problem":

(i) It is very simple to be formulated: Let $(X_n)_{n\in\mathbb{N}}$ be a sequence of iid random variables on a probability space $(\Omega,\mathcal{S},P)$ such that $P(X_1=1) = P(X_1=-1) = {}^1/_2$ and let $S_n := \sum_{i=1}^{n} X_i$. One observes the sequence $(X_n)_{n\in\mathbb{N}}$ term by term and can decide to stop at any time point; when stopping with X_n one receives the reward S_n/n. What stopping rule will maximize the expected reward?

(ii) The problem has an intuitive interpretation and obvious generalizations.

(iii) Even this simple problem is partially unsolved e.g. neither the exact value V^* nor an explicit optimal stopping time are known.

Obviously it is impossible to get an expected reward >1; on the other hand Bellman and Dreyfus obtained by computer calculations - namely solving a backward induction with horizon 1000 (see [C/R]) - as lower bound $V^* \geq 0.5850$. Chow and Robbins [C/R] were able to show that $V^* < 0.98$.

The investigations during the attempts to solve the S_n/n problem have led to considerable progress in the general theory of optimal stopping (see e.g. [C/R/S], Ch. 4.7, [Si], [Sp], [K1], [K2], [Dv], [Da], [T/B/O], [M/S]).

Our goal is to give - in a more general context - an improvement of the crude estimation

(1) $$0.5850 \leq V^* < 0.98$$

(which shows that the lower bound is, as it might be expected, rather good).

2. General results

Let $(X_n)_{n\in\mathbb{N}}$ be a sequence of non-degenerate iid real-valued bounded random variables, in particular $M:=\text{ess sup } X_1<\infty$, (for the general propositions (2.1)-(2.3) it would be sufficient to assume, that the X_n are real-valued with $E|X_1|^\beta<\infty$ for some $\beta>1$) and

$$S_n:=\sum_{i=1}^{n} X_i \quad \forall n\in\mathbb{N}, \quad S_0:=0, \quad 0/0:=0.$$

Let T be the set of all stopping times τ (i.e. $\tau: (\Omega,\mathcal{S},P) \longrightarrow (\overline{\mathbb{N}}_0, P(\overline{\mathbb{N}}_0))$ s.t. $\{\tau=n\}\in\mathcal{S}_n:=\sigma(X_1,\dots,X_n)$ for all $n\in\mathbb{N}_0$ and $P(\tau<\infty)=1$; clearly $\mathcal{S}_0=\{\emptyset,\Omega\}$)). For $n\in\mathbb{N}$, $s\in\mathbb{R}$ and $\tau\in T$ let

$$V_n(s):= \sup_{\tau\in T} E\,\frac{s+S_\tau}{n+\tau}$$

$$V(\tau):=ES_\tau/\tau$$

and

(*) $$V^*:=V_0(0):=\sup_{\tau\in T} V(\tau).$$

Each V_n is isotonic and convex. From [Sh], ch.2 and [C/R/S], Th.4.11 (resp. [Da] for the general case) one obtains

(2.1) For the problem (*) of optimal stopping there exists an optimal stopping rule τ^*, i.e. a $\tau^*\in T$ such that $V(\tau^*) = V^*$.

(2.2) (Forward induction)
$V_n(s) = \max\{s/n, EV_{n+1}(s+X_1)\}$, $n\in\mathbb{N}_0$, $s\in\mathbb{R}$ (with $s=0$ if $n=0$).

(2.3) τ^* from (2.1) may be chosen as

$$\tau^*=\inf\{n\in\mathbb{N}_0: S_n/n = V_n(S_n)\} \text{ with } \inf\emptyset:=\infty.$$

Thus it is optimal to stop, if $s_n/n \geq EV_{n+1}(s_n+X_1)$.
In particular the problem is "in principle" solved; moreover it is known (see [Dv], [Sp]) that for $EX_1=0$, Var $X_1=1$ the "bounds" of τ^* grow as $\sqrt{n}$. But these results are not sufficient to yield the (numerical) value or an explicit optimal stopping rule.

Therefore it seems reasonable to "approximate" the (infinite) problem by problems with bounded stopping rules which may - at least in principle - be solved by backward induction.

3. An improved upper bound for the S_n/n problem using the method of Chow/Robbins

Let for $P(X_1=1) = P(X_1=-1) = {}^1/_2$, $n \in \mathbb{N}_0$ and $N \in \mathbb{N}$

$$T^{(N)} := \{\tau \in T:\ 0 \leq \tau \leq N\},$$

$$V_n^N(s) := \sup_{\tau \in T^{(N)}} E\left(\frac{(s+S_\tau)^+}{n+\tau}\right).$$

Then there exists (see [C/R]) a minimal optimal stopping rule $\tau_{s,n}^{N,*} \in T^{(N)}$ which may be determined in the usual way:

$$\gamma_N^N(s,n) := \frac{(s+S_N)^+}{n+N}$$

$$\gamma_m^N(s,n) := \max\left\{\frac{(s+S_m)^+}{n+m},\ E(\gamma_{m+1}^N(s,n) \mid S_m)\right\}, \quad 0 \leq m \leq N-1$$

$$\tau_{s,n}^{N,*} = \inf\left\{m \in \mathbb{N}_0:\ \frac{(s+S_m)^+}{n+m} = \gamma_m^N(s,n)\right\} \quad (\leq N).$$

The connection with the initial problem is given by

$$V_n(s) = \lim_{N \to \infty} V_n^N(s).$$

Using the constants $b_n^N(s)$, $a_n^N(s)$ and $a_n(s)$ as defined by Chow/Robbins [C/R] one obtains

(3.1) $$\tau_{s,n}^{N,*} = \inf\{m \leq N:\ a_{n+m}^{n+N}(s+S_m) = 0\}$$

(3.2) $$a_N^N(s) = 0 \qquad \forall s \in \mathbb{Z}$$

$$a_n^N(s) = \left[\frac{1}{2}\, a_{n+1}^N(s+1) + \frac{1}{2}\, a_{n+1}^N(s-1) + \right.$$

$$\left. + \frac{1}{2}\, \frac{(s+1)^+}{n+1} + \frac{1}{2}\, \frac{(s-1)^+}{n+1} - \frac{s^+}{n}\right]^+$$

(3.3) $$a_n(s) = \lim_{N \to \infty} a_n^N(s).$$

(3.4) $$V_n(s) = \max\left(\frac{1}{2}\, a_{n+1}(s+1) + \frac{1}{2}\, a_{n+1}(s-1) + \frac{(s+1)^+}{2(n+1)} + \frac{(s-1)^+}{2(n+1)},\ \frac{s^+}{n}\right),$$

in particular

$$V^* = V_0(0) = \frac{1}{2} + \frac{1}{2}\, a_1(-1).$$

Using (3.2) one obtains

$$a_n^N(s) \le \frac{1}{2}\, a_{n+1}^N(s+1) + \frac{1}{2}\, a_{n+1}^N(s-1) \quad \text{for } s \neq 0,$$

$$a_n^N(0) = \frac{1}{2}\, a_{n+1}^N(1) + \frac{1}{2}\, a_{n+1}^N(-1) + \frac{1}{2(n+1)},$$

hence

$$\begin{aligned} a_1^N(-1) &= \frac{1}{2}(a_2^N(0) + a_2^N(-2)) = \frac{1}{4}(a_3^N(1) + 2a_3^N(-1) + a_3^N(-3) + \frac{1}{3}) \\ &\le \dots \\ &\le \sum_{n=1}^{[(N-1)/2]} \binom{2n-1}{n-1} \left(\frac{1}{4}\right)^n \frac{1}{2n+1} \end{aligned}$$

and therefore ([Ku])

$$\begin{aligned} a_1(-1) &\le \sum_{n=1}^{\infty} \binom{2n-1}{n-1} \left(\frac{1}{4}\right)^n \frac{1}{2n+1} \\ &= \frac{1}{4}\left(\sum_{n=0}^{\infty} \frac{(2n)!}{n!(n+1)!} \left(\frac{1}{4}\right)^n - 2 \sum_{n=0}^{\infty} \frac{1}{2n+3} \frac{(2n)!}{n!(n+1)!} \left(\frac{1}{4}\right)^n\right). \end{aligned}$$

Remembering our forefathers' knowledge on hypergeometric resp. elliptic functions and special series one finds

$$\begin{aligned} \sum_{n=1}^{\infty} \binom{2n-1}{n-1} \left(\frac{1}{4}\right)^n \frac{1}{2n+1} &= \sum_{n=1}^{\infty} \frac{1}{2} \frac{((0.5)_n)^2}{n!(1.5)_n} = \\ &= \frac{1}{2}\left(\frac{\Gamma(1.5)\Gamma(0.5)}{\Gamma(1)\Gamma(1)} - 1\right) \quad \text{according to [A/S] 15.1.20,} \end{aligned}$$

respectively

$$\sum_{n=0}^{\infty} \frac{(2n)!}{n!(n+1)!} \left(\frac{1}{4}\right)^n = 2 \qquad \text{according to [Ha], 5.24.15}$$

$$\sum_{n=0}^{\infty} \frac{1}{2n+3} \frac{(2n)!}{n!(n+1)!} \left(\frac{1}{4}\right)^n = 2\left(1 - \frac{\pi}{4}\right) \quad \text{according to [A/H] 6.915(2),}$$

thus $$a_1(-1) \le \frac{\pi}{4} - \frac{1}{2}$$

i.e. using (3.4)

(2) $$0.5850 \le V^* \le \frac{1}{4} + \frac{\pi}{8} < 0.6427 \qquad \text{([Ku]).}$$

By a more detailed discussion of the $a_n^N(s)$ the upper bound can be further (numerically) improved; e.g.

(i) Since $\frac{1}{2}\, a_{n+1}^N(0) \ge \frac{1}{4} \frac{1}{n+2} > \frac{1}{n(n+1)}$ for $5 \le n < N$,

for $a_n^N(1) = [\frac{1}{2}\, a_{n+1}^N(2) + \frac{1}{2}\, a_{n+1}^N(0) - \frac{1}{n(n+1)}]^+$ the index + may be omitted.

(ii) Since $a_4^N(0) = \frac{1}{2} a_5^N(1) + \frac{1}{2} a_5^N(-1) + \frac{1}{10} \geq \frac{1}{840} + \frac{1}{56} + \frac{1}{10}$,

$a_3^N(1) \leq \frac{1}{2} a_4^N(2) + \frac{1}{2} a_4^N(0) - 0.0595$

etc. Using (i) and (ii) one obtains e.g.

(3) $$0.5850 \leq V^* \leq 0.6278,$$

but here seem to be "natural" limits for further improvements.

4. Bounds obtained by estimating hitting probabilities

Having in mind the difficulties of this special approach, the first author changed over to the following general method for the model in 2. starting from (2.2) and (2.3): Let $N \in \mathbb{N}$ be fixed and assume that $V_N^l, V_N^u: \mathbb{R} \longrightarrow \mathbb{R}$ are measurable, locally bounded functions with

$$V_N^l \leq V_N \leq V_N^u .$$

Define inductively for $i \in \{l,u\}$, $n<N$, $s \in \mathbb{R}$

(4.0) $$V_n^i(s) := \max\{s/n, EV_{n+1}^i(s+X_1)\}.$$

Then each V_n^i is measurable, and since X_1 is bounded, locally bounded again. By induction we get for $n \leq N$

(4.1) $$V_n^l \leq V_n \leq V_n^u,$$

in particular

(4.1)' $$V_0^l(0) \leq V^* \leq V_0^u(0) .$$

Let further for $i \in \{l,u\}$

$$\tau^{*i} := \inf\{n<N: S_n/n = V_n^i(S_n)\}$$

with $\inf \emptyset := N$. Then from (4.1) and (2.3) and $V_n^i(s) \geq s/n$

(4.2) $$\tau^{*l} \leq \min\{N, \tau^*\} \leq \tau^{*u}.$$

We now want to determine practicable lower and upper bounds V_N^l, resp. V_N^u. The case of lower bound is simple (cf.[C/R/S]). Observe that by the law of iterated logarithm

$$P((s+S_n)/(N+n) \geq EX_1 \text{ for some } n \in \mathbb{N}_0) = 1,$$

thus $\tau_0 := \inf\{n \in \mathbb{N}_0: (s+S_n)/(N+n) \geq \max(s/N, EX_1)\}$ is in T. Therefore we choose

$$V_N^1(s) := \max\{s/N,\ EX_1\} \leq V_N(s).$$

To get an upper bound we have to estimate $E\,\frac{s+S_\tau}{N+\tau}$ from above. Let

$$Y_s := \sup_{n\in\mathbb{N}_0} \frac{s+S_n}{N+n}.$$

Then $(s+S_\tau)/(N+\tau) \leq Y_s$ a.e., thus $V_N(s) \leq EY_s$. Observing that $Y_s \geq y_s := \max(s/N,\ EX_1)$ a.e. we get (cf. [Hi], Lemma 25.3)

$$EY_s = E(Y_s - y_s) + y_s = y_s + \int_0^\infty P(Y_s - y_s > t)\,dt$$

$$= y_s + \int_{(y_s;M)} P(Y_s > t)\,dt, \text{ if } s/N \leq M.$$

Clearly this is true even if $s/N > M$ (then $(y_s;M) = \emptyset$). We now estimate $P(Y_s > t)$ from above. Let $t \in (y_s;M)$. We get

$$P(Y_s > t) = P\Big(\sup_{n\in\mathbb{N}_0} \frac{s+S_n}{N+n} > t\Big) = P\Big(\sup_{n\in\mathbb{N}_0} (S_n - nt) > Nt - s\Big).$$

Put $Z_n(t) := X_n - t$, $S_n'(t) := \sum_1^n Z_i(t) = S_n - nt$ and $d_s(t) := Nt - s$. Let for $u \in \mathbb{R}$

$$\varphi_t(u) := \ln Ee^{uZ_1(t)} = \ln E(e^{uX_1}) - ut.$$

Since X_1 is bounded, φ_t is finite. Further $\varphi_t(0) = 0$

$$\varphi_t'(0) = EZ_1(t) = EX_1 - t < 0$$

and φ_t is strictly convex (cf. [Nv], IV.4), and $\lim_{u\to\infty} \varphi_t(u) = \infty$, since

$$\varphi_t(u) \geq \ln E(1_{\{X_1>t\}} e^{u(X_1-t)}) \uparrow \ln E(\infty \cdot 1_{\{X_1>t\}}) = \infty$$

and $P(X_1 > t) > 0$.

Thus there is exactly one $u(t) > 0$ with $\varphi_t(u(t)) = 0$ and then $\varphi_t'(u(t)) > 0$. By Wald's identity ([Nv], IV.4.19) with

$$\nu_t := \inf\{n \in \mathbb{N}_0 :\ S_n'(t) \geq Nt - s\}$$

we get

$$1 = \int_{[\nu_t<\infty]} \exp(u(t) S'_{\nu_t}(t))\,dP \geq P(\nu_t < \infty) \cdot \exp(u(t) d_s(t)) \geq$$

$$\geq P\Big(\sup_{n\in\mathbb{N}_0} S_n'(t) > d_s(t)\Big) \exp(u(t) d_s(t)),$$

since $\{\sup_{n\in\mathbb{N}} S_n'(t) > d_s(t)\} \subseteq \{\nu_t < \infty\}$.

Thus for $t \in (y_s; M)$

$$P(Y_s > t) = P(\sup_{n \in \mathbb{N}} S_n'(t) > d_s(t)) \leq \exp(-u(t) \cdot d_s(t)). \tag{4.3}$$

Clearly u is measurable (its graph is measurable); thus from (4.3) we get

Lemma 1: Let $u\colon (EX_1; M) \longrightarrow (0;\infty)$ be defined by $Ee^{u(t)X_1} = e^{tu(t)}$. Then u is measurable and with $y_s := \max(EX_1, s/N)$

$$V_N(s) \leq V_N^u(s) := y_s + \int_{(y_s;M)} \exp[-u(t)\cdot(Nt-s)]dt .$$

Remark:
It is easy to show (by dominated convergence) that $V_N^u(s) \longrightarrow y_s = V_N^{\ell}(s)$ uniformly in s as $N \longrightarrow \infty$. Thus, if $N \longrightarrow \infty$, both $V_0^{\ell}(0)$ and $V_0^u(0)$ in (4.1)' converge to V^*.

5. Improved bounds for the S_n/n problem

We now apply the results of section 4 to the S_n/n stopping problem of the introduction. Here $P(X_1=1) = P(X_1=-1) = 1/2$, hence $M=1$, $EX_1=0$ and $y_s=s^+/N$. Lemma 1 reduces to

Corollary 2: Let $u\colon (0;1) \longrightarrow (0;\infty)$ be defined by

$$\cosh u(t) = e^{tu(t)}$$

for each t. Then for $s = -N, -N+2, \ldots, N$

$$V_N(s) \leq V_N^u(s) = s^+/N + \int_{s^+/N}^{1} e^{-u(t)(Nt-s)}dt. \tag{5.1}$$

The equation $\cosh u(t) = e^{tu(t)}$ can be solved numerically. It turns out that $t \longrightarrow \rho(t) := e^{-u(t)}$ is decreasing and convex with $\rho(0+) = 1$ and $\rho(1-) = 0$. Thus ρ can be easily estimated from above by a piecewise linear function ρ^*. This has been implemented in a program.
Estimating $s^+/N + \int_{s^+/N}^{1} \rho^*(t)^{Nt-s}dt \geq V_N^u(s)$ from above, we got upper bounds $V_N^{u*}(s)$. Similarly, the lower bounds $V_N^{\ell}(s) = s^+/N$ were implemented. Using (4.0) we got from (4.1)' with N = 8000

$$0.585736 \leq V^* \leq 0.586098. \tag{4}$$

Further using (4.2) bounds τ^{*l} and τ^{*u} for the optimal stopping time τ^* have been calculated. Below is a table of "control limits" c_n^* for $1 \le n \le 100$. τ^* is then given by

$$\tau^* = \inf\{n \in \mathbb{N}: S_n > c_n^*\},$$

i.e. it is optimal to stop at n at the latest, if the number of successes s_n is larger than the control limit c_n^*. For n=28, 79 and 100 these control limits could not be determined exactly.

Table of control limits c_n^*

n	1	2	3	4	5	6	7	8	9	0
	-1	0	1	0	1	0	1	0	1	2
10	1	2	1	2	1	2	3	2	3	2
20	3	2	3	2	3	2	3	2..4	3	4
30	3	4	3	4	3	4	3	4	3	4
40	3	4	5	4	5	4	5	4	5	4
50	5	4	5	4	5	4	5	4	5	6
60	5	6	5	6	5	6	5	6	5	6
70	5	6	5	6	5	6	5	6	5..7	6
80	7	6	7	6	7	6	7	6	7	6
90	7	6	7	6	7	6	7	6	7	6..8

In particular, if $X_1 = -1$, we never stop before n=4.

6. References

[A/H] Adams, E. and R. Hippisley: Smithonian Mathematical Formulae and Tables of Elliptic Functions. Washington 1947 (2nd ed.).

[A/S] Abramowitz, M., I. Stegun: Handbook of Mathematical Functions. Dover, N.Y. 1965.

[C/R] Chow, Y.S. and H. Robbins: On optimal stopping rules for S_n/n. Illinois J. Math. 9(1965), 444-454

[C/R/S] Chow, Y.S., H. Robbins and D. Siegmund: Great Expectations: The Theory of Optimal Stopping. Houghton Mifflin, Boston 1971.

[Da] Davis, B.: Moments of random walk having infinite variance and the existence of certain optimal stopping rules for S_n/n. Illinois J. Math. 17(1973), 75-81.

[Dv] Dvoretzky, A.: Existence and properties of certain optimal stopping rules. Proc. Fifth Berkeley Symp. Math. Statistics and Prob. (1967), Vol. I, 441-452.

[Ha] Hansen, E.: A Table of Series and Products. Prentice Hall, 1975.

[Hi] Hinderer, K.: Grundbegriffe der Wahrscheinlichkeitstheorie. Springer, Berlin u.a.; 1972.

[K1] Klass, M.: Properties of optimal extended-valued stopping rules for S_n/n. Ann. Prob. 1(1973), 719-757.

[K2] Klass, M.: A survey of the S_n/n problem. Statistical Inference and Related Topics (ed. M. Puri), Academic Press, N.Y. (1975), 179-201.

[Ku] Kuhlmann, M.: Optimale Stopregeln für Durchschnittsauszahlungen. Unpublished Diplomarbeit Münster, 1982.

[M/S] McCabe, B. and L. Shepp: On the supremum of S_n/n. Ann. Math. Stat. 41(1970), 2166-2168.

[Nv] Neveu, J.: Dicrete-Parameter Martingales. North-Holland, Amsterdam 1975.

[Sp] Shepp, L.: Explicit solutions to some problems of optimal stopping. Ann. Math. Stat. 40(1969), 993-1o1o.

[Sh] Shiryayev, A.: Optimal Stopping Rules. Springer, Berlin u.a. 1978.

[Si] Siegmund, D.: Some problems in the theory of optimal stopping rules. Ann. Math. Stat. 38(1967), 1627-1640.

[T/B/O] Thompson, M., A. Basu and W. Owen: On the existence of the optimal stopping rule in the S_n/n problem where the second moment is infinite.
Ann. Math. Stat. 42(1971), 1936-1942.

SELECTION OF SOLUTIONS BY ALGORITHMS

Peter Kosmol
Christian-Albrechts-Universität
Kiel

Suppose you have chosen a method for the solution of a problem which may have more than one solution, then you have made automatically a selection amongst possible solutions. If we replace a problem by a sequence of approximating problems, whose solutions can be interpreted as solutions of variational inequalities (optimization problems, equations, saddle- and equilibrium point problems), then the solutions we obtain, are the solutions of a two stage variational inequality. The inherent difficulty consists in finding the appropriate variational inequality. The numerical behaviour of the method depends on this "second stage inequality".

It is a similar approach as used in probability theory for the central limit theorem, where the normal distribution describes the "second stage". Firstly, we want to give some examples.

E1) A problem of Polya.
Polya proved that every cluster point of the sequence of best L_p-approximations ($p \in \mathbb{N}$) of an element in C[a,b] with respect to a finite-dimensional subspace V of C[a,b] is always a best Chebyshev-approximation. He asked: Is the sequence always convergent? After more than 40 years J. Descloux 1963 ([1]) constructed a counterexample. For the analogous question in $\mathbb{R}^n$ he gives a positive answer: The sequence converges to the strict approximation introduced by J. Rice. In the case p=1 there is a positive answer for arbitrary probability spaces (T,Σ,μ) and finite dimensional convex subsets V of $L_1(\mu)$. For $p \to 1$ the minimal solutions converge to the minimal L_1-solution that has maximal entropy, i.e. maximizes the function ([3])

$$g(v) := - \int_T |v| \log |v| d\mu \ .$$

The best L_1-approximation with respect to the 1-dimensional subspace of the constant functions is a median. Landers and Rogge ([7]) suggested to call the limit of the L_p-approximations $(p \to 1)$ the natural median.

E2) Is it possible to obtain similar results for approximation solutions of equations or saddle point problems?

E3) So, e.g. the solutions of the system of equations $Ax = b$ with

$$A = \begin{pmatrix} 1 & 1 \\ 2 & 2 \end{pmatrix} \text{ and } b = (1,2)^T \text{ are } \{(r,1-r) \mid r \in \mathbb{R}\}$$

The regularization $(A + \alpha I)x = b$ by the unit matrix I and $\alpha \in \mathbb{R}_+ \setminus \{0\}$ gives an unique solution $(\frac{1}{3+\alpha}, \frac{2}{3+\alpha})^T$ that converges to $(\frac{1}{3}, \frac{2}{3})^T$ for $\alpha \to 0$. What is the relation of the vector $(\frac{1}{3}, \frac{2}{3})$ and the data (A,b,I)?

E4) There are even problems whose "solutions" cannot be interpreted but as the limit of the sequence of solutions for approximating problems. An interesting example is the well-known problem from optics (cf. books for calculus of variations):

minimize $f(y) := \int_0^a \frac{\sqrt{1+\dot{y}^2(t)}}{y(t)} dt$ subject to $y \in C^1(0,a]$, $y(0)=0, y(a)=b$, $y \geq 0$. It is obvious that this problem cannot have a minimal solution in the usual sense, since the function f becomes ∞ for all feasible points, because:

$$\int_0^a \frac{\sqrt{1+\dot{y}^2}}{y} \geq \int_0^a \frac{\dot{y}}{y} = \ln y \Big|_{0+}^{a} = \infty .$$

1. Stability for variational inequalities

Let X be a topological space and $\varphi : X \times X \to \mathbb{R}$.

Def. 1. Sets of solutions of variational inequalities

$$S_1(\varphi,X) := \{x \in X \mid \varphi(x,y) \geq 0 \quad \text{for all } y \in X\}$$
$$S_2(\varphi,X) := \{x \in X \mid \varphi(y,x) \leq 0 \quad \text{for all } y \in X\}$$

Def. 2. Lower semi continuous convergence

The sequence of functions $(f_n : X \to \mathbb{R})_{n \in \mathbb{N}}$ is called lower semicontinuous (resp. upper semi continuous) convergent to $f : X \to \overline{\mathbb{R}}$ if (f_n) converges pointwise to f and for every convergent sequence (x_n) with $\lim x_n = x$ we have

$$\underline{\lim}_{n\to\infty} f_n(x_n) \geq f(x) \qquad (\text{resp. } \overline{\lim}_{n\to\infty} f_n(x_n) \leq f(x)).$$

(notation: l.s.c.-convergence).

Def. 3. Kuratowski-convergence of sets

Let $(M_n)_{n \in \mathbb{N}}$ be a sequence of subsets of X. Then we denote

$$\overline{\lim_{n \in \mathbb{N}}}\, M_n := \{y \in X \mid k \in \mathbb{N},\ n_k \in \mathbb{N},\ n_k < n_{k+1},\ x_{n_k} \in M_{n_k},\ \lim_k x_{n_k} = y\}$$

$$\underline{\lim_{n \in \mathbb{N}}}\, M_n := \{y \in X \mid \exists n_o \in \mathbb{N},\ \forall n \geq n_o : y_n \in M_n \text{ and } \lim_n y_n = y\}$$

We say that $(M_n)_{n \in \mathbb{N}}$ converges to M if

$$\overline{\lim}\, M_n = \underline{\lim}\, M_n = M \neq \emptyset$$

(notation: $M = \lim M_n$).

Proposition 1: Let $(\varphi_n : X \times X \to \mathbb{R})_{n \in \mathbb{N}}$ be a sequence of functions that converges l.s.c. (resp. u.s.c.) to $\varphi_o : X \times X \to \mathbb{R}$ and let $(C_n)_{n \in \mathbb{N}}$ be a sequence of subsets of X that converge to C_o. Then we have

$$\overline{\lim_{n \in \mathbb{N}}}\, S_1(\varphi_n, C_n) \subset S_1(\varphi_o, C_o)$$

(resp. $\overline{\lim}\, S_2(\varphi_n, C_n) \subset S_2(\varphi_o, C_o)$).

Proof: Let $x_{n_k} \in S_1(\varphi_{n_k}, C_{n_k})$ and $x_{n_k} \xrightarrow[k \to \infty]{} \bar{x}$. For each $y \in C$ there is by definition 3 a sequence (y_n) that converges to y and $y_n \in C_n$ for $n \geq n_o$. Thus

$$\varphi_{n_k}(x_{n_k}, y_{n_k}) \geq 0.$$

By lower semi continuous convergence we get

$$\varphi_o(\bar{x}, y) \geq 0$$

i.e. $\bar{x} \in S_1(\varphi_o, C_o)$.

Corollary. Let $(\varphi_n : X \times X \to \mathbb{R})_{n \in \mathbb{N}}$ be a monotone sequence of l.s.c. functions that converges pointwise to a l.s.c. function φ_o and $\lim_{n \in \mathbb{N}} C_n = C_o$. Then we have

$$\overline{\lim_{n \in \mathbb{N}}}\, S_1(\varphi_n, C_n) \subset S_1(\varphi_o, C_o).$$

Proof: By ([5]) the convergence is l.s.c.

Remark: If we have for all $n \in \mathbb{N}$ that $C_n = C_o$ then it suffices to assume l.s.c. convergence for all $x \in X$ of $\varphi_n(\cdot,x)$ to $\varphi(\cdot,x)$. For this we use the notation 1 - l.s.c. convergence.
The following generalization of the principle of uniform boundedness for convex-concave and componentwise convex continuous operators helps to check the assumption of Proposition 1.

Def.: A family F of convex cones in a normed space Y is called uniformly normal if the union

$$\bigcup_{C \in F} \{(B+C) \cap (B-C)\}$$

is bounded where B is the unit ball in Y.

THEOREM 2: Let X_j, $j=1,\dots,n$ be Banach spaces and let U_j, $j=1,\dots,n$ be an open, convex subset of X_j. Let Y be a normed space that contains a uniformly normal family $\{C_{ij} \mid i \in I,\ j \in \{1,\dots,n\}\}$, (I arbitrary index set) of convex cones.
Moreover, in the set $F = \{A_i : U_1 \times \dots \times U_n \to Y\}_{i \in I}$ of operators let each component A_{ij} be C_{ij}-convex continuous and let the family $\{A_i\}_{i \in I}$ be pointwise norm-bounded. Then every point in $U_1 \times \dots \times U_n$ has a neighbourhood on which $\{A_i\}_{i \in I}$ is uniformly bounded and equi-Lipschitzian.

Proof: We prove the theorem by induction. For $n = 1$ it is the Theorem 1 of [4]. Suppose now that we have shown the result for n-1. For uniform boundedness on a neighbourhood of a point $U := U_1 \times \dots \times U_n$ it suffices to show:
For all sequences $x_k = (x_{k,1},\dots,x_{k,n})_{k \in \mathbb{N}}$ in U that converge to $\bar{x} = (\bar{x}_1,\dots,\bar{x}_n)$ and all sequences $(A_k)_{k \in \mathbb{N}}$ in F $(\|A_k(x_k)\|)_{k \in \mathbb{N}}$ is bounded.
The norm in $X_1 \times \dots \times X_n$ is given by $\|\cdot\|_{X_1} + \dots + \|\cdot\|_{X_n}$. For all $z \in \overset{\smile}{U} := U_1 \times \dots \times U_{n-1}$ $\{A_k(z,\cdot) \mid k \in \mathbb{N}\}$ is pointwise bounded and by [4] equicontinuous in $\bar{x}_n$. Because of $x_{k,n} \xrightarrow[k\to\infty]{} \bar{x}_n$

(1) $$\{A_k(z,x_{k,n})\}_{k \in \mathbb{N}}$$

is bounded for all $z \in \overleftarrow{U}$, i.e. the family $\{A_k(\cdot, x_{k,n})\}_{k \in \mathbb{N}}$ is pointwise bounded and by induction hypothesis equicontinuous in $(\overline{x}_1, \ldots, \overline{x}_{n-1})$. Therefore we have because of

$$(x_{k,1}, \ldots, x_{k,n-1}) \xrightarrow[k\to\infty]{} (\overline{x}_1, \ldots, \overline{x}_{k-1})$$

that

$$A_k(x_{k,1}, \ldots, x_{k,n}) - A_k(\overline{x}_1, \ldots, \overline{x}_{n-1}, x_{k,n}) \xrightarrow[k\to\infty]{} 0.$$

By (1) follows the case of uniform boundedness. By this there are open neighbourhoods V_j in U_j, $j=1,\ldots n$, and $\lambda \in \mathbb{R}$ such that for all $v_j \in V_j$ and all $A \in F$ we have

$$\| A(v_1, \ldots, v_n) \| \leq \lambda .$$

For $\hat{U} = V_1 \times \ldots \times V_{n-1}$ we consider the family

$$\{A(\cdot, v) : \hat{U} \to Y \mid A \in F,\ v \in V_n\}$$

It is pointwise bounded. For a $x_o \in \hat{U}$ there is by induction hypothesis a neighbourhood $W \subset \hat{U}$ of x_o and $\alpha_1 \in \mathbb{R}_+$ such that for all $u_1, u_2 \in W$ and for all $v \in V_n$ we have

$$\|A(u_1, v) - A(u_2, v)\| \leq \alpha_1 \|u_1 - u_2\| .$$

In the same way we conclude that the set $\{A(w, \cdot) : V_n \to Y \mid w \in V_1, \ldots \times V_{n-1}, A \in F\}$ is pointwise bounded and by [4] there is a $\overleftarrow{V} \subset V_n$ and $\alpha_2 \in \mathbb{R}_+$ such that for all $v_1, v_2 \in \overleftarrow{V}$ and $u \in \hat{U}$

$$\|A(u, v_1) - A(u, v_2)\| \leq \alpha_2 \|v_1 - v_2\| .$$

For all $(x,y), (u,v) \in W \times \overleftarrow{V}$ and $\alpha = \max\{\alpha_1, \alpha_2\}$ we have for all $A \in F$
$\|A(u,v) - A(x,y)\| \leq \|A(u,v) - A(x,v)\| + \|A(x,v) - A(x,y)\| \leq \alpha[\|u-x\| + \|v-y\|] = \alpha \ \|(u,v) - (x,y)\|$.

Remarks

1) In Theorem 2 the special case $n = 1$ and $C_{i1} = \{0\}$ for all $i \in I$ is the uniform boundedness principle of Banach for linear operators.

2) The family $\{A_i\}_{i \in I}$ is equicontinuous.

3) Let $I = \mathbb{N}$ and $(A_i)_{i \in \mathbb{N}}$ be pointwise convergent to A. Then the convergence is continuous. Indeed, suppose that $x_i \to x_o$ then by Theorem 2 there is a $n_o \in \mathbb{N}$ and a $L \in \mathbb{R}_+$ so that for all $i \geq n_o$

$$\|A_i x_i - A x_i\| \leq \|A_i x_i - A_i x_o\| + \|A_i x_o - A x_o\| \leq L \ \|x_i - x_o\| + \|A_i x_o - A x_o\| \xrightarrow[i\to\infty]{} 0.$$

4) Theorem 2 generalizes the analogous results for convex functions ([3]), concave-convex functions ([8]) and componentwise convex functions ([9]).

Two stage optimization problems

Let (f_n,T), $n \in \mathbb{N}$ be optimization problems and $M(f_n,T) := \{x \in T \mid f_n(x) = \inf f(T)\}$. In this section we study the set $\overline{\lim\limits_{n\in\mathbb{N}}} M(f_n,T)$ a little bit closer. Its elements can be viewed as solutions of a two stage optimization problem.

Proposition 3: Let T be a topological space, $f : T \to \mathbb{R}$ and for the sequence of functions $(f_n : T \to \mathbb{R})_{n\in\mathbb{N}}$ we assume that $\overline{\lim\limits_{n\in\mathbb{N}}} M(f_n,T) \subset M(f,T)$. Moreover, let $(\gamma_n)_{n\in\mathbb{N}}$ be a sequence of monotone non decreasing functions such that there is a function $g : T \to \overline{\mathbb{R}}$ and $\gamma_n(f_n-f)$ l.s.c.-convergent to g. Then we have

$$\overline{\lim_{n\in\mathbb{N}}} M(f_n,T) \subset M(g,M(f,T)).$$

Proof: Let $y \in M(f,T)$ and $\overline{x} = \lim x_{n_i}$ with $x_{n_i} \in M(f_{n_i},T)$. We have

$$[f_{n_i}(x_{n_i}) - f_{n_i}(y)] + [f(y) - f(x_{n_i})] \leq 0$$

$$f_{n_i}(x_{n_i}) - f(x_{n_i}) \leq f_{n_i}(y) - f(y)$$

$$\gamma_{n_i}(f_{n_i}(x_{n_i}) - f(x_{n_i})) \leq \gamma_{n_i}(f_{n_i}(y) - f(y)).$$

The l.s.c. convergence implies

$$g(\overline{x}) \leq g(y).$$

By computation we found that the differentiable approximation

$$\sum_{i=1}^{n} [\,|x_i| - \frac{1}{k} \ln(\frac{1}{k} + |x_i|)\,], \qquad k \in \mathbb{N}$$

of the L_1-norm in $\mathbb{R}^n$ gives good results. Choosing $\gamma_k(s) := -\exp(-ks)$ we obtain for the second stage

$$g(x) = - \prod_{i=1}^{n} |x_i|.$$

Two stage variational inequalities

The following scheme helps to find variational inequalities describing the second stage. Let X be a topological space. Let $B_n, n \in \mathbb{N} \cup \{0\}$ be a subset of X that is being viewed as the set of solutions of a problem (P_n).

Proposition 4: Suppose

1) $\overline{\lim_{n\in\mathbb{N}}} B_n \subset B_o$

2) There is a sequence $(\varphi_n : X \times X)_o^\infty$ with $B_n \subset S_1(\varphi_n, X)$ for $n \in \mathbb{N}$ and $B_o \subset S_2(\varphi_o, X)$

3) There is a sequence of mappings $(D_n : X \times X \to \mathbb{R}_+)_{n\in\mathbb{N}}$ such that

$$D_n(\cdot)\cdot(\varphi_n - \varphi_o)$$

converges 1 - l.s.c. to a mapping $h : X \times X \to \mathbb{R}$. Then we have

$$\overline{\lim_{n\in\mathbb{N}}} B_n \subset S_1(h, B_o).$$

Proof: Let $x \in B_o$ and $x_n \in B_n$ with $x_n \to \bar{x}$. Then we have

$$\varphi_n(x_n, x) \geq 0 \quad \text{and} \quad \varphi_o(x_n, x) \leq 0.$$

Thus

$$(\varphi_n - \varphi_o)(x_n, x) \geq 0$$

and

$$D_n(x_n, x)\cdot(\varphi_n - \varphi_o)(x_n, x) \geq 0.$$

By 1 - l.s.c. convergence of $D(\cdot)\cdot(\varphi_n - \varphi_o)$ to h it follows that

$$h(\bar{x}, x) \geq 0 .$$

In this context we are interested in those $\varphi : X \times X \to \mathbb{R}$ for which holds

(E) $\qquad S_1(\varphi, X) \subset S_2(\varphi, X).$

This property is obviously satisfied by monotone φ ([2]). $\varphi : X \times X \to \mathbb{R}$ is called monotone if we have for all $x, y \in X$ that

$$\varphi(x,y) + \varphi(y,x) \leq 0.$$

In particular, we have

(1) optimization problems

Let (f,X) be a optimization problem and $M(f,X)$ be the set of minimal solutions of f on X. For

$$\varphi(x,y) := f(y) - f(x)$$

we have obviously

$$S_1(\varphi,X) = S_2(\varphi,X) = M(f,X).$$

(2) equations of monotone operators

Let X be a normed space. A mapping $T : X \to X^*$ is called monotone, if we have

$$<Tx - Ty, x - y> \geq 0$$

for all $x,y \in X$. Let $\varphi(x,y) := <Tx, y-x>$. Then we have: φ is monotone and the set of solutions of the equation

$$Tx = 0$$

is $S_1(\varphi,X)$. By monotonicity it follows $S_1(\varphi,X) \subset S_2(\varphi,X)$. By such considerations we obtain the following proposition.

Proposition 5: Let X,Y be normed spaces and suppose that the sequence of mappings $(A_n \cdot X \to Y)_0^\infty$ satisfies

$$\overline{S} := \overline{\lim_{n\in\mathbb{N}}} \{x \in X \mid A_n x = 0\} \subset \{x \in X \mid A_0 x = 0\}.$$

Moreover, suppose that there is a sequence $(a_n)_{n\in\mathbb{N}}$ of positive numbers and a mapping $B : Y \to X^*$ with $B(0) = 0$ such that

(i) $B \circ A_0 : X \to X^*$ is monotone

(ii) There is a $D : X \to X^*$ such that for

$h_n(x,y) := <a_n(BA_n - BA_0)(x), y - x>$ and $h(x,y) := <Dx,y-x>$ h_n converges 1-l.s.c. to h.

Then we have for $\overline{x} \in \overline{S}$

$$<D\overline{x},x-\overline{x}> \geq 0 \quad \text{for all } x \in \{x \mid A_0 x = 0\} .$$

Proof: For $n \in \mathbb{N} \cup \{0\}$ we put $\varphi_n(x,y) := <B(A_n(x)), y-x>$ and apply Proposition 4.

In the special case of linear operators we may assume positive semi definiteness instead of monotonicity. For $a_n, n \in \mathbb{N}$, we may choose e.g. $1/\|BA_n - BA_o\|$. The 1-l.s.c. convergence is assured by Theorem 2. If $A_n = A_o + \alpha_n I$ and B such that BA_o is positive semi definite then we have $\bar{x} \in \overline{\lim_{n \in \mathbb{N}}} \{x \in X \mid A_n x = 0\}$

(*) $\quad \langle B\bar{x}, x-\bar{x}\rangle \geq 0 \quad$ for all $x \in \{x \mid A_o x = 0\}$

In example E3) we may choose

$$B = \begin{pmatrix} 1-2a, & a \\ 1-2b, & b \end{pmatrix} \quad a,b \in \mathbb{R}$$

For these matrices we have always $(\frac{1}{3},\frac{2}{3})$ as solution of the variational inequality (*).

References

[1] J. Descloux: Approximation in L_p and Tschebycheff approximation. SIAM J. Appl. Math. 11 (1963) 1017-1026.

[2] J. Gwinner: Nichtlineare Variationsungleichungen mit Anwendungen. Haag + Herchen, 1978.

[3] P. Kosmol: Optimierung konvexer Funktionen mit Stabilitätsbetrachtungen. Dissertationes Mathematicae CXL, 1976.

[4] P. Kosmol: On Stability of Convex Operators. In "Optimization and Operations Research" Lect. Notes in Econom. and Math. Systems 157, 173-179, 1978.

[5] P. Kosmol: Zweistufige Lösungen von Optimierungsaufgaben. In "Mathematische Systeme in der Ökonomie", hrsg. von M.J. Beckmann, W. Eichhorn, W. Krelle, Athenäum, 1983.

[6] P. Kosmol: Bemerkungen zur Brachistochrone. To appear in "Abhandlungen aus dem Mathematischen Seminar der Universität Hamburg".

[7] D. Landers and L. Rogge: The natural median. The Annals of Probability 9, 1981.

[8] G. Pallas: Gleichgradige Stetigkeit von Familien konkav-konvexer Funktionen. To appear in Mathematische Nachrichten.

[9] H.H. Thomsen: Gleichgradige Stetigkeit von Funktionenfamilien mit Anwendungen bei Mehrstufigen Optimierungsaufgaben. Diplomarbeit, Mathematisches Seminar der Universität Kiel, 1983.

INTRODUCTION TO STOCHASTIC SCHEDULING PROBLEMS

Rolf H. Möhring*
Franz J. Radermacher**

ABSTRACT:

The paper gives an introduction to some recent developments in stochastic scheduling, covering quite general nonpreemptive models. The approach is mainly intuitive, using a lot of illustrative examples and referring to other papers for proofs. Subjects treated are the characterization of all existing strategies, the identification of interesting subclasses of strategies, results on the optimality, stability and monotonicity behaviour and, finally, insights into the special nature of exponential models, for which hints to some basic open questions are also included.

INTRODUCTION:

Stochastic scheduling problems have been quite intensively studied in recent years in applied probability theory, operations research and computer science in the framework of e.g. networks of queues, project networks and computer modelling. A good survey on several aspects of this field may be found in the proceedings volume [3], together with some hints to the great variety of models that have to be considered to cover the different practical applications. Important aspects of such applications are the degree of knowledge of the data, the time horizon and the flexibility in handling jobs. While in computer-related applications information is often quite low and flexibility (via paging techniques) is quite high [16], [17], in applications in the building and construction industry it is often the other way round. Therefore, in the first case preemptive exponential models [30], [35], [36] will be of importance, while in the second case, general nonpreemptive models have to be taken into account. Such general nonpreemptive models have been studied extensively in [8], [12], [20], [21], [26], [34] and have led to quite deep insights into the

* Lehrstuhl für Informatik IV, RWTH Aachen, 51 Aachen, West Germany
**Lehrstuhl für Informatik und Operations Research, Universität Passau, 8390 Passau, West Germany

theoretical nature of such problems, including the establishment of interesting connections with the field of stochastic dynamic optimization [1], [7], [30]. As the mentioned papers are quite involved, we will try here to give an intuitive introduction to the whole field, using several illustrative examples, omitting proofs and concentrating on conceptual aspects.

The organization of the paper is as follows: Section I contains a short discussion of the model. In Section II, the set of all strategies is characterized by a functional as well as by a stochastic dynamic optimization type description. Subclasses of strategies, having analytical properties such as being convex, uniformly continuous or monotonically increasing are characterized in Section III by combinatorial properties. In doing so, the "world" of strategies is structured to a high degree. In Section IV, optimality criteria are given and the stability and monotonicity behaviour of the model is discussed. Finally, in Section V, the connection with exponential models is made explicit , including a quite general optimality result as well as hints to some basic open questions in this field.

I. DESCRIPTION OF THE MODEL

Stochastic scheduling problems as discussed in this paper are specified by a tuple $[A,O_o,N,P,\kappa]$ consisting of five different types of data (cf. also Example 2.1):

$A=\{\alpha_1,\ldots,\alpha_n\}$ denotes the set of jobs or activities that are to be scheduled. Jobs are to be executed without interruption (nonpreemptive case),

O_o is a precedence relation (poset) on A, representing technological precedence constraints or time sequencing conditions,

$N=\{N_1,\ldots,N_k\}$ is a clutter(i.e. a system of pairwise incomparable sets) of O_o-independent subsets of A, representing those minimal sets of technologically independent jobs that are not allowed to be scheduled simultaneously at any time. N is called the system of forbidden sets. It can be shown that arbitrary time independent resource constraints can be represented this way [23].

P is a distribution on $(\mathbb{R}^n_>, \mathcal{B}^n_>)$, i.e. on the system of Borel sets on the n-vectors of positive reals, representing the joint distribution of activity durations $(x_1,\ldots,x_n) \in \mathbb{R}^n_>$, where $x_i := x(\alpha_i)$ denotes the duration of job α_i, $i=1,\ldots,n$. The realization of x becomes known only gradually in an on-line fashion during the execution of the project and constitutes the stochastic nature of the problem. For technical reasons, the expected duration of each job should exist, i.e. $\mathbb{E}_P[\Sigma]<\infty$, where $\Sigma: \mathbb{R}^n_> \to \mathbb{R}^1_>$ denotes the "sum" of real numbers,

$\kappa: \mathbb{R}^n_> \to \mathbb{R}^1_\geqslant$ denotes any regular measure of performance, i.e. κ is a montonically increasing function associating with any vector $(t_1,\ldots,t_n)$ of completion times for the activities $\alpha_1,\ldots,\alpha_n$ a project cost $\kappa(t_1,\ldots,t_n)$. κ is usually assumed to be (universally) measurable and linearly bounded (i.e. bounded on $\mathbb{R}^n_>$ by a linear function). For applications, κ should also be easily computable. Typical examples are $\kappa=\max$ (project duration), $\kappa=\Sigma$ (flow time), $\kappa=\Sigma_i\, w_i \cdot t_i$ (weighted flow time); other examples such as maximum tardiness $\max\{0, t_\alpha - d_\alpha \mid \alpha\in A\}$ are defined via due dates $d_\alpha \in \mathbb{R}^1_\geqslant$, $\alpha\in A$, which represent for each job a given individual upper bound on the intended completion time.

Given this framework, the aim of scheduling is to schedule all jobs $\alpha\in A$ in a nonpreemptive way (i.e. without ever interrupting a job execution), such that the precedence and time conditions given by O_o are respected, and such that at no time $t\in\mathbb{R}^1_\geqslant$, a forbidden set is under performance. This has to be done under limited information concerning the job durations. Solutions therefore have to be strategies (in the sense of stochastic dynamic optimization), defining the project execution in a consistent way w.r.t. all "possible" realizations of job durations. From a decision theoretical point of view, this constitutes a risk situation. As the following example shows, this risk is non-trivial, i.e. a pointwise optimal way of scheduling w.r.t. all $x\in\mathbb{R}^n_>$ is, in general, not possible. That means that the deficit concerning the a priori information on $x\in\mathbb{R}^n_>$ makes it impossible in most cases to construct a strategy from pointwise (i.e. for each x) optimal solutions (schedules). At the same time, it distinguishes stochastic scheduling problems from the study of the average behaviour of deterministic scheduling problems [27], which, at most, can deliver certain lower bounds [23].

EXAMPLE 1.1:

Let $[A,O_o,N,P,\kappa]$ be as follows: $A=\{1,2,3\}$; $\mathcal{Q}_o=\emptyset$ [where $\mathcal{Q}_o$ denotes the covering relation associated with O_o], $N=\{\{1,2,3\}\}$, $P=\frac{1}{3}(\varepsilon_{x^1}+\varepsilon_{x^2}+\varepsilon_{x^3})$ with $x^1=(1,2,3)$, $x^2=(3,1,2)$, $x^3=(2,3,1)$ [where ε_x, for $x\in\mathbb{R}^n_>$ arbitrary, denotes the singular distribution $\varepsilon_x(B)=1$ for $x\in B$ and $\varepsilon_x(B)=0$ for $x\notin B$, $B\in\mathcal{B}^n_>$ arbitrary], $\kappa=\max$ (project duration).

Let us first consider the deterministic case, i.e. assume that all activity durations are known in advance. Taking into account the required nonpreemptiveness, any job $\alpha\in A$ will have to be started at some time $T(\alpha)\in\mathbb{R}^1_\geqslant$ and will then be completed at time $T(\alpha)+x(\alpha)$, i.e. the whole way of scheduling will be completely determined by the vector $(T(\alpha_1),\ldots,T(\alpha_n))\in\mathbb{R}^n_\geqslant$ of starting times of the respective jobs. It is easily seen, that the possible starting time vectors, the so-called feasible schedules for (A,O_o,N,x), are exactly characterized by the following two properties:

$$T(\alpha)+x(\alpha)\leqslant T(\beta) \quad \text{whenever } (\alpha,\beta)\in O_o, \alpha\neq\beta$$
$$N\not\subseteq\{\alpha\in A \mid T(\alpha)\leqslant t<T(\alpha)+x(\alpha)\} \quad \text{for all } t\in\mathbb{R}^1_\geqslant, \text{ all } N\in N.$$

The project cost associated with T is given by $\kappa(T,x):=\kappa(T(\alpha_1)+x(\alpha_1),\ldots,T(\alpha_n)+x(\alpha_n))$ and thus the deterministic optimal value is

$$\rho(\kappa,x):=\inf\{\kappa(T,x) \mid T \text{ is a feasible schedule}\}.$$

Concentrating now on the considered example, we have three independent jobs needing identical machines for their execution, where, however, only 2 machines are available. It is easily seen, that for all three duration vectors, there is a way of scheduling, such that all jobs can be completed by time 3 (as a rule, start the longest job at time zero). Thus we have $\rho(\kappa,x^i)=3$ for $i=1,2,3$.

Consider now the stochastic version. At time zero, we can start at most two jobs. Independently of our choice, we will miss the job with the longest duration with probability $1/3$. Our way of scheduling will then be unfavourable and lead to a completion time of 4, thus yielding an expected project duration of $3\,1/3$.

The risk situation, described in Example 1.1, can be handled in the standard decision theoretical way. That means that if κ is properly interpreted (e.g. modified in advance to reflect individual utilities or preferences), minimizing expected project cost (over suitable classes of strategies) becomes the reasonable optimization aim [12], [14], [32].

Let, in an informal way, τ denote such a subclass of strategies. For any $\Pi\in\tau$ and any realized $x\in\mathbb{R}^n_>$, the completion time of all jobs and thus the associated cost value, here denoted by $\kappa(\Pi,x)$, will be defined. Assume that the function $\kappa(\Pi,\cdot)$ will have the needed measurability properties, so that the associated expected project cost $\mathbb{E}_P[\kappa(\Pi,\cdot)]$ w.r.t. a given duration distribution P is defined. We are then, among other things, interested in the associated <u>optimal value</u> $\rho^\tau(\kappa,P) := \inf\{\mathbb{E}_P[\kappa(\Pi,\cdot)] \mid \Pi\in\tau\}$. Insights into the behaviour of this optimal value are wanted for general classes of strategies as well as for subclasses that are important from an applicational point of view. Interesting questions that will be covered in this paper concern the <u>existence</u> of optimal strategies, the <u>stability behaviour</u> w.r.t. perturbations of κ and P and the <u>monotonicity behaviour</u>, particularly for replacement of P by a stochastically greater distribution P'. Note that dealing with these questions would be almost hopeless, if the set τ of interesting or available strategies would somehow depend on κ and P. Certainly, this would also make the handling of real-life problems almost impossible, as for the continuous data types κ and P, there is often no chance of practically obtaining the exact values. Thus altogether, arriving at a set of available strategies that is independent of κ and P and that constitutes no undue restriction of available options, is a central issue in stochastic scheduling. As we will see next, this goal can be achieved. The obtained set of general strategies will only depend on the discrete and quite robust data types O_o and N. In particular, it will give the set of general strategies even for the case, where nothing about κ and P is known at all.

Note finally, that for arriving at reasonable sets of strategies, it can be advantageous to make use of a natural DOMINANCE RELATION among strategies. To this end, write $\Pi\leqslant\Pi'$ for strategies Π and Π', if the relation $\Pi[x](\alpha)\leqslant\Pi'[x](\alpha)$ is true for all $x\in\mathbb{R}^n_>$ and all $\alpha\in A$, i.e. if each job is started (and thus completed) no later according to Π as according to Π', independent of x. Certainly, $\Pi\leqslant\Pi'$ implies $\mathbb{E}_P[\kappa(\Pi,\cdot)]\leqslant\mathbb{E}_P[\kappa(\Pi',\cdot)]$ for all P and κ and therefore enables us to forget about Π' if necessary.

II. GENERAL STRATEGIES

Let a scheduling problem $[A,O_o,N,P,\kappa]$ be given. Let us study the effect of using any strategy (in whatever way it is defined) after completion of the whole project, i.e. after the realization of the duration vector x. Obviously, the situation will then be the same as in the deterministic case described in Example 1.1, i.e. the required nonpreemptiveness will guarantee that the whole project execution is completely determined by the vector $(T(\alpha_1),\ldots, T(\alpha_n))\in\mathbb{R}^n_{\geq}$ of starting times of the jobs, with $(T(\alpha_1)+x(\alpha_1),\ldots,T(\alpha_n)+x(\alpha_n))$ giving the vector of completion times. Again, the possible vectors of starting times are characterized by the fact that they are schedules for (A,O_o,x) [i.e. fulfill $T(\alpha)+x(\alpha)\leqslant T(\beta)$ whenever $(\alpha,\beta)\in O_o,\alpha\neq\beta$] and that they are feasible w.r.t. N, [i.e. fulfill $N\nsubseteq\{\alpha\in A|T(\alpha)\leqslant t<T(\alpha)+x(\alpha)\}$ for all $N\in N$ and any time $t\in\mathbb{R}^1_{\geq}$]. Thus, in an a posteriori interpretation, a strategy Π will be a special function Π: $X \to \mathbb{R}^n_{\geq}$, where $X\subseteq\mathbb{R}^n_{>}$ is the set of duration vectors, for which the strategy is defined, and Π gives, for any such $x\in X$, the associated feasible schedule $\Pi[x]=(\Pi[x](\alpha_1),\ldots,\Pi[x](\alpha_n))$ in a consistent way.

The just described interpretation is called the FUNCTIONAL APPROACH to stochastic scheduling problems. Of course, we will have to impose some regularity conditions on the respective functions to allow practical execution. Certainly, (universal) measurability [·], [7] is the weakest condition to ask for; it will imply the (universal) measurability of $\kappa(\Pi,\cdot)$: $\mathbb{R}^n_{>} \to \mathbb{R}^1_{\geq}$ and thus allow us to use the notion of expected project cost associated with a strategy in the sense described above. An additional restriction coming from practical considerations will also be discussed in this Section, viz. that of being an ELEMENTARY STRATEGY, meaning that jobs are either started at time zero or at the completion times of other jobs. Other restrictions on Π, coming e.g. from analytical or combinatorial requirements will be discussed in Section III. The major question then concerns the identification of a consistency condition that makes a function a strategy, i.e. that reflects the dynamic nature and the use of incomplete information that are typical for on-line stochastic scheduling problems. In this context, a major difficulty is created by all P-dependent strategies, i.e. strategies which are only defined on some arbitrary (universally) measurable set X with $P(X)=1$; cf. e.g. Example 1.1, where it is sufficient from a practical point of view to define a strategy Π on the set $X=\{x^1,x^2,x^3\}$ only. Certainly, if we could not avoid w.l.o.g. all those locally defined strategies, we could never achieve the intended independence of κ and P. Consequently, we aim now at strategies defined on $\mathbb{R}^n_{>}$, i.e. strategies that give the scheduling procedure for all possible duration vectors $x\in\mathbb{R}^n_{>}$, and simultaneously hope and look for an extension operator, which somehow extends every locally defined strategy to the whole set $\mathbb{R}^n_{>}$ and thus justifies the intended approach. We will deal with such an extension construction below. Before, we discuss a small example, that helps in deriving the needed consistency condition.

EXAMPLE 2.1:

Let $[A,O_o,N]$ be as follows: $A=\{\alpha_1,\alpha_2,\alpha_3,\alpha_4,\alpha_5,\alpha_6\}$, $O_o=\{(\alpha_2,\alpha_4);(\alpha_2,\alpha_5);(\alpha_3,\alpha_6);(\alpha_4,\alpha_6)\}$, $N=\{\{\alpha_2,\alpha_3\},\{\alpha_3,\alpha_4,\alpha_5\}\}$; cf. Figure 1.

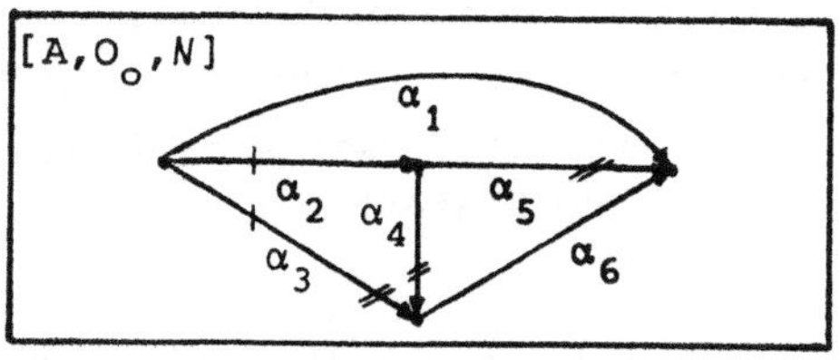

Figure 1

Given the general framework described above, we can w.l.o.g. start job α_1 at time zero and will then at some time have to start either job α_2 or job α_3. After that no other job can be started before α_2 or α_3 ends, respectively. With the completion of the respective job, the other one may be started. If we schedule job α_3 first, α_2 is the only available job at the time of completion of α_3. However, if job α_2 is scheduled first, jobs α_3,α_4 and α_5 are available afterwards. Of course, this set cannot be scheduled simultaneously, i.e. at most two of these jobs can be started after the completion of job α_2.

(1) Consider first the function $\Pi^1: \mathbb{R}^6_> \to \mathbb{R}^6_\geq$, defined by $\Pi^1(x_1,x_2,x_3,x_4,x_5,x_6)=(0,0,x_2,x_2+x_3,x_2+x_3+x_4,x_2+x_3+x_4)$.

We will see that Π^1 is a strategy. In fact Π^1 leads to the following consistent way of scheduling, visualized in Figure 2.

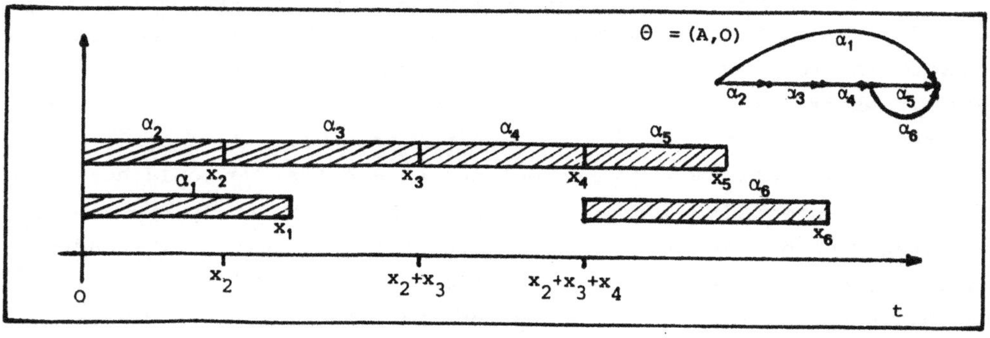

Figure 2

The underlying idea is that we start job α_2 at time zero and wait for its completion at time x_2, then start job α_3 and wait for its completion at time x_2+x_3, then start job α_4 and wait for its completion at time $x_2+x_3+x_4$ and finally, start the two remaining jobs. In doing so, the precedence relations $(\alpha_2,\alpha_4),(\alpha_2,\alpha_5),(\alpha_2,\alpha_6),(\alpha_3,\alpha_6),(\alpha_4,\alpha_6)$ are all respected, independently of the realization of x. Also, at no time $t\in\mathbb{R}^1_{\geq}$, a forbidden set is under performance; in fact, jobs α_5 and α_6 are the only two resource consuming jobs, ever executed at the same time.

Certainly, there are no problems with Π^1 being consistent, as the information, needed to make scheduling decisions (i.e. needed in order to start a particular job) is always available in time. Also, Π^1 is obviously an <u>elementary</u> strategy. Furthermore, Π^1 is particularly well-behaved, as it is e.g. a <u>convex</u>, <u>uniformly continuous</u>, <u>monotonically increasing</u> and <u>positive homogeneous</u> function; in fact, Π^1 is even <u>linear</u>. As we will see in Section III, this nice analytical behaviour is closely related to the combinatorial property of Π^1 being a so-called <u>ES-strategy</u>. In fact, Π^1 exactly represents the <u>earliest start</u> scheduling procedure w.r.t. the (feasible) partial order (A,O) given in Figure 2.

(2) Consider next the function $\Pi^2 : \mathbb{R}^6_> \to \mathbb{R}^6_\geq$, defined by

$$\Pi^2(x_1,x_2,x_3,x_4,x_5,x_6) = \begin{cases} (0,0,x_2,x_2,x_2+\min(x_3,x_4),x_2+\max(x_3,x_4)) & x_2 \leq 10 \\ (0,0,x_2,x_2+\min(x_3,x_5),x_2,x_2+\max(x_3,x_4+\min(x_3,x_5))) & x_2 > 10 \end{cases}$$

Π^2 is also a strategy. The underlying idea is essentially given by the observation that, after the completion of job α_2 we start jobs α_3 and α_4 if we observe $x_2\leq 10$ and we start instead jobs α_3 and α_5 if we observe $x_2>10$. The remaining jobs are scheduled as early as possible. Obviously, Π^2 is <u>elementary</u> and <u>dominates</u> Π^1, i.e. we have $\Pi^2\leq\Pi^1$. Furthermore, Π^2 is positive homogeneous but has none of the other analytical properties listed in (1).

(3) Consider next the function $\Pi^3 : \mathbb{R}^6_> \to \mathbb{R}^6_\geq$, defined by

$$\Pi^3(x_1,x_2,x_3,x_4,x_5,x_6) = \begin{cases} (0,0,x_1,x_1+\min(x_3,x_5),x_1,x_1+\max(x_3,x_4+\min(x_3,x_5))) & x_2\leq x_1\leq 10 \\ (0,0,10,10,10+\min(x_3,x_4),10+\max(x_3,x_4)) & x_2\leq 10<x_1 \\ \Pi^1[x] & \text{otherwise} \end{cases}$$

Π^3 is also a strategy. The underlying idea is that we start according to Π^1 but later behave differently if x_2 is smaller than x_1 and smaller than 10. In this case, we do not make a decision on scheduling a job from the set $\{\alpha_3,\alpha_4,\alpha_5\}$ until either job α_1 ends or time 10 is reached without α_1 being completed. While in the first case we start α_2 and α_5 at time x_1, we start α_2 and α_4 at time 10 otherwise. The remaining jobs are scheduled as early as possible. Obviously, Π^3 dominates Π^1 but not Π^2; also Π^2 does not dominate Π^3. Note that Π^3 is <u>not</u> elementary and has none of the analytical properties mentioned in (1). Still there are problems for which Π^3 is optimal while no elementary strategy has this property.

(4) Consider finally the function Π^4: $\mathbb{R}^6_> \to \mathbb{R}^6_\geq$, defined by

$$\Pi^4(x_1,x_2,x_3,x_4,x_5,x_6) = \begin{cases} (0,0,x_2,x_2+x_3,x_2+x_3+x_4,x_2+x_3+x_4) & x_5 \leq x_6 \\ (0,0,x_2+x_4,x_2,x_2+x_3+x_4,x_2+x_3+x_4) & x_6 > x_5 \end{cases}$$

Π^4 is again a nicely behaved piecewise linear function, aiming at doing earliest start scheduling according to Π^1 if $x_5 \leq x_6$ and analogously with the roles of jobs α_3 and α_4 permuted if $x_5 > x_6$. Obviously, this function cannot be a strategy, as after the completion of job α_2, there is no way of knowing in which order to schedule α_3 and α_4, due to the fact that it is impossible to know the "future" values x_5 and x_6 already at that time.

Example 2.1 demonstrated the nature of the functional approach. Of course, this concept does not really make transparent the strategic ideas hidden in a strategy. In this respect, the <u>stochastic dynamic optimization</u> approach discussed below is much more instructive. However, the functional approach is highly useful when investigating <u>analytical properties</u> and <u>stability</u> as well as in all cases where <u>limits of sequences of strategies</u> play a role, particularly in connection with the proof of results on the <u>existence of optimal strategies</u>, as is done in Section IV.

We now give the CONSISTENCY CONDITION, which reflects the dynamic nature of those functions Π: $\mathbb{R}^n_> \to \mathbb{R}^n_\geq$ that are strategies. Intuitively, this condition should guarantee that a decision to start a certain job $\beta \in A$ at some time $t \in \mathbb{R}^1_\geq$ w.r.t. some duration vector $x \in \mathbb{R}^n_>$, depends only on the "<u>t-past</u>" of x, i.e. on the information on x available at time t. Of course, observed starting and completion times before t as well as insights into the "future" behaviour of x, coming e.g. from <u>stochastic dependences</u> and <u>conditional distributions</u>, may also be of importance, but inductively, such information should already be implicitly determined by the t-past of x.

DEFINITION:

(1) Let $\Pi: \mathbb{R}^n_> \to \mathbb{R}^n_\geqslant$ be a function and $x,y \in \mathbb{R}^n_>$. Call y <u>t-similar</u> to x (w.r.t. Π), iff for all $\alpha \in A$

$$\Pi[x](\alpha)+x(\alpha) \leqslant t \Rightarrow x(\alpha) = y(\alpha)$$
$$\Pi[x](\alpha) \leqslant t < \Pi[x](\alpha)+x(\alpha) \Rightarrow y(\alpha) > t - \Pi[x](\alpha)$$

(2) Let $\Pi: \mathbb{R}^n_> \to \mathbb{R}^n_\geqslant$ be a function. Call Π <u>consistent</u> (or realizable), iff $\Pi[x](\beta)=t$ for arbitrary $x \in \mathbb{R}^n_>$ and $\beta \in A$ implies $\Pi[y](\beta)=t$ for all y t-similar to x (w.r.t. Π).

The given notion of consistency has turned out to reflect precisely the intended behaviour, even in a framework where no measurability conditions are considered. A thorough discussion of this matter is given in [26]. The basic result consists in Theorem 1.5 in [26] which states, that <u>t-similarity</u> is an <u>equivalence relation</u> on $\mathbb{R}^n_>$ for all $t \in \mathbb{R}^1_\geqslant$ iff Π is consistent. Note that, in general, t-similarity needs neither be a symmetric nor a transitive relation on $\mathbb{R}^n_>$. For instance in Example 2.1 (4), y = (2,1,3,3,2,1) is 3-similar to x = (2,1,4,1,1,2) w.r.t. Π^4 but not the other way round. Of course, Π^4 is not consistent. For example, we have $\Pi^4[x](\alpha_3)=1 \neq \Pi^4[y](\alpha_3)$ though x and y are mutually 1-similar w.r.t. Π^4. The main insights available are then the following two results:

(1) If $\Pi: \mathbb{R}^n_> \to \mathbb{R}^n_\geqslant$ is not consistent, there are $x,y \in \mathbb{R}^n_>$, $\beta \in A$ and $t \in \mathbb{R}^n_\geqslant$ such that x,y are mutually t-similar, $\Pi[x](\alpha)=\Pi[y](\alpha)$ for all $\alpha \in A$ with $\Pi[x](\alpha)<t$ or $\Pi[y](\alpha)<t$ but still $\Pi[x](\beta)=t$ and $\Pi[y](\beta)>t$, i.e. there is a different scheduling behaviour based on the same observed past, something practically impossible; cf. the example just given to demonstrate the missing consistency of Π^4.

(2) If $\Pi: \mathbb{R}^n_> \to \mathbb{R}^n_\geqslant$ is consistent and $\Pi[x](\alpha)=t$ for some $\alpha \in A, t \in \mathbb{R}^n_\geqslant$, then also $\Pi[y](\alpha)=t$ for all $y \in \mathbb{R}^n_>$ that are t-similar to x. Thus scheduling decisions to start a particular job $\alpha \in A$ at a particular time $t \in \mathbb{R}^1_\geqslant$ are made identically on the whole t-equivalence class of all those duration vectors compatible with the observed t-past. The proof of this observation mainly uses the fact, that t-similarity of y with x implies $(t+\varepsilon)$-similarity of y with x for a suitable (small) $\varepsilon>0$. Practically it means

that, given a t-past of an unknown duration vector x, we can extend this vector arbitrarily into the future and then use the resulting $y \in \mathbb{R}^n_>$ to base our decision to start a particular job β at time t on whether or not $\Pi[y](\beta)=t$. Combining everything said so far, we arrive at the functional description of strategies as used e.g. in [8], [20], [21], [26].

DEFINITION: A function $\Pi: \mathbb{R}^n_> \to \mathbb{R}^n_\geqslant$ is a strategy for a stochastic scheduling problem $[A, O_o, N, P, \kappa]$ iff the following four conditions are fulfilled:

(Sto 1) $\Pi[x](\alpha)+x(\alpha) \leqslant \Pi[x](\beta)$ for all $(\alpha,\beta) \in O_o, \alpha \neq \beta$, all $x \in \mathbb{R}^n_>$

(Sto 2) $N \not\subseteq \{\alpha \in A \mid \Pi[x](\alpha) \leqslant t < \Pi[x](\alpha)+x(\alpha)\}$ for all $t \in \mathbb{R}^1_\geqslant$, all $N \in N$

(Sto 3) If $\Pi[x](\beta)=t$ for $\beta \in A, x \in \mathbb{R}^n_>$ and $t \in \mathbb{R}^1_\geqslant$ then $\Pi[y](\beta)=t$ for all y t-similar to x w.r.t. Π

(Sto 4) Π is universally measurable and avoids total idleness, i.e. periods (before project completion) with no job under performance.

Here (Sto 1) means that $\Pi[x]$ has to be a schedule for (A, O_o, x) for any $x \in \mathbb{R}^n_>$, while (Sto 2) is the required feasibility of these schedules w.r.t. N. (Sto 3) is the consistency condition just discussed and (Sto 4) the weakest form of regularity, considered in the framework of stochastic scheduling. Note that a measurability condition has to be imposed explicitly. This is not necessary w.r.t. the required non-idleness condition. In fact, as is shown in Theorem 1.7 in [26], there exists for any Π' fulfilling (Sto 1) - (Sto 4) up to non-idleness, some Π fulfilling (Sto 1) - (Sto 4), such that $\Pi \leqslant \Pi'$, i.e. Π dominates Π'. The idea behind the proof is that in periods of total idleness there is neither progress in job execution nor in the collection of information (i.e. no transition to another conditional distribution). Consequently, using a sequence of left shifts in order to eliminate the idle times does not really change the dynamic behaviour and therefore leads to the wanted dominating strategy Π. Note that by definition, elementarity will exclude total idleness. The main advantage of guaranteeing non-idleness finally is that this property implies the validity of $\Pi[x](\alpha)+x(\alpha) \leqslant \sum_{\alpha \in A} x(\alpha)$ for all $\alpha \in A$, all $x \in \mathbb{R}^n_>$. Thus the completion times of all jobs turn out to be linearly bounded in x, implying, under the general assumptions made, that $\mathbb{E}_P[\kappa(\Pi,\cdot)]<\infty$ for all strategies.

Strategies are defined <u>independently</u> of P and κ. As was discussed above, this definition needs a justification in form of some <u>extension operation</u>, that shows how to come from locally defined so-called P-STRATEGIES, i.e. strategies defined on some (universally) measurable set $X \in \mathcal{B}^n_>$, to strategies defined on $\mathbb{R}^n_>$ that are extensions of the original ones. Note first, that P-strategies might be properly defined by restricting conditions (Sto 1) to (Sto 4) to the considered sets X. The intuitive approach to an extension is then as follows: Consider some $y \notin X$; one can show that there is some time $t^*>0$, such that exactly for all $t<t^*$, y will be t-similar to some $x \in X$. This will necessitate certain scheduling decisions. Only after we reach t^*, we will have some freedom in defining the extension. A very convenient way is to wait until all scheduled jobs are completed and then to schedule all elements from the set $B \subseteq A$ of remaining jobs (if case $B \neq \emptyset$) one after the other according to a <u>fixed</u> linear order on B, respecting O_o ; cf. the following example.

<u>EXAMPLE 2.2</u>: Let $[A, O_o, N, P, \kappa]$ be as in Example 1.1. Obviously, it is sufficient to give an optimal scheduling procedure for the set $X = \{x^1, x^2, x^3\}$ of duration vectors only. By what has been said, the function $\Pi(y_1, y_2, y_3) = (0, 0, \min(y_1, y_2))$, restricted to X, would be a solution. It leads to the three schedules given in Figure 3.

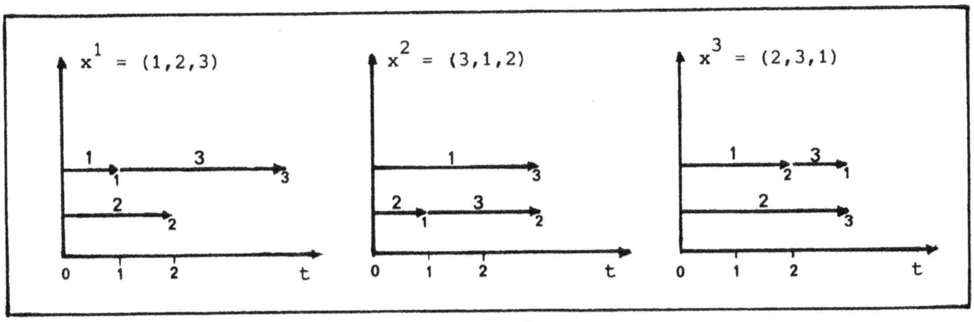

Figure 3

Using the extension operation just described leads to the following strategy Π',

$$\Pi' = \begin{cases} (0,0,\min(y_1,y_2)) & \text{if } \min(y_1,y_2)=1 \text{ or} \\ & \quad \min(y_1,y_2)=y_1=2 \\ (0,0,\max(y_1,y_2)) & \text{otherwise} \end{cases}$$

Note that all duration vectors are 0-similar, so that we will have to start with jobs 1 and 2 at time 0. Now if $\min(y_1, y_2) < 1$ we obviously have $t^*=\min(y_1,y_2)$, i.e. exactly from that time on, y will never be similar with any element from X. By our rule, we will then wait until $\max(y_1,y_2)$ and start job 3. If $\min(y_1,y_2)=1$, the case $y_1<y_2$ will mean 1-similarity with x^1, the case $y_2<y_1$ 1-similarity with x^2 and $y_1=y_2$ no more similarity with elements from X. In any case, we will have to schedule job 3 at time 1. If $1<\min(y_1,y_2)<2$, we again have $t^*=\min(y_1,y_2)$ and will wait until $\max(y_1,y_2)$ before starting job 3. If $\min(y_1,y_2)=2=y_1$ we will be 2-similar with x^3 and thus start job 3. In all other cases, we will have $t^*=2$ and start job 3 at time $\max(y_1,y_2)$.

It should be mentioned here that the technical problems in proving that the given construction defines a strategy are non-trivial. Major questions concern the independence of the first part of the scheduling rule from the choice of t-similar representatives as well as the consistency of the resulting function. Furthermore, there occur some difficulties with the measurability condition, due to the necessity to use projections of Borel sets. Exactly here, universal measurability becomes the appropriate notion [1],[7]. The next theorem (cf. Theorem 1.8 in [26]) gives the main insight presently available.

THEOREM 2.3: Let $[A,O_o,N]$ be given and $\emptyset \neq X \in \mathcal{B}^n_>$. Let $\Pi: X \to \mathbb{R}^n_\geqslant$ be a measurable function, fulfilling (Sto 1) - (Sto 4) w.r.t. X. Then Π can be extended to a strategy Π'. If Π is elementary, the same can be guaranteed for Π'.

The proof follows the ideas given above. From a practical point of view, the result is sufficiently general. For if anyone wishes to consider some universally measurable Π'' locally defined on some universally measurable set X'' (with $P(X'')=1$ for the considered P) one can proceed as follows: Restrict Π'' by standard arguments to some measurable function Π' defined on some $X' \in \mathcal{B}^n_>$ fulfilling $X' \subseteq X''$ as well as $P(X')=1$. Obviously $\mathbb{E}_P[\kappa(\Pi',\cdot)]=\mathbb{E}_P[\kappa(\Pi'',\cdot)]$. Now extend Π' to Π according to Theorem 2.3. Of course, we have $\mathbb{E}_P[\kappa(\Pi,\cdot) = \mathbb{E}_P[\kappa(\Pi',\cdot)$ and therefore have realized the objective value associated to Π'' by a strategy Π. Π is an extension of Π'' up to some possible minor modifications on a set of P measure zero. Note finally, that there is up to now no result available that allows a restriction to Borel-measurable strategies. The problem is how to modify a universally measurable strategy slightly so that it remains a strategy but becomes measurable. In any case this seems to be an interesting OPEN QUESTION for anybody who prefers to do stochastic scheduling in the framework of Borel-measurability.

Now, that the basic functional notion of a strategy is available, we may ask for properties of this set of functions. Two results, concerning the LIMIT BEHAVIOUR (cf. [12]) and the DOMINANCE BEHAVIOUR (cf. [26]) are contained in the next theorem.

THEOREM 2.4: Let $[A,Q_o,N]$ be given.

(1) The associated set of strategies is closed against pointwise limits, i.e. if $(\Pi^n)_{n\in\mathbb{N}}$ is a sequence of strategies converging pointwise against some limit function Π, then Π is a strategy itself. If the $(\Pi^n)_{n\in\mathbb{N}}$ are elementary, the same is true for Π.

(2) The associated set of strategies is bounded w.r.t. dominance, i.e. to any strategy Π there is some $\leqslant$-minimal strategy Π' fulfilling $\Pi'\leqslant\Pi$. If Π is elementary, the same can be guaranteed for Π'.

The proof of (1) strongly uses the following observation: Let $\Pi[x](\alpha_o)=t$ and put $\Pi^n[x](\alpha_o)=t_n, n\in\mathbb{N}$, with $t_n\to t$. Assume that y is t_o-similar to x(w.r.t. Π). Then there is some $j_o\in\mathbb{N}$ such that y is also t_j-similar to x(w.r.t. Π^j) for all $j\geqslant j_o$. Using this property, the proof is quite straightforward. From a technical point of view, property (1) will be of great use in arriving at optimality criteria in Section IV. In this context, examples of convergent sequences of strategies will also be given (e.g. Examples 3.7 and 4.4).

The proof of (2) is more difficult. Note first that one might want to apply Zorn's Lemma. One would then have to show that any (maybe uncountable) decreasing family $(\Pi^i)_{i\in I}$ of strategies is bounded from below. It is not difficult to see along the lines of the proof of (1) that the (existing) lower limit function $\Pi:=\inf_{i\in I}\Pi^i$ fulfills (Sto 1) - (Sto 3) and is idle-time free. The boundedness of special subclasses of strategies (such as elementary or convex or monotonically increasing strategies) now follows immediately, as all these properties are inherited by Π from the family $(\Pi^i)_{i\in I}$. With continuity or (universal) measurability however, things are different. Of course, if one could choose a countable approximating subsequence $(\Pi^i)_{i\in J}, J\subseteq I$, (universal) measurability would follow immediately. The choice of such a subsequence is possible, as long as for at least some $x\in\mathbb{R}^n_>$ and some $\alpha\in A, \Pi^i[x](\alpha)>\Pi[x](\alpha)$ holds for all $i\in I$. However, if this condition is not fulfilled, there are indeed examples, for which Π is no longer (universally) measurable. This does not contradict the statement of Theorem 2.4. (2).

It only says, that Zorn's Lemma will not lead to the general result in the way indicated. In fact, a very involved construction, using the iterative decomposition of strategies, discussed below, is needed to proof this result.

The insights obtained so far with the functional approach allow an equivalent reformulation in terms of STOCHASTIC DYNAMIC OPTIMIZATION, cf. [1] [7] [30]. This second approach is extremely useful for many reasons, e.g. in stimulating additional insights into the theoretical behaviour of the model, in guiding to the appropriate optimality criteria and, above all, in leading to insights into the iterative decomposition of strategies into substrategies for subproblems as discussed below. With respect to an appropriate stochastic-dynamic-optimization-type description, the given "streamlined" functional notion of a strategy, in particular property (Sto 3), yield the "right" state and action spaces as follows:

The state at time $t \in \mathbb{R}^1_{\geqslant}$ can be described by t itself, the set $B^* \subseteq A$ of activities finished no later than t together with their starting times and durations and, finally, the set $B \setminus B^*$ of activities started before t but not completed by time t, together with their starting times. This state space is of course uncountable. Actions taken at any decision point t have to depend in a (universally) measurable way on the history up to time t and are of the type $(B(t),t^*)$. Here, $B(t)$ is the (possibly empty) set of jobs started at time t as part of the action taken, where of course the possible choices of this set are restricted via conditions (Sto 1) and (Sto 2), i.e. all predecessors of jobs from $B(t)$ must already be completed (i.e. must belong to B^*) and forbidden sets must be avoided (i.e. $N \not\subseteq B(t) \cup (B \setminus B^*)$ must be true for all $N \in \mathcal{N}$). Furthermore, $t^* \in (t,\infty]$ is any (out of uncountably many) future moments of time (cf. Example 2.1 (3)), fixed as part of the action taken at t. This time serves as a preliminary next decision time, i.e. starting from the first decision point $t=0$, where w.l.o.g. $B(t) \neq \emptyset$, the next decision point is given iteratively as $t^+ := \min \{t^*; \Pi[x](\alpha)+x(\alpha) \mid \alpha \in (B \setminus B^*) \cup B(t)\}$, i.e. if there is no completion in the time interval $(t,t^*]$, then t^* gives the next decision point. In this case, i.e. if $\min \{\Pi[x](\alpha)+x(\alpha) \mid \alpha \in (B \setminus B^*) \cup B(t)\} > t^*$ we can, taken into account (Sto 3), assume $B(t^*) \neq \emptyset$. Note that as we can avoid total idleness, we will have to consider at most 2n-1 decision points. Of course, special classes of strategies will be characterized by special assumptions concerning the choice of actions

(B(t),t*). In particular, elementary strategies are characterized by the fact, that w.l.o.g. $t^* = \infty$ for all actions (B(t),t*).

The interpretation of stochastic scheduling problems, just given, allows an iterative description of a strategy by means of induced substrategies defined on smaller sets of activities by conditioning on the first job completion. This decomposition is discussed in [20] in great details and is essentially used in the induction proofs of all main results, particularly the APPROXIMATION THEOREM, given in Section IV. The mere strategy-oriented part of this decomposition is given next; a discussion of examples follows subsequently.

Thus let now Π denote any strategy. Due the type of possible actions just described, we will start with a first decision (B_o,t_1), i.e. start the jobs in B_o at time $t_o := 0$ and postpone the next decision either to the first job completion if it occurs before t_1, or to time t_1 otherwise. Here, as part of an iterative procedure, we will usually assume that certain prescribed jobs belong to B_o, i.e. have to be started at time t = 0. Then the measurable set $Z_o := \{x \in \mathbb{R}^n_> \mid x(\alpha) \leq t_1$ for some $\alpha \in B_o\}$ gives all duration vectors for which one or more jobs from B_o end before t_1. The different possible cases of certain jobs from B_o being completed first are distinguished by introducing for each non-void $E \subseteq B_o$ the measurable set $Z_{o,E} := \{x \in Z_o \mid x(\alpha) = x(\beta)$ for $\alpha, \beta \in E$ and $x(\alpha) < x(\beta)$ for $\alpha \in E$, $\beta \in B_o \setminus E\}$. Then the subproblem induced by some $x \in Z_{o,E}$ is defined on the subset $A \setminus E$ of jobs and, because of the required non-preemptiveness, has the set $B_o \setminus E$ as the set of prescribed starting jobs.

If $t_1 = \infty$ (e.g. always for elementary strategies), then $Z_o = \mathbb{R}^n_>$, and no other subproblems occur. Otherwise, i.e. for $x \notin Z_o$, we make the next decision (B_1,t_2) at time t_1, where $B_1 \neq \emptyset$ is the set of jobs that are started at time t_1, and $t_2 > t_1$ is the next decision point in case there is no completion up to t_2. Then the measurable set $Z_1 := \{x \in \mathbb{R}^n_> \mid t_1 < x(\alpha)$ for all $\alpha \in B_o$ and $x(\alpha) \leq t_2$ for some $\alpha \in B_o$ or $t_1 + x(\alpha) \leq t_2$ for some $\alpha \in B_1\}$ contains all duration vectors for which the first job completion occurs in $]t_1,t_2]$. We will again distinguish those jobs which are first completed by putting $Z_{1,E} := \{x \in Z_1 \mid x(\alpha) = x(\beta) = x(\gamma) + t_1 = x(\delta) + t_1$ for all $\alpha, \beta \in B_o \cap E$ and $\gamma, \delta \in B_1 \cap E$ and $x(\alpha) < x(\beta)$ for $\alpha \in B_o \cap E$, $\beta \in B_o \setminus E$ or for $\alpha \in B_1 \cap E$ and $\beta \in B_1 \setminus E\}$.

Proceeding iteratively in this way, we obtain a finite sequence of decisions $(B_o,t_1),(B_1,t_2),\ldots,(B_\ell,t_{\ell+1})$, where $0 < t_1 < t_2 < \ldots < t_\ell < t_{\ell+1} = \infty$ because of the finiteness of A. Put $D_o := B_o, D_r := B_r \cup D_{r-1}, r = 1,\ldots,\ell$, and $Z_r := \{x \in \mathbb{R}^n_> \mid t_r < t_j + x(\alpha)$ for all $\alpha \in B_j$, $j = 1,\ldots,r-1$ and $t_j + x(\alpha)$

$\leqslant t_{r+1}$ for some $\alpha \in B_j$ and some $j = 1,\dots,r\}$. Z_r contains all $x \in \mathbb{R}^n_>$ for which the first job completion occurs in $]t_r, t_{r+1}]$, $r = 1,\dots,\ell$. We again distinguish those jobs that are completed first by defining accordingly the sets $Z_{r,E}$ for all non-void $E \subseteq D_r$.

Altogether this leads to a recursive CANONICAL DECOMPOSITION of a strategy Π by means of a partition of $\mathbb{R}^n_>$ into a finite number of measurable sets $Z_{r,E}$, $r = 0,\dots,\ell$, $\emptyset \neq E \subseteq D_r$ with the following properties: On each $Z_{r,E}$ there is no completion up to t_r, all jobs $\alpha \in D_r = B_0 \cup B_1 \cup \dots \cup B_r$ are being performed since time t_j if $\alpha \in B_j$, and the first completion of a job occurs in $]t_r, t_{r+1}]$. Then the random variable Y that gives the first completion time is of the form $Y = X_\alpha + t_j$ on $Z_{r,E}$ for any $\alpha \in E \cap B_j$, $j = 1,\dots,r$.

Taking into account now the induced <u>conditional distributions</u>, associated with each subproblem, leads to the intended basis for induction arguments in proofs for e.g. optimality criteria, cf. [26]. We do not go into further details here but close this Section on general strategies with examples that demonstrate the nature of the iterative decomposition and the stochastic-dynamic-optimization-type description of strategies.

<u>EXAMPLE 2.5</u>:

We discuss here strategies Π^1, Π^2 and Π^3 of Example 2.1 w.r.t. a description in the framework of stochastic dynamic optimization and w.r.t. the iterative decomposition into subproblems.

(1) For Π^1 we start at time $t_0 = 0$ with the first action $(\{\alpha_1,\alpha_2\},\infty)$. The next decision point is $t_1 = \min(x_1,x_2)$. Depending on whether $x_1 < x_2$ or $x_1 = x_2$ or $x_1 > x_2$, we get into the different subproblems already at this second decision point. If $x_1 < x_2$, the second action is $(\emptyset,\infty)$, leading to the third decision point x_2, third action $(\{\alpha_3\};\infty)$, fourth decision point x_2+x_3, fourth action $(\{\alpha_4\},\infty)$, fifth decision point $x_2+x_3+x_4$, fifth decision $(\{\alpha_5,\alpha_6\},\infty)$ and sixth decision point $x_2+x_3+x_4+\min(x_5,x_6)$. Now if $x_5 \neq x_6$, the last decision will be $(\emptyset,\infty)$; otherwise, the project is already completed at the sixth decision point.

If instead $x_2 \leqslant x_1$, we proceed analogously, where at the completion point x_1 the associated action will be $(\emptyset,\infty)$ (if x_1 is different from the completion time of any other job).

(2) For Π^2 we also start at time $t_0 = 0$ with the first decision $(\{\alpha_1,\alpha_2\},\infty)$ and have the next decision point $t_1 = \min(x_1,x_2)$. Now if

$x_1 < x_2$, the action chosen at time t_1 is $(\emptyset,\infty)$, leading to the decision point x_2, where the action is $(\{\alpha_3,\alpha_4\},\infty)$ if $x_1 \leq 10$ and $(\{\alpha_3,\alpha_5\},\infty)$ otherwise. All further actions are, from that time on, chosen in an earliest-start-type manner. If instead $x_2 < x_1$, we proceed accordingly (i.e. take the action $(\{\alpha_3,\alpha_4\},\infty)$ if $x_2 \leq 10$ and $(\{\alpha_3,\alpha_5\},\infty)$ otherwise, whereas the action at the later occuring decision point x_2, given that this value does not coincide with any other completion time, is $(\emptyset,\infty)$.

(3) For Π^3, the situation is somewhat more involved then for Π^2. The essential difference to Π^2 is given by the handling of the case $x_2 \leq \min\{x_1, 10\}$. In that case, our action at the first decision point $t_1 = x_2 < 10$ is $(\emptyset, 10)$. The next decision point then is $\min\{10, x_1\}$. If $x_1 \leq 10$, the action taken is $(\{\alpha_2,\alpha_5\},\infty)$, while otherwise, the action is $(\{\alpha_3,\alpha_4\},\infty)$. All future startes and actions again are given by earliest start scheduling.

III. SPECIAL CLASSES OF STRATEGIES

Up to now, the only REGULARITY CONDITIONS, imposed onto strategies, have been (universal) measurability and, in some cases, elementarity. However, from an applicational point of view, there is a great variety of additional assumptions that might be considered. Essentially, there are three types of conditions, that will be discussed below. First of all, there are combinatorial properties of strategies, such as being induced by a poset or by a selection, which lead to the classes of ES-, MES- and preselective strategies. Secondly, there are procedural concepts such as using priority rules that lead, among other things, to list scheduling strategies and set strategies. Thirdly, there are analytical properties, such as being λ^n-a.e. continuous or (uniformly) continuous or convex or subadditive or monotonically increasing that lead to still other classes of strategies. We will have a close look into this "universe" of classes of strategies and will find a surprising coincidence between the different types of approaches; cf. also Figure 8 at the end of this Section. Also, we will try to distinguish these classes w.r.t. their theoretical behaviour and numerical tractability. Main aspects of these discussions will be the existence of the associated optimum value and its relation e.g. to the overall optimal value, the boundedness of the respective classes w.r.t. dominance, the stability behaviour w.r.t. small perturbations of the data, and, finally, the monotonicity behaviour. In doing so, the following principles are used:

Dealing with a class of strategies, we may always restrict attention to the $\leqslant$-minimal elements of this class (w.r.t. dominance) as long as every strategy in the class is dominated by some $\leqslant$-minimal strategy in the class. If we can restrict attention to finite sets of strategies, we can certainly guarantee the existence of optimal solutions, whatever cost function and duration distribution is given. Concerning stability, the available insights (cf. Section IV) imply that a really satisfactory behaviour can only be expected if one can restrict attention to finite sets of continuous strategies. If only quasi-stability, i.e. stability for duration distributions with Lebesgue densities is required, finite sets of λ^n-a.e. continuous strategies will already do. Finally, if one can restrict attention to monotonically increasing (convex and monotonically increasing) strategies, one will find a nice monotonicity behaviour with regard to transition to stochastically greater (stochastically greater in the convex sense) duration distributions, cf. Section IV.

We begin with the discussion of earliest start scheduling, which constitutes one of the most common tools in applications of scheduling theory, e.g. in the building and construction industry [4],[18],[22]. Intuitively, this approach consists in assigning a precedence relation $\Theta = (A,O)$ to the jobs by which the project is executed in the sense that a job is started when its predecessors are finished, i.e. the associated "earliest start" schedule is defined as:

$$ES_\Theta[x](\alpha) := \begin{cases} 0 & \alpha \text{ minimal in } \Theta \\ \max\limits_{\substack{(\beta,\alpha)\in O \\ \alpha \neq \beta}} \{ES_\Theta[x](\beta)+x(\beta)\} & \text{otherwise} \end{cases}$$

Note that the earliest start schedule, associated with (A,O), can be carried out in an on-line fashion without having any previous knowledge of activity durations, and yields a pointwise optimal (thus cost minimal) schedule w.r.t. (A,O) and the realized durations, whatever (maybe not precisely known) regular cost function applies.

DEFINITION:

Call a strategy Π for $[A,O_o,N]$ an ES-strategy, if there is a partial order $\Theta = (A,O)$, such that $\Pi[x](\alpha) = ES_\Theta[x](\alpha)$ holds for all $\alpha\in A$ and all $x\in\mathbb{R}^n_>$.

It is well known [23],[25] that ES_Θ is a strategy iff Θ is feasible, i.e. if $O_o \subseteq O$ and $N \notin U(\Theta)$ for all $N \in \mathcal{N}$, where $U(\Theta)$ denotes the system of Θ-independent sets. Intuitively speaking, this means that ES strategies avoid simultaneous performance of forbidden sets by introducing a new precedence constraint $(\alpha_N, \beta_N) \in O$ with $\alpha_N \neq \beta_N$, $\{\alpha_N, \beta_N\} \subseteq N$ for each $N \in \mathcal{N}$. This means that the conflict on each forbidden set is solved in a universal way (i.e. in the same way for all $x \in \mathbb{R}^n_>$) by letting a particular job from this set wait for the completion of a particular other job from the set.

Due to their nice structure, there are a number of algorithmic methods, based on simulation, available for dealing with ES-strategies, cf. [12],[23],[25], though one is of course working with NP-hard optimization problems. Also, the class of ES strategies is dominated by $\leqslant$-minimal ES strategies, which correspond to the $\subseteq$-minimal feasible posets. (Note however, that these strategies are usually still not $\leqslant$-minimal w.r.t. all strategies.). It is well known, that for suitable κ and P, any such $\leqslant$-minimal ES strategy may yield the unique optimal strategy within this class, cf. [24],[26].

Because of the given recursive description, ES strategies on $\mathbb{R}^n_>$ are elementary and are sublinear (thus convex and subadditive), uniformly continuous, monotonically increasing and positive homogeneous (in all components). Obviously, the class is finite, implying that the associated optimum value $\rho^{ES}(\kappa,P)$ is attained for all P and κ. In fact, $\rho^{ES}(\kappa,P)$ coincides with the overall optimal value $\rho(\kappa,P)$ in the case of singular distributions (deterministic case), this being one of the reasons for the importance of feasible partial orders in the theory of deterministic scheduling [23],[19]. Given the fact that ES strategies are continuous and that there is only a finite number of such strategies, they form a stable class in the sense of Section IV. Furthermore, as they are convex and monotonically increasing, the monotonicity behaviour is particularly nice, even in the dependence case. All these properties add to the importance of the class of ES strategies, so much the more, as this class will later turn out to give exactly the convex strategies.

EXAMPLE 3.1:

Let $[A, O_o, \mathcal{N}]$ be as in Example 2.1. There are 7 $\leqslant$-minimal feasible posets for this problem, four of which are given in Figure 4 by arrow diagrams, together with the newly introduced precedence relations on the respective forbidden sets $\{\alpha_2,\alpha_3\}$ and $\{\alpha_3,\alpha_4,\alpha_5\}$. The associated $\leqslant$-minimal ES-strategies are also given in a functional description:

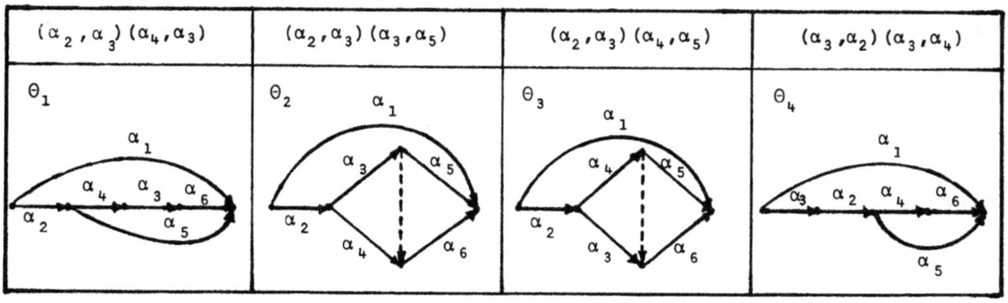

Figure 4

$\alpha \in A$	α_1	α_2	α_3	α_4	α_5	α_6
$ES_{\Theta_1}[x](\alpha)$	O	O	x_2+x_4	x_2	x_2	$x_2+x_3+x_4$
$ES_{\Theta_2}[x](\alpha)$	O	O	x_2	x_2	x_2+x_3	$x_2+\max(x_3,x_4)$
$ES_{\Theta_3}[x](\alpha)$	O	O	x_2	x_2	x_2+x_4	$x_2+\max(x_3,x_4)$
$ES_{\Theta_4}[x](\alpha)$	O	x_3	O	x_2+x_3	x_2+x_3	$x_2+x_3+x_4$

Note that ES_{Θ_1} and ES_{Θ_4} are <u>linear</u> functions. In fact this is true exactly if Θ is a <u>forest of outtrees</u>. This also applies to strategy Π^1 in Example 2.1 (1), which is of course an ES strategy for the problem under discussion and which is dominated e.g. by ES_{Θ_2} and ES_{Θ_3}.

The next class of strategies discussed is the class of <u>MES-strategies</u>, which is a proper extension of the class of ES strategies. The basic notion is as follows:

DEFINITION:

Call a strategy $\Pi := \Pi_\Phi$ for $[A, O_0, \mathcal{N}]$ an <u>MES strategy</u>, if there is a set Φ of feasible posets, such that $\Pi[x](\alpha) = \min\{ES_\Theta[x](\alpha) \mid \Theta \in \Phi\}$ holds for all $\alpha \in A$ and all $x \in \mathbb{R}^n_>$.

Like ES strategies, MES strategies are <u>combinatorially</u> defined and appealing from an applicational point of view. In fact, the use of

MES strategies may be interpreted as a variant of earliest start scheduling, viz. employing in an on-line fashion a set of "compatible" earliest start schedules, while, according to the realized duration vector $x \in \mathbb{R}^n_>$, the set of still considered precedence relations is gradually reduced down to one particular poset. A thorough discussion of MES and preselective strategies, including aspects of the algorithmic treatment, is given in [8], [9]. We restrict ourselves here to some short remarks.

First of all, the bounding behaviour is extremely nice, cf. Theorem 3.8 and Figure 7. In particular, the $\leq$-minimal strategies of this class are well characterized and each such strategy turns out as the only optimal strategy within this class for suitably chosen κ and P, cf. [24], [26]. Given the definition of MES strategies as "minimum" over certain ES strategies, many of the nice properties of ES strategies immediately carry over to this case. E.g., all MES strategies are elementary and are uniformly continuous, monotonically increasing and positively homogeneous on $\mathbb{R}^n_>$ (in all components). Note that sublinearity, convexity and subadditivity characterize precisely the borderline with the ES strategies, and that there are MES strategies that are not ES strategies, iff $|N|>2$ for some $N \in \mathcal{N}$. Also, the class of MES strategies is finite, implying that the associated optimum value $\rho^{MES}(\kappa,P) \leq \rho^{ES}(\kappa,P)$ is attained for all P and κ. Of course, also $\rho^{MES}(\kappa,P)$ coincides with the overall optimal value in the case of singular distributions. Also, we are dealing again with a stable class and find a satisfying monotonicity behaviour in case of transition to stochastically greater duration distributions, even in the dependence case.

EXAMPLE 3.2:

Consider the scheduling problem in Example 3.1:

(1) If we put $\Phi:=\{\Theta_1,\Theta_2\}$, then Π_Φ is not a strategy. To see this, take for instance $x(\alpha)=1$ for all $\alpha \in A$. Then $ES_{\Theta_1}[x]=(0,0,1,2,1,3)$, $ES_{\Theta_2}[x]=(0,0,1,1,2,2)$ and therefore $\Pi_\Phi[x]=(0,0,1,1,1,2)$. Thus jobs $\alpha_3,\alpha_4,\alpha_5$ are all started at time 1, leading to a contradiction to (Sto 2).

(2) If we put $\Phi=\{\Theta_1,\Theta_4\}$, then again Π_Φ is not a strategy. For whatever duration vector is given, jobs α_1,α_2 and α_3 are all started at time 0, leading to a contradiction to (Sto 2).

(3) If we put $\Phi=\{\Theta_2,\Theta_3\}$, then Π_Φ is a strategy. Its functional representation is as follows:

$\Pi_\Phi[x](\alpha) = (0,0,x_2,x_2,x_2+\min(x_3,x_4),x_2+\max(x_3,x_4))$.

The idea behind this strategy is to start with jobs α_1 and α_2 at time 0 and wait for the completion of job α_2. Then start jobs α_3,α_4 and as soon as one of these two jobs is completed, job α_5 follows. Finally, as soon as both jobs α_3 and α_4 are completed, α_6 is started. Note that a contradiction to (Sto 2) is avoided by the following conflict-solving rule: On the forbidden set $\{\alpha_2,\alpha_3\}$, job α_3 waits for the completion of α_2, while on the forbidden set $\{\alpha_3,\alpha_4,\alpha_5\}$, job α_5 waits for the completion of either α_3 or α_4.

Example 3.2 contains major hints to the nature of MES strategies, cf. also [8]. Indeed it turns out that a function Π_Φ is a strategy, iff it fulfills (Sto 2), i.e. the type of contradiction occuring in (1) and (2) is the only possible. Furthermore, the fulfillment of (Sto 2) is indeed equivalent to the behaviour observed in (3), i.e. to the existence of a selection of waiting jobs from the forbidden sets. In fact, this is what motivated the introduction of the notion of preselectivity, that is given next.

DEFINITION:

Let $[A,O_o,N]$ with $N = \{N_1,\ldots,N_k\}$ be given and $s = (\alpha_1,\ldots,\alpha_k)$ be an associated selection, i.e. $\alpha_j \in N_j$ for $j = 1,\ldots,k$. Call a function Π: $\mathbb{R}^n_> \to \mathbb{R}^n_\geqslant$ preselective with selection s, iff $\min\{\Pi[x](\beta)+x(\beta) \mid \beta \in N_j \setminus \{\alpha_j\}\} \leq \Pi[x](\alpha_j)$ holds for all $x \in \mathbb{R}^n_>$.

It is interesting to note that preselectivity is a rather general principle, which leads to an interesting, uncountably infinite and quite unstructured class of strategies. However, as we will see below, it not only contains the MES strategies, but also such interesting, (analytically defined) classes as the sublinear, subadditive, convex, monotonically increasing, uniformly continuous, linear, (super)additive and concave strategies [26]. It turns out that the class of preselective strategies can nicely be handled. The reason is that it coincides essentially with the MES strategies in the sense of dominance. I.e. MES strategies are preselective and each preselective strategy is dominated by at least one particular s-induced (preselective) MES strategy, where the s-induced strategies are defined as follows:

$\Pi_s := \Pi_{\Phi_s}$, where $\Phi_s := \{\Theta = (A,O) \mid O_o \subseteq O$ and for $j=1,\ldots,k$ there is $\beta_j \in N_j \setminus \{\alpha_j\}$ such that $(\beta_j,\alpha_j) \in O\}$.

I.e. the idea is to take all feasible partial orders Θ that are compatible with a given selection, i.e. that solve the conflict on the forbidden sets in such a way, that on each such set N_j, the preselected waiting job α_j waits for the completion of at least one particular other job β_j of the respective set. Exactly if $\Phi_s \neq \emptyset$, the associated MES-strategy Π_{Φ_s} exists. As is shown in [8], the property $\Pi_{\Phi_s} \leq \Pi_{\Phi_{s'}} \Longleftrightarrow \Phi_{s'} \subseteq \Phi_s$ holds. Thus the $\subseteq$-maximal sets Φ_s of partial orders, s being a selection, induce the <u>$\leq$-minimal MES</u> or <u>preselective strategies</u>, which are of great further interest, cf. Theorem 3.8 and Figure 7.

<u>EXAMPLE 3.3:</u>

Consider the situation of Example 3.1 and let Θ^1, Θ^2 and Θ^3 denote the posets given in Figure 5 by arrow diagrams:

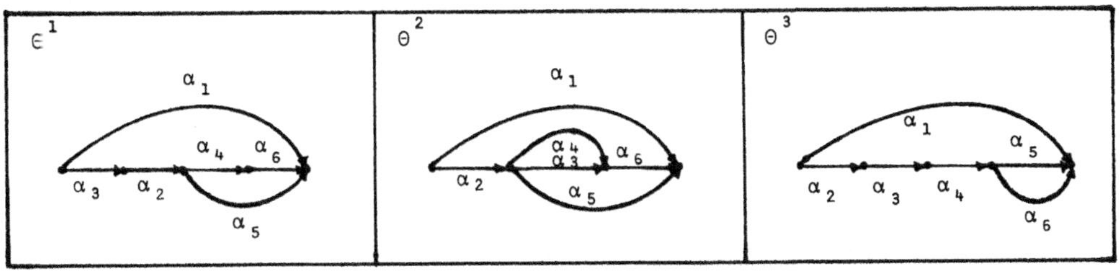

Figure 5

There are 6 selections $s_1 = (\alpha_2,\alpha_3), s_2 = (\alpha_2,\alpha_4), s_3 = (\alpha_2,\alpha_5), s_4 = (\alpha_3,\alpha_3), s_5 = (\alpha_3,\alpha_4), s_6 = (\alpha_3,\alpha_5)$. Note that if we select α_2 as the waiting job on $N_1 = \{\alpha_2,\alpha_3\}$, we have to add the precedence constraint (α_3,α_2) to Θ_o, which leads to the poset Θ^1 in **Figure** 5. Obviously, jobs α_4 and α_5 then act already as waiting jobs on $N_2 = \{\alpha_3,\alpha_4,\alpha_5\}$, i.e. we have $\Phi_{s_2} = \Phi_{s_3} = \{\Theta = (A,O) \mid O^1 \subseteq O\}$. Thus the MES-strategy $\Pi_{\Phi_{s_2}}$ coincides with ES_{Θ^1} (which is in fact ES_{Θ_4} in Example 3.1), and this strategy is a <u>$\leq$-minimal</u> MES strategy. Also, $\Phi_{s_1} = \emptyset$ is obvious, i.e. there is <u>no</u> preselective strategy with selection s_1.

If, alternatively, α_3 becomes the waiting job on $N_1=\{\alpha_2,\alpha_3\}$, the resulting poset after introducing the precedence constraint (α_2,α_3) is Θ^2. Now it is easily verified, that any of the associated selections s_4, s_5 and s_6 leads to a <u>$\leq$-minimal</u> MES-strategy. Note that Φ_{s_5} and Φ_{s_6} both contain the poset Θ^3, which is in fact the poset Θ occuring in Figure 2 in Example 2.1. Note further that $\Phi_{s_6} = \{\Theta = (A,O) \mid$

$O_2 \subseteq O$ or $O_3 \subseteq O\}$, where O_2 and O_3 belong to the partial orders Θ_2 and Θ_3 in Example 3.1. Thus $\Pi_{\Phi_{S6}} = \Pi_{\Phi}$ in Example 3.2.(3); in particular $\Pi_{\Phi_{S6}}$ is not an ES-strategy.

Very much different from the COMBINATORIALLY defined classes of strategies, discussed so far, are strategies defined via (parallel) PRIORITY RULES. The idea is to give, at any decision time t, a linear ordering L(t) (the priority ordering) on the set of jobs not yet started. If L(t) is compatible with L(O) for all decision times, the rule is said to be static, if L(t) may vary with t, it is said to be dynamic. In a strategy induced by a priority rule, actions taken at some time t (starting from t = O) consist in starting (from the set of jobs available at t) in order of decreasing priority as many jobs as possible in terms of precedence and resource constraints. So, at any decision time t, a maximal set of jobs is started that is lexicographically smallest w.r.t. the priority ordering L(t).

COROLLARY 3.4:

Let a strategy Π be induced by a priority rule. Then

(1) Π is elementary

(2) Π is a $\leqslant$-minimal strategy; in fact, $\Pi[x]$ is even a $\leqslant$-minimal feasible schedule for all $x \in \mathbb{R}^n_>$.

Note that (1) follows immediately from the definition of priority rules, while (2) reflects exactly the essential aspect of the whole approach, viz. its greedyness. Whenever there is a machine available that might be used, it is used immediately regardless of possible benfits arising from postponing the decision on whether to start a particular job or not for a while (deliberate idleness of machines).

It should be mentioned that in order to arrive at a strategy by using a dynamic priority rule, the priority orderings L(t) may only vary in a way compatible with the information about x available at time t. The most general orderings of that type considered here are set-type priority rules as discussed below. In fact, in literature one is usually mostly interested in constant priority rules (list scheduling strategies), for which (good) performance bounds have in some cases been obtained; cf. [5],[6].

We will see below that priority induced strategies are not a very reasonable class of strategies to deal with. They are of course easily implemented and have the properties mentioned in Corollary 3.4, which are the direct consequences of their greedyness. It is also true, that in special exponential scheduling problems, even the overall optimum strategy is of that type, cf. Section V. On the other hand, due to the greedyness involved, this class will in general not lead to the optimum value even for the deterministic case and will at most have a restricted stability behaviour. Furthermore, the analytical and monotonicity behaviour will be quite unsatisfying, even in the deterministic case. In fact, this is what is known as GRAHAM ANOMALIES in the deterministic framework [6]; cf. also the following example and the discussion at the end of this section.

EXAMPLE 3.5:

(1) Consider the situation of Example 2.1 and take the constant priority list 1>2>3>4>5>6. Then the resulting strategy is obviously the MES strategy Π_Φ discussed in Example 3.2. In particular, this strategy has nice analytical properties.

(2) Consider instead the scheduling problem, given in Figure 6.

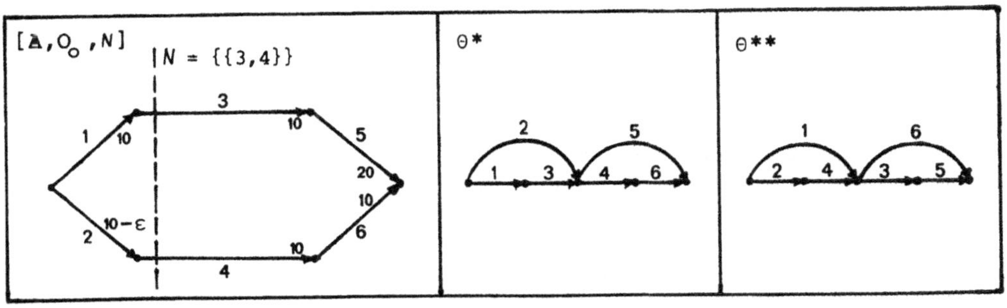

Figure 6

Here, there is only one decision to be made, viz. whether to start job 3 before job 4 or the other way round. The associated (dynamic) priority-induced strategies are defined independently of the priority rule, except for the case $x_1 = x_2$. Giving job 3 a higher priority than job 4 leads to the following induced strategy:

$$\Pi[x]:= \begin{cases} ES_{\Theta*}[x] & x_1 \leq x_2 \\ ES_{\Theta**}[x] & \text{otherwise} \end{cases}$$

Note that, in this example (which $\varepsilon>0$ being small), it is preferable to start job 3 before job 4. However due to their greedyness, every priority-induced strategy will do the converse, given that job 2 ends shortly before job 1. All such strategies will therefore not be optimal. Certainly, increasing the duration vector to $(10, 10+\varepsilon, 10, 10, 20, 10)$ will decrease the achieved project duration from $50-\varepsilon$ time units to 40 time units. Furthermore, there will be an discontinuity when appropriately approaching the duration vector (10,10,10,10,20,10), independently of whether job 3 has a higher priority than job 4 or not.

Given the fact that priority-induced strategies have a poor analytical behaviour and, due to their greedyness, often even miss the deterministic optimum value while on the other side behaving nicely in some exponential models, the question was for an extension of this class that shows a better overall behaviour. The aim was to somehow find an integration of MES and priority-induced strategies into a finite class of strategies, starting from a common feature of both approaches. This common feature is given by the fact that, in any case, decisions made at some point only depend on the set of already completed jobs and the set of jobs still being performed. In fact, this idea led to the following definition [21]:

DEFINITION:

Call a strategy Π for $[A,O_o,N]$ a set strategy, if Π is elementary and if the action $B(t)$ taken at any decision point $t \in \mathbb{R}^1_{\geq}$ depends only on the sets B^* and $B \setminus B^*$ of jobs already finished or being performed at that time.

It is easy to see that all MES strategies are set strategies, as are all dynamic priority-induced strategies which are set-type, i.e. which determine the priority list $L(t)$ only in dependence of the sets B^* and $B \setminus B^*$. Thus in particular, strategy Π in Example 3.5(2) is a set strategy. Note, however, that strategies Π^2 and Π^3 in Example 2.1 are not set strategies, as the decisions taken strongly depend on whether $x_2 \leq 10$ or not.

A thorough discussion of set strategies is given in [21]. Certainly, as the class is finite, the associated optimum value $\rho^{SET}(\kappa,P)$, for which $\rho^{SET}(\kappa,P)<\rho^{MES}(\kappa,P)$ is possible, is attained for all P and κ. Again, $\rho^{SET}(\kappa,P)$ coincides with the overall optimal value $\rho(\kappa,P)$ in the case of singular distributions as well as in exponentional models (cf. Section V), i.e. set strategies generalize this nice feature of certain list scheduling strategies in special cases to all exponential models. Furthermore, the bounding behaviour of set strategies is nice, i.e. any such strategy is bounded by some $\leqslant$-minimal one and any such $\leqslant$-minimal strategy is also $\leqslant$-minimal w.r.t. all strategies.

As was already mentioned, the analytical behaviour will in general not be completely satisfying, implying a bad monotonicity behaviour in the stochastic case, cf. Section IV. However, the observation from Example 3.5 (2), viz. a possible representation as piecewise composition of ES strategies remains possible; in fact, this is the content of the following theorem, cf. [21]:

THEOREM 3.6:

Let Π be a set strategy for $[A,O_0,N]$. Then there exists a partition of $\mathbb{R}^n_>$ into finitely many non-empty sets $Z_1,\ldots,Z_m$ such that

(i) each Z_i is a (not necessarily closed) convex polyhedron (even a cone)

(ii) for each Z_i there exists a (unique, feasible) partial order (even an interval order) $\Theta_i=(A,O_i)$ such that $\Pi[x] = ES_{\Theta_i}[x]$ for all $x\in Z_i$, $i = 1,\ldots,m$.

Theorem 3.6 means that every set strategy behaves as an ES strategy on each of finitely many convex polyhedra forming a partion of $\mathbb{R}^n_>$; cf. e.g. the two associated polyhedra $\{x\in\mathbb{R}^6_> \mid x_1\leqslant x_2\}$ and $\{x\in\mathbb{R}^6_> \mid x_1>x_2\}$ in Example 3.5 (2). This means, that any such strategy, thus any list scheduling strategy, is piecewise well-behaved, i.e. is convex (thus subadditive), monotonically increasing and positive homogeneous on each of the finitely many open sets $Z_i\setminus H, i = 1,\ldots,m$, where H denotes the union of the finitely many hyperplanes that are the boundaries of the sets $Z_i, i = 1,\ldots,m$. Consequently, bad analytical behaviour (and thus GRAHAM ANOMALIES) are restricted to the closed set H, which has obviously Lebesgue measure zero. Thus all such strategies are λ^n-almost everywhere continuous, implying at least a kind of quasi-stable behaviour, viz. stability in case of duration distributions with a Lebesgue density, cf. Theorem 4.6.

We discuss now a third and particularly appealing approach to reasonable classes of strategies, viz. defining them by ANALYTICAL

PROPERTIES such as being convex or continuous or monotonically increasing. The natural notion to start with, also from a stability point of view, is continuity. Surprisingly enough, this class as a whole will turn out to be extremely unsuited for any use in real-life contexts.

We may start from the fact, that any preselective strategy is dominated by a nice MES strategy, which is elementary, uniformly continuous, monotonically increasing, positive homogeneous and, w.l.o.g., $\leqslant$-minimal. Thus concerning continuous strategies that are also preselective, the situation is nice. More interesting is the question for continuous strategies that are not preselective. Certainly, if $|N| = 2$ for all $N \in \mathcal{N}$, there is no way to avoid the introduction of a fixed precedence relation on each forbidden set in order to be continuous, i.e. continuity then will be equivalent to being an ES-strategy. However, as soon as $|N|>2$ for some $N \in \mathcal{N}$, where N does not contain all minimal elements in Θ_o, there exist continuous strategies, that are not preselective. We demonstrate the construction method in the example, given next. The idea is to change the role of the waiting job in dependence of the observed duration of some minimal element, not in N, and achieve continuity by having two waiting jobs for certain duration vectors.

EXAMPLE 3.7:

Consider again the scheduling problem of Example 2.1, where $N_2 = \{\alpha_3,\alpha_4,\alpha_5\}$ fulfills $|N_2|>2$ and does not contain all minimal elements of Θ_o. Consider now the following, iteratively defined strategy Π_ε, where $0<\varepsilon<1$:

Start at time 0 with action $(\{\alpha_1,\alpha_2\};\infty)$. Base the future actions on the completion time x_2 of job α_2. For $0<x_2\leqslant 10-\varepsilon$, let α_5 act as a preselected waiting job on N_2, i.e. take the action $(\{\alpha_3,\alpha_4\},\infty)$ at time x_1 and do earliest start scheduling afterwards. For $10+\varepsilon\leqslant x_2$, let analogously act α_4 as a preselected waiting job. For $x_2 = 10$, let both jobs α_4 and α_5 wait for the completion of job α_3. Use the time intervals $(10-\varepsilon,10)$ and $(10,10+\varepsilon)$ for continuous transitions from one situation to the other. I.e. for $10-\varepsilon<x_2<10$, start only job α_3 at time x_2, let α_5 wait for the completion of job α_3, and postpone the start of job α_4 to time $x_2 + \frac{x_2-10+\varepsilon}{10-x_2}$, if α_3 is not completed before that time, or to the completion time x_2+x_3 of job α_3 otherwise. Similarly, for $10<x_2<10+\varepsilon$, start only job α_3 at time x_2, let α_4 wait for the completion of job α_3, and postpone the start of job α_5 to time

$x_2 + \frac{10+\varepsilon-x_2}{x_2-10}$, if α_3 is not completed before that time, or to the completion time x_2+x_3 of job α_3, otherwise. Obviously, the resulting strategy is continuous and not preselective.

Example 3.7 demonstrated, that there exist quite nasty continuous strategies. It is not hard to see that such nasty behaviour is really an unavoidable consequence of giving up preselectivity. As can intuitively be guessed from Example 3.7, any such strategy will show a certain "pole-behaviour" at some point $x \in \mathbb{R}^n_>$ (here: all $x \in \mathbb{R}^n_>$ with $x_1 = 10$ and "large" durations on N_2). This means, in particular, that such strategies can neither be uniformly continuous nor elementary (note that the postponed starting times of jobs α_4 and α_5 cannot generally be realized as completion times of other jobs). In fact, any such strategy can also not be $\leqslant$-minimal. To see this for the case of Example 3.7, put $\varepsilon = 1/j, j \in \mathbb{N}$, and consider the sequence $\Pi_j := \Pi_{1/j}, j \in \mathbb{N}$, which obviously is monotonically decreasing in the sense of Theorem 2.4 and approximates a lower bounding strategy Π, that is discontinous and consists in selecting the following waiting jobs on N_2: α_5 if $x_2<10$, both α_4 and α_5 if $x_2=10$ and, finally, α_4 if $x_2>10$. Note that this indicates that the boundary of the set of non-preselective, continuous strategies will consist of discontinuous strategies. This will straightforwardly imply, that the restricted optimum value $\rho^{CON}(P,\kappa)$ is generally not attained on the class of continuous strategies and that the stability behaviour as well as the monotonicity behaviour will generally be bad.

The last hints given indicate that the class of all continuous strategies is a very unsuited class to work with. There are quite involved theorems [26] available that show that the behaviour found in Example 3.7 is actually of a general nature. These results, which will be published elsewhere, are briefly discussed next.

THEOREM 3.8: CONTINUOUS-BOUND THEOREM

Let $[A,O_0,N]$ be a scheduling problem and Π be any associated strategy. Then the following statements are equivalent:

(1) Π is continuous and $\leqslant$-minimal w.r.t. all strategies

(2) Π is continuous and $\leqslant$-minimal w.r.t. all continuous strategies

(3) Π is a $\leqslant$-minimal preselective strategy

(4) Π is a $\leqslant$-minimal MES-strategy

(5) $\Pi = \Pi_{\Phi_s}$, where s is a selection, such that Φ_s is $\subseteq$-maximal.

The behaviour given in Theorem 3.8 is visualized in Figure 7. Note that the two (special) classes of preselective strategies and continuous strategies are not contained in each other but overlap. The MES strategies are contained in both classes. All preselective strategies and all MES strategies are bounded by the finitely many (preselective) MES strategies of type Π_{Φ_s}, s selection with Φ_s $\subseteq$-maximal. Continuous strategies are also bounded by these finitely many continuous strategies, as long as they are preselective. If a continuous strategy is not preselective, it is not dominated by a $\leqslant$-minimal continuous strategy, i.e. we can find a decreasing countably infinite sequence of continuous strategies dominating it. The existing lower bound of this sequence in the sense of Theorem 2.4 is of course <u>not</u> continuous.

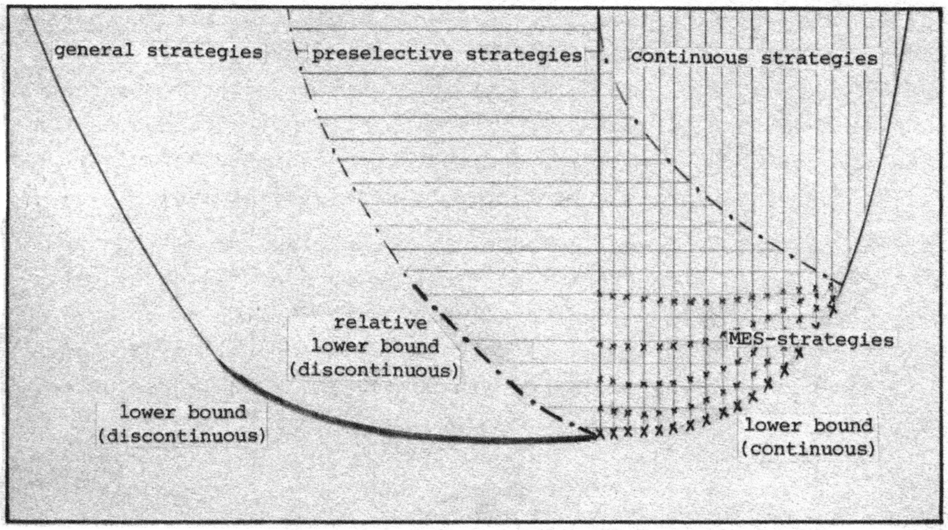

Figure 7

<u>THEOREM 3.9</u>: FIRST CHARACTERIZATION THEOREM

(1) The classes of <u>monotonically increasing</u>, <u>uniformly continuous</u>,

continuous and elementary, $\leqslant$-minimal continuous strategies can all essentially be identified with the classes of MES or preselective strategies, i.e. any of these strategies is dominated by some MES strategy, which simultaneously has all the properties mentioned.

(2) The class of continuous and elementary strategies is exactly the class of MES strategies.

This First Characterization Theorem generalizes many of the aspects discussed in connection with Example 3.7. It includes the surprising observation, that in the "universe" of strategies, the quite uncomparable properties of being preselective or uniformly continuous or continuous and elementary or monotonically increasing are all essentially equivalent and imply each other, together with positive honogeneity. Also, there are essentially only finitely many strategies of this type. These essential strategies may be characterized by being continuous and elementary.

Some hints to the proof techniques follow below. Before, we give a similar result for the case of ES strategies.

THEOREM 3.10: SECOND CHARACTERIZATION THEOREM

(1) The classes of sublinear, convex, subadditive strategies can all essentially be identified with the class of ES strategies, i.e. any of these strategies is dominated by some ES strategy, which simultaneously has all properties mentioned.

(2) The class of sublinear and the class of convex strategies is exactly the class of ES strategies.

The Second Characterization Theorem tells us that also the properties of being sublinear or convex or subadditive can essentially be identified in the "universe" of strategies and lead to the finite class of ES strategies, thus also implying positive homogeneity. Both Characterization Theorems show an interesting INTERPLAY between COMBINATORIAL and ANALYTICAL properties of strategies, which considerably restrict the interesting parts of the "universe" of strategies that need to be considered. We give a concise overview over that "universe" below in Figure 8 and discuss some consequences of the given results for GRAHAM ANOMALIES afterwards. A sort of interpretation of the given results from an applicational point of view focussing on the use of either MES or set strategies is contained in the summary of this paper. Additional results, covering e.g. concave strategies, are given in [26]. Some hints to the proof techniques involved follow next.

One main idea for proving the CHARACTERIZATION THEOREMS is to concentrate on the conflict solving mechanism on forbidden sets $N \in \mathcal{N}$. This is done by starting with any duration vector $x \in \mathbb{R}^n_>$ and by studying simultaneously all duration vectors $x^n, n \in \mathbb{N}$, obtained from x by enlarging the duration of jobs in N by n time units. For increasing $n \in \mathbb{N}$, the scheduling situation will be characterized by the fact, that at some time $t \in \mathbb{R}^1_>$, certain jobs are completed while only jobs from the forbidden set N will be under performance. It can be obtained, that some jobs in N will not start before at least one job in N is completed, i.e. some jobs in N will act as locally selected waiting jobs. We denote the set of these selected elements by $S(N,x)$. As for instance Example 3.7 indicates, the local waiting jobs may vary with x (i.e. for $x_2 = 1$, $S(\{\alpha_3,\alpha_4,\alpha_5\},x) = \{\alpha_5\}$ while for $x_2 = 11$, $S(\{\alpha_3,\alpha_4,\alpha_5\},x) = \{\alpha_4\}$. However, as soon as $\bigcap_{x \in \mathbb{R}^n_>} S(N,x) \neq \emptyset$ for all $N \in \mathcal{N}$, i.e. as soon as there is at least one common waiting job (in each $N \in \mathcal{N}$), for all $x \in \mathbb{R}^n_>$, we are dealing with a preselective strategy. Using this fact, it is not difficult to see that, if for any forbidden set $N \in \mathcal{N}$, at least one of the following conditions (I1) and (I2) holds

(I1) $\qquad x \leq y \Rightarrow S(N,x) \subseteq S(N,y)$

(I2) $\qquad x \geq y \Rightarrow S(N,x) \subseteq S(N,y)$

then Π is preselective.

Starting now with a continuous strategy and assuming that for some $N \in \mathcal{N}$ (I1) (or analoguously (I2)) does not apply, leads, for some $z = \lambda \cdot x + (1-\lambda)y$ with $0 < \lambda < 1$, to a "pole-behaviour" as discussed in connection with Example 3.7, i.e. leads to a contradiction to uniform continuity, continuity together with elementarity and $\leq$-minimal continuity. Thus all three conditions imply preselectivity. W.r.t. monotonically increasing strategies Π, (I1) applies. To see this, assume the existence of some $\alpha \in S(N,x) \setminus S(N,y)$. Obviously, $x^n \leq y^n$. It is not difficult to see then, that $n \leq \Pi[x^n](\alpha) \leq \Pi[y^n](\alpha) = \Pi[y](\alpha)$ should be true for all $n \in \mathbb{N}$, which is impossible; thus Π is preselective. Altogether, the proof of (1) in the First Characterization Theorem follows.

W.r.t. (1) in the Second Characterization Theorem, similar arguments then just mentioned guarantee the validity of (I1) and (I2) for sublinear and convex strategies and of (I2) for subadditive strategies. These observations yield preselectivity, i.e. the existence of general waiting elements on each forbidden set. Furthermore now, subadditivity already implies that there must be particular jobs in the respective forbidden sets, for whose completion the waiting jobs wait for all $x \in \mathbb{R}^n_>$. That means, that the conflict on all forbidden sets is solved by the introduction of fixed precedence constraints implying the statement of (1).

Concerning now the stronger versions in (2), one first observes that convexity (and thus sublinearity) implies elementarity. Thus the question is, why elementarity together with convexity or continuity implies being an ES or an MES strategy. The main problem in proving this is that a particular convex (continuous) and elementary strategy need not be identical with the dominating ES(orMES)strategy,constructed in the just described proof technique. Take for instance the convex strategy Π^1 in Example 2.1. Applying the given proof technique might lead us to the introduction of the precedence constraints (α_2,α_3) on N_1 and (α_3,α_5) or (α_4,α_5) on N_2, thus to strategies ES_{Θ_2} and ES_{Θ_3} in Example 3.1. Both these strategies properly dominate Π^1 and are therefore of no direct use in deciding whether Π^1 is an ES strategy or not. The reason for this difficulty is of course, that Π^1 is not a $\leq$-minimal strategy in the respective class. The idea is therefore in all cases under consideration to associate with any considered strategy the <u>"strongest" compatible poset</u> Θ_o' (with $(\alpha,\beta) \in \Theta_o'$ for $\alpha \neq \beta :\Leftrightarrow \Pi[x](\alpha) + x(\alpha) \leq \Pi[x](\beta)$ for all $x \in \mathbb{R}^n_>$) and the <u>"strongest" system of forbidden sets</u> N' (i.e. N forbidden iff $N \in \mathfrak{U}(\Theta_o')$ and there is no $x \in \mathbb{R}^n_>$ and no $t \in \mathbb{R}^1_\geq$, such that w.r.t. x, all jobs in N are under performance at time t). E.g. for Π^1 in Example 2.1., Θ_o' would be the partial order Θ given in Figure 2, and N' would be empty.

The stronger versions of both Characterization Theorems then follow by arguing w.r.t. $[\Theta_o', N']$, for which the considered strategies are still convex or continuous and elementary. By parts (1) the strategies are again dominated by certain ES or MES strategies (now for $[\Theta_o', N']$, where in the present situation <u>equality</u> with these dominating strategies can be shown with similar arguments as in (1). Altogether, this implies the proof of parts (2).

The following Figure 8 summerizes some of the insights into the "universe" of strategies, discussed in this paper. The additional information from Theorems 3.8 - 3.10 should also be seen in this context.

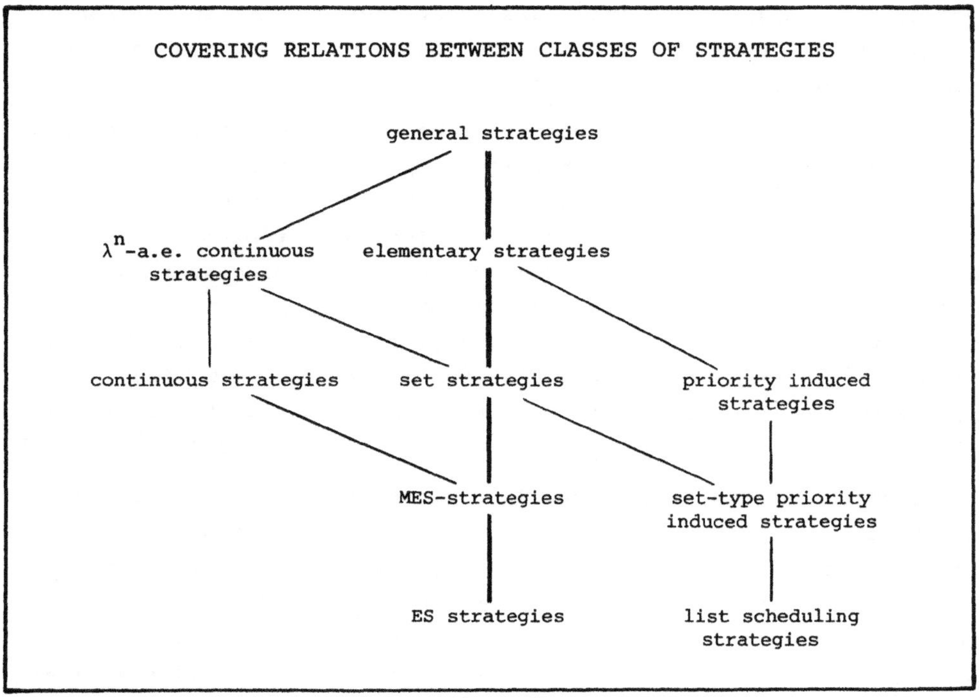

Figure 8

We close this Section with a few concluding remarks on GRAHAM ANOMALIES, i.e., - to be more precise in this context -, on the bad monotonicity and continuity behaviour of certain list scheduling strategies. These anomalies, cf. also Example 3.5, have led to some discussion in the literature, as they seem to be contra-intuitive. In fact, intuition is correct here as far as the deterministic optimum value is concerned. For as this value $\rho(\kappa,x)$ is representable as $\rho(\kappa,x)=\min\{\kappa(ES_\Theta[x]+x) \mid \Theta$ is a feasible partial order$\}$, cf. Example 1.1, this value is a nicely behaved function [23]. In particular, it is monotonically increasing and, if κ is (uniformly) continuous, so in $\rho(\kappa,\cdot)$. Thus anomalies are not something associated with the optimum value function but instead something associated with the quite unmotivated (but sometimes advertised) restriction to the use of greedy strategies, i.e. to list schedules.

Now concerning anomalies of this particular type, Corollary 3.4 together with Theorem 3.9 imply that such priority induced strategies have no anomalies iff they are MES strategies. Thus, in particular, anomalies concerning monotonicity and continuity always occur together. There are cases like (1) in Example 3.5, where no such anomalies occur. The usual case is however different, cf. Example 3.5 (2). The only partial comfort available in this context is the statement of Theorem 3.6, viz. that the nasty discontinuities are restricted to a set of Lebesgue measure zero.

Note finally, that in m-machine models, i.e. if Θ_o is trivial and $N = \{B \subseteq A \mid |B| = m+1\}$ with $1 \leq m < |A|$; all list scheduling strategies are MES strategies and thus have no anomalies (cf. Theorem 2.31 in [26]). This is important insofar as it implies a satisfying stability behaviour for those special exponential models for which certain list scheduling strategies have turned out to be overall optimal; cf. Section V. In fact, the given result extends to m-machine models for which Θ_o is a forest of intrees [28]. A proof of this result within the context of this paper leads, for a priority ordering that is e.g. compatible with Θ_o (i.e. which gives higher priorities to predecessors), to the observation that the priority induced strategy is just the MES strategy Π_{Φ_s} induced by selecting from any $\subseteq$-minimal forbidden set the job with the lowest priority. This explicit representation yields of course continuity, monotonicity and positive homogeneity, even w.r.t. each individual completion time (and not just project duration). But furthermore, it also implies a decreasing optimum value for increasing numbers of machine while using a particular fixed priority list, i.e. the exclusion of another type of anomalies, sometimes discussed in literature [6]. Altogether, this quite straightforward way to quite deep insights into the behaviour of rather involved list scheduling strategies should act as an indication to the argumental potential that is contained in the quite broad analysis of subclasses of strategies as discussed in this section.

IV. RESULTS ON OPTIMALITY, STABILITY AND MONOTONICITY

When dealing with stochastic models, three types of questions are usually of particular interest. One concerns the existence of optimal strategies, one the stablility behaviour w.r.t. small pertubations of the data and one the more qualitative behaviour e.g. of the optimum value w.r.t. monotonic variations of the system parameters. In the context of this paper, we will refer briefly to all three aspects and do this for the classes of all strategies and all elementary strategies as well as for the classes of set, MES and ES strategies. The particular choice of classes is motivated from the insights obtained in Section III, i.e. we restrict our comments to those classes that seem, at least for the time being, to be of the greatest interest from a theoretical as well as from an applicational point of view. Our main references are [20],[26], where the subjects discussed here are covered in greater detail.

Concerning the EXISTENCE OF OPTIMAL STRATEGIES, there is trivially a positive answer for the finite classes of set, MES and ES strategies. We may therefore concentrate on general or elementary strategies. The situation then becomes more involved. One might first try to use general results available. In exponential models as considered e.g. in [3], general results from semi-Markov decission theory (cf. e.g. [29]) actually yield a positive answer. However for the general case, the existing general results from stochastic dynamic optimization (cf. Theorem 17.12 in [7]) lead to positive answers only under quite restrictive assumptions, cf. [12], and are therefore not really sufficient. Still, these general results lead to indications as to what kind of conditions should be considered and what direction of argumentation should be tried. Following this line, quite deep insights are possible. They are based on quite interesting features of stochastic scheduling problems that deliver powerful tools for proofs. Maybe the most import feature of this type is captured in the following theorem:

THEOREM 4.1: APPROXIMATION THEOREM

Let $[A,O_o,N,P,\kappa]$ be arbitrary and $(\Pi^j)_{j\in\mathbb{N}}$ be a sequence of strategies (of elementary strategies) for $[A,O_o,N]$ such that $(E_P[\kappa(\Pi^j,\cdot)],j\in\mathbb{N} \downarrow a\in\mathbb{R}^1_>$. Then there exists a sequence $(\overset{*}{\Pi}{}^j)_{j\in\mathbb{N}}$ of strategies (of elementary strategies) such that $(E_P[\kappa(\overset{*}{\Pi}{}^j,\cdot)])_{j\in\mathbb{N}} \downarrow a'\in\mathbb{R}^1_>$ with $a'<a$ and such that $\overset{*}{\Pi} := \lim_{j\to\infty} \overset{*}{\Pi}{}^j$ exists pointwise.

The proof of Theorem 4.1 is given in [20],[26] and is quite complicated. We restrict ourselves here to a few remarks, to give an idea of how the special features of stochastic scheduling problems enter into the proof. In doing so, we concentrate on the general case; it should however be apparent, how the case of elementary strategies fits into this scheme.

The proof relies heavily on the special type of actions occuring in stochastic scheduling problems and on the iterative decomposition into subproblems, discussed in Section III. So given the sequence $(\Pi^j)_{j\in\mathbb{N}}$ of strategies, we first consider the associated canonical decompositions.

Let $(B_o^j,t_1^j)_{j\in\mathbb{N}}$ denote the respective first decisions. Due to the finiteness of A, a particular set B_o equals B_o^j for infinitely many $j \in \mathbb{N}$. We can go over to the respective subsequence, i.e. assume w.l.o.g. $B_o^j = B_o$ for all $j \in \mathbb{N}$. Now consider the set $(t_1^j)_{j \in \mathbb{N}}$, which has some accumulation point t_1 ($t_1 = \infty$ is possible). We again choose a subsequence of $(\Pi^j)_{j \in \mathbb{N}}$ such that the respective t_1^j converge against t_1 and let (B,t_1) be our first decision w.r.t. Π (which has to be interpreted appropriately if $t_1 = 0$). It turns out that if we can choose the converging sequence t_1^j in such a way that infinitely many members are greater than t_1, we can even w.l.o.g. replace the Π^j by certain strategies $\hat{\Pi}^j$, for which t_1^j and t_1 coincide. So the critical case is $t_1^j \uparrow t_1$ (cf. also Example 4.4 below). Altogether, an iterative application of this procedure enables us to assume, possibly after some "inessential" modifications of the given $(\Pi^j)_{j \in \mathbb{N}}$, that the canonical decomposition for all strategies in the approximating sequence is of the form $((B_o,t_1^j),(B_1,t_2^j),\ldots,(B_\ell,t_{\ell+1}^j))_{j \in \mathbb{N}}$, where $t_i^j \uparrow t_i$ for $i = 1,\ldots,\ell$. Of course, the sequence $(B_o,t_1),\ldots,(B_\ell,t_{\ell+1})$ will act as the canonical decomposition for the wanted limit strategy.

At that point the main intuitive argument for the validity of Theorem 4.1 schould have become apparent, viz. how the special nature of scheduling problems allows for manipulating the sequence $(\Pi^j)_{j \in \mathbb{N}}$ in such a way, that at least up to the first job completion, there is guaranteed a convergent behaviour of the modified sequence $(\overset{*}{\Pi}{}^j)_{j \in \mathbb{N}}$ of strategies, while still attaining the objective value. The rest of the proof then is very technical and has to make the necessary manipulations for the use of an inductive argument. That includes changes on the subproblem level to force the inductive assumption also onto these problems. Not surprisingly, such changes involve technical difficulties with guaranteeing (universal) measurability. However, these technical problems should not conseal the essential reason for the given result, which is given above.

It is worthwhile to study the statement of the Approximation Theorem very carefully. It covers the surprising result that, given an approximating sequence $(\mathbb{E}_P[\kappa(\Pi^j,\cdot)])_{j \in \mathbb{N}} \downarrow a$, i.e. a monotonically decreasing sequence of real numbers (approaching the optimum value from above) which are expected cost associated with certain strategies, that enables us to assume w.l.o.g. that $(\Pi^j)_{j \in \mathbb{N}}$ is itself a convergent sequence of functions. By Theorem 2.4, the associated limit strategy Π exists. All results on the existence of optimal strategies now are actually of the form that they imply Π to be an optimal strategy, i.e. imply that $\mathbb{E}_P[\kappa(\Pi,\cdot)] = a$. So what we essentially will have to do is to find conditions, under which $(\Pi^j)_{j\in\mathbb{N}} \to \Pi$ implies $\mathbb{E}_P[\kappa(\Pi,\cdot)] \leq \lim_{j\to\infty} \mathbb{E}_P[\kappa(\Pi^j,\cdot)]$. Similarly, a counterexample to the existence of an optimal strategy must yield $\mathbb{E}_P[\kappa(\Pi,\cdot)] > \lim_{j\to\infty} \mathbb{E}[\kappa(\Pi^j,\cdot)]$, cf. also Example 4.4. The two main theorems on the existence of optimal strategies follow next, cf. [20],[26]. The first one states that, within the set of elementary strategies, there is always an optimal one. The second gives quite general conditions, under which there is an overall optimal strategy.

THEOREM 4.2:

Let $[A,Q_0,N,P,\kappa]$ be any stochastic scheduling problem. Then the optimum value $\rho^{ELE}(\kappa,P)$ w.r.t. the class of elementary strategies is attained on this class.

The proof of Theorem 4.2 starts with the convergent sequence $(\Pi^j)_{j\in\mathbb{N}} \to \Pi$ described above and uses the following, easily obtained property of elementary strategies: Given any elementary strategy $\overline{\Pi}$, any $x\in\mathbb{R}^n_>$ and any $\alpha\in A$, either $\overline{\Pi}[x](\alpha) = 0$ or $\overline{\Pi}[x](\alpha) = \sum_{\beta\in B} x(\beta)$, where B is some non-void subset of A. Due to the finiteness of A, there are only finitely many such sets B, and therefore only finitely many choices to define $\overline{\Pi}[x](\beta)$. Taking into account that $\lim_{j\to\infty} \Pi^j[x](\alpha) = \Pi[x](\alpha)$ for all $\alpha\in A$ and $x\in\mathbb{R}^n_>$ therefore implies that the sets $Z_\ell := \mathbb{R}^n_> \setminus \{x\in\mathbb{R}^n_> \mid \Pi^j[x](\alpha) = \Pi[x](\alpha)$ for all $\alpha\in A$, all $j\geq\ell\}$, $\ell\in\mathbb{N}$, form a decreasing sequence of (universally) measurable sets approaching $\emptyset$, i.e. $Z_\ell \downarrow \emptyset$. Using the $\emptyset$-continuity of probability measures yields $\lim_{\ell\to\infty} P(Z_\ell) = 0$. Therefore, all strategies Π^j, j sufficiently large, differ from Π only on a set of arbitrary small measure. The fact that $E_P[\kappa(\Pi,\cdot)]<\infty$ then immediately yields $\mathbb{E}_P[\kappa(\Pi,\cdot)] = \lim_{j\to\infty} \mathbb{E}_P[\kappa(\Pi^j,\cdot)]$, i.e. the optimality of Π.

THEOREM 4.3:

Let $[A,Q_0,N,P,\kappa]$ be a stochastic scheduling problem. There is an (overall) optimal strategy for this problem, if any of the following properties applies:

(1) κ is lower semi-continuous.

(2) P is finite-discrete.

(3) P has a Lebesgue density.

The proof of Theorem 4.3 again starts from a convergent sequence $(\Pi^j)_{j\in\mathbb{N}}$ $\to\Pi$ as described above. It is not so difficult to see that for continuous κ, $\lim_{j\to\infty} \mathbb{E}_P [\kappa(\Pi^j,\cdot)] = \mathbb{E}_P [\kappa(\Pi,\cdot)]$. Using this result and the fact that the lower semi-continuous functions bounded from below can be approximated from below by a monotonically increasing sequence $(\kappa_j)_{j\in\mathbb{N}}$ of continuous functions yields the wanted inequality $\mathbb{E}_P [\kappa(\Pi,\cdot)] \leq \lim_{j\to\infty} \mathbb{E}_P [\kappa(\Pi^j,\cdot)]$, which implies the statement of Theorem 4.3(1).

To prove Theorem 4.3(2), one may show by induction, that only a finite set of strategies induced by the finite-discrete distribution P needs to be considered. Consequently, the sequence $(\Pi^j)_{j\in\mathbb{N}}$ will become stationary.

The proof of Theorem 4.3(3) includes two main observations. First, using the canonical decomposition of strategies as basis for an induction proof, one can show that the distributions $P_{(\Pi^j[x]+x)}$, $j\in\mathbb{N}$ of completion time vectors will have a Lebesgue density, if P has this property. Secondly, one can show that any regular cost function κ, using the fact that it is monotonically increasing on $\mathbb{R}^n_>$, is λ^n-a.e. continuous. Applying now results on weak convergent sequences of distributions [2], here $(P_{(\Pi^j[x]+x)})_{j\in\mathbb{N}}$, and the fact that κ is uniformly integrable w.r.t. this sequence, yields the wanted property $\lim_{j\to\infty} \mathbb{E}_P [\kappa(\Pi^j,\cdot)] = \mathbb{E}_P [\kappa(\Pi,\cdot)]$.

Note that Theorem 4.3 is quite general, due to the fact that there are counterexamples to the existence of optimal strategies already for the case of infinite-discrete P and upper semi-continuous κ. Complicated examples of this type allow even to guarantee stochastical independence of job durations [20]. A less complicated example, exploiting stochastic dependences, is given next.

EXAMPLE 4.4:

Let $[A,O_o,N]$ be given by $A = \{1,\ldots,5\}$, O_o as given in Figure 9 by an arrow diagramm and $N = \{\{2,3\}\}$.

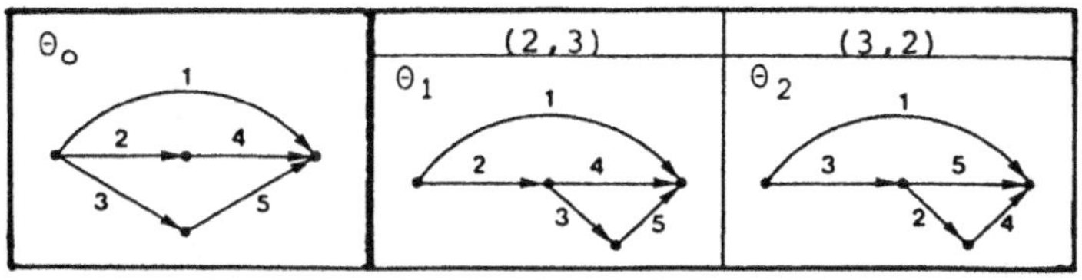

Figure 9

Let $P = \frac{3}{\pi^2} \sum_{j=1}^{\infty} \frac{1}{j^2} \cdot \varepsilon_{y_j} + \frac{1}{2} \varepsilon_z$ [with ε_x, for $x \in \mathbb{R}^n_>$ arbitrary, denoting the singular distribution $\varepsilon_x(B) = 1$ for $x \in B$ and $\varepsilon_x(B) = 0$ for $x \notin B$, $B \in \mathbb{B}^n_>$ arbitrary], where $y_j = (2-1/j, 10, 10, 20, 10)$ and $z = (2, 10, 10, 10, 20)$, and let κ denote the bounded, upper semi-continuous cost function

$$\kappa(t_1,\ldots,t_5) := \begin{cases} \max(t_1,\ldots,t_5) & \text{if } \max(t_1,\ldots,t_5) \leq 100 \text{ and } t_2 < 22 \\ 100 & \text{otherwise.} \end{cases}$$

Note that this example is structured as follows: The only decision that has to be made is whether to start job 2 before job 3 or conversly. If we make this decision at time zero, we arrive at the earliest start strategies ES_{Θ_1} or ES_{Θ_2} (where Θ_1 and Θ_2 are given by arrow diagrams in Figure 9), which both have the associated expected cost 35. This is obivious, as the example is made in such a way that in 50 % of all cases (viz. if duration vectors of type $y_j, j \in \mathbb{N}$ are realized) 2 should precede 3, while in the other 50 % cases (viz. if z is realized) it should be the other way round.

Now due to the involved stochastic dependences, it is possible to learn about the future realizations by observing the duration of job 1. This leads to studying all strategies $(\Pi^j)_{j \in \mathbb{N}}$ having the first decision $(\{1\}, 2-1/j)$, and putting 2 before 3 if job 1 ends no later than $2-1/j$, and acting the other way round, otherwise. I.e.,until time $2-1/j$, strategy Π^j tries to learn about the future by observing job 1. It is not so difficult to compute that the associated expected cost fulfill $\mathbb{E}_P[\kappa(\Pi^j,\cdot) \downarrow a$, where $a \approx 31.56$ is the optimum value. It is in fact also the optimum value for κ' = max (project duration).

The statement of the Approximation Theorem applies directly, viz. the sequence $(\Pi^j)_{j \in \mathbb{N}}$ converges against a limit strategy Π, which is elementary, starts with action $(\{1\}, \infty)$ and puts job 2 before 3, if $x_1 = 2-1/j$ for some $j \in \mathbb{N}$ and behaves the other way round, otherwise. This limit strategy is in fact optimal for κ'=max. However, for the cost function κ considered here, we will in 50% of all cases come up with t_2=22, which yields the high cost value κ=100 and in our case implies, that there exists no optimal strategy. In particular, we have $\lim_{j\to\infty} \kappa(\Pi^j,\cdot) < \kappa(\Pi,\cdot)$ which is, as was demonstrated above, necessary for non-existence of optimal strategies. Note also, that the canonical decompositions occurring here fulfill $t_j = 2-1/j \uparrow t=2$, i.e. are exactly of the type, predicted in connection with the Approximation Theorem.

The next topic discussed is STABILITY. This means the behaviour of system parameters such as expected costs, the optimum value, the property of being an optimal strategy and so forth w.r.t. small perturbations of the data. From an applicational point of view, this question is of particular importance w.r.t. "continuous" data types (here: distribution P and cost function κ), because there is, in general, no way to avoid at least small differences in practical data estimation. I.e. estimated data and "real" data will differ at least slightly and the model should be such that such differences only result in small differences in the system parameters. To be more precise, we will study now the behaviour of system parameters w.r.t. smooth approximations $(P_j)_{j\in\mathbb{N}} \to P$, viz. weakly convergent approximations with $\Sigma : \mathbb{R}^n_> \to \mathbb{R}^1_>$, defined by $\Sigma(x_1,\ldots,x_n) = x_1+\ldots+x_n$, being uniformly integrable w.r.t. $(P_j)_{j\in\mathbb{N}}$, and simultaneous uniformly convergent approximations $\kappa_j \to \kappa$. As the following example shows, there is, for general or elementary strategies, still a great instability, in spite of the very smooth type of approximation considered.

EXAMPLE 4.5:

Let $[A,O_o,N]$ be given by $A = \{1,\ldots,5\}$, O_o as given in Figure 10 by an arrow diagram and $N = \{\{2,3\}\}$.

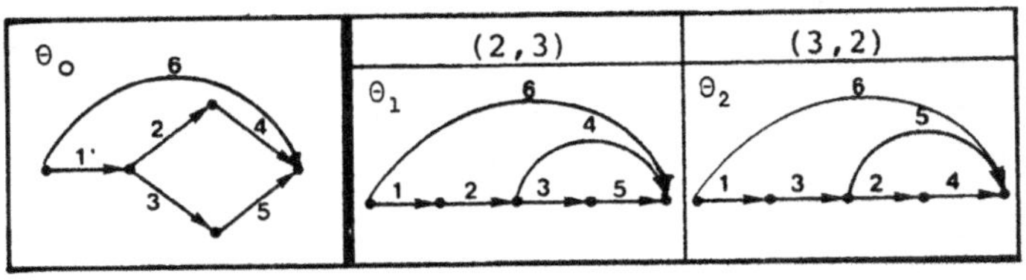

Figure 10

Obviously, ES_{Θ_1} and ES_{Θ_2}, with Θ_1,Θ_2 as given in Figure 10, are strategies for the problem under discussion. They may be combined to yield the following (incontinuous) set strategy

$$\Pi[x] := \begin{cases} ES_{\Theta_1}[x] & x(1)<x(6) \\ ES_{\Theta_2}[x] & x(1)\geq x(6) \end{cases}$$

Let P_j, $j\in\mathbb{N}$ be similarly defined to the situation in Example 4.4, i.e. $P_j = \frac{1}{2}\varepsilon_{x_j^1} + \frac{1}{2}\varepsilon_{x^2}$, where $x_j^1 := (2-1/j,2,2,4,2,2)$ and $x^2 := (2,2,2,2,4,2)$ and put $\kappa_j \equiv \kappa = \max$ (project duration). Then Π is optimal w.r.t. (κ,P_j) for all $j\in\mathbb{N}$. In fact, Π is even pointwise optimal for P_j-almost all duration vectors, owing to the fact that with the completion of activity 1, there is no further uncertainty about the future. We therefore have $\rho(\kappa,P_j) = \mathbb{E}_{P_j}[\kappa(\Pi,\cdot)] = 8-1/2j$, $j\in\mathbb{N}$.

By construction, the sequence $(P_j)_{j\in\mathbb{N}}$ converges weakly against $P = \frac{1}{2}\varepsilon_{x^1}+\frac{1}{2}\varepsilon_{x^2}$, where $x^1 = (2,2,2,4,2,2)$ and x^2 is as above. Also, Σ (and even all its powers Σ^m, $m\in\mathbb{N}$) is uniformly integrable w.r.t. $(P_j)_{j\in\mathbb{N}}$. Nevertheless, the associated optimal value is now given by $\mathbb{E}_P[\kappa(\Pi,\cdot)] = \mathbb{E}_P[\kappa(ES_{\Theta_1},\cdot)] = \mathbb{E}_P[\kappa(ES_{\Theta_2},\cdot)] = 9$, owing to the fact that the completion time of activity 1 gives absolutely no information about the future for P-almost all duration vectors.

Altogether, we have $\rho(\kappa,P) = 9 \neq 8 = \lim_{j\to\infty} \rho(\kappa,P_j)$, i.e. the instability of the objective value (for Π), as well as of the overall optimum value. The instability of being an optimal strategy can similarly be obtained.

Example 4.5 has demonstrated that stochastic scheduling problems have a bad tendency to an instable behaviour, whether one is dealing with general, or elementary or even with the quite restricted set strategies. The reason is, that much information about the future can e.g. be contained in a distribution by means of two different duration realizations - regardless of how small the difference may be -, and that discontinuous strategies can, in certain cases, strongly exploit this information. The effects are - not surprisingly - particularly strong for discrete distributions involving stochastic dependences and constitute a serious problem for practical applications.

A more detailed discussion of the matter, as done in [20], [26], reveals the fact that only a restriction to certain continuous strategies will overcome this difficulty. As was discussed in the context of Example 3.7, this does not mean that the set of all continuous strategies would be a reasonable set to deal with. In fact, as was demonstrated there, the natural wish to consider with each continuous strategy all continuous strategies dominating it would immediately yield instability as soon as we consider non-preselective continuous strategies.

Thus taking into account Theorem 3.8, a really satisfying stability behaviour and a reasonable completeness w.r.t. dominance will lead immediately to the class of MES strategies, which is the greatest class of the type wanted. On this class, we then have all the mentioned stability behaviour of expected cost, of the optimum value and of being a (near-)optimal strategy that were discussed above.

We finally mention, that a restricted type of stability (quasi-stability) can be achieved for finite sets of λ^n-a.e. continuous strategies. This type of stability is restricted to duration distributions, that have a Lebesgue density and covers many interesting classes of problems like e.g. exponential models. As was discussed in connection with Theorem 3.6, set strategies have this restricted type of stability. To give a better feeling for the kind of results existing in this contexts, we close our comments on this subject by giving the corresponding theorem from [21]:

THEOREM 4.6:

The class of set strategies is quasi-stable, i.e., given $[A,O_o,N,P,\kappa]$, where P has a Lebesgue-density, the following properties hold for each weakly convergent sequence $(P_j)_{j\in\mathbb{N}} \to P$ of joint distributions for which $\Sigma(x_1,\ldots,x_n) := x_1+\ldots+x_n$ is uniformly integrable, and for each uniformly convergent sequence $(\kappa_j)_{j\in\mathbb{N}} \to \kappa$ of cost functions:

1. For any set strategy Π:
   - (i) $(P_j)_{\kappa_j(\Pi,\cdot)}$ converges weakly to $P_{\kappa(\Pi,\cdot)}$.
   - (ii) $\lim_{j\to\infty} \mathbb{E}_{P_j}[\kappa_j(\Pi,\cdot)] = \mathbb{E}_P[\kappa(\Pi,\cdot)]$.
2. W.r.t. optimality:
   - (i) $\lim_{j\to\infty} \rho^{SET}(\kappa_j,P_j) = \rho^{SET}(\kappa,P)$.
   - (ii) Let Π^j denote, for any $\varepsilon > 0$ and any $j\in\mathbb{N}$, a set strategy that is ε-optimal in this class w.r.t. (κ_j,P_j). Then there is $j_o\in\mathbb{N}$ such that Π^j is ε-optimal in this class for all $j > j_o$.
   - (iii) If Π is an optimal set strategy w.r.t. infinitely many $(\kappa_j,P_j)_{j\in\mathbb{N}}$, then Π is also optimal w.r.t. (κ,P). Furthermore, there is an optimal set strategy for (κ,P) having this property.

We conclude this section with some hints concerning the MONOTONICITY BEHAVIOUR, which is one of the most important qualitative aspects to discuss in stochastic models; cf. e.g. [33]. Note that among the data changes that might be considered, more precedence constraints or more forbidden sets or pointwise greater cost functions immediately lead to non decreasing expected cost and optimum values, as the classes of e.g. ES, MES, set, elementary or general strategies shrink while the expected cost for each remaining strategy increases. So all these data changes, even if done simultaneously, behave nicely from a monotonicity point of view. [Note that this does not mean that using a particular priority ordering and considering the induced strategies, the associated expected cost will not decrease in the above situation. The possibility of this strange Graham anomaly is due to the fact, that the induced strategies may be different. However each of the (possibly) two resulting strategies has the discribed behaviour].

Thus altogether, the main monotonicity behaviour to study concerns the transition to stochastically greater duration distributions. Here, given distributions P,Q on $(\mathbb{R}^n_>, \mathcal{B}^n_>)$, P is called stochastically smaller than Q (write $P \leqslant Q$), iff $\mathbb{E}_P[f] \leqslant \mathbb{E}_Q[f]$ for all monotonically increasing $f: \mathbb{R}^n \to \mathbb{R}^1$. In the independence case, i.e. if $P = \bigotimes_{i=1}^n P_i$ and $Q = \bigotimes_{i=1}^n Q_i$, $P \leqslant Q$ iff $P_i \leqslant Q_i$ for all $i = 1,\ldots,n$, meaning that the property of being stochastically smaller can be reduced to the one-dimensional case. For this case, the survival function $1-F_P$, F_P being the distribution function of P, yields a simple test criterion, viz. $P \leqslant Q$ iff $1-F_P \leqslant 1-F_Q$ on $\mathbb{R}^1$. Note that the notion of being stochastically smaller can in fact be associated to everywhere smaller realizations [13] and thus catches one of the really basic aspects of monotonicity in a stochastic framework. There is a less strict notion, viz. being stochastically smaller in the convex sense [33] (write $P \underset{c}{\leqslant} Q$), which means $\mathbb{E}_P[f] \leqslant \mathbb{E}_Q[f]$ for all monotonically increasing and convex $f: \mathbb{R}^n \to \mathbb{R}^1$ and which is also of some use for practical applications in scheduling.

Now due to the basic definitions given, the assumption $P \leqslant Q$ (or $P \underset{c}{\leqslant} Q$) for duration distributions will certainly imply the intended monotonicity whenever we are dealing with monotonically increasing (or monotonically increasing and convex strategies), even in the dependence case. Taking into account the Characterization Theorems 3.9 and 3.10, this guarantees a nice behaviour essentially within the classes of either MES or ES strategies. The following theorem captures this observation:

THEOREM 4.7:

Let $[A,O_o,N,P,\kappa]$ and $[A,O',N',P',\kappa']$ be stochastic scheduling problems such that $O_o \subseteq O'$, $N \subseteq N'$ and $\kappa \leqslant \kappa'$ on $\mathbb{R}^n_>$. Then every strategy for $[A,O_o',N']$ is also a strategy for $[A,O_o,N]$. Furthermore:

(1) If $P \leqslant Q$ and Π is a monotonically increasing strategy for $[A,O',N']$, then $E_P[\kappa(\Pi,\cdot)] \leqslant E_{P'}[\kappa'(\Pi,\cdot)$, i.e. in particular $\rho^{MES}_{\Theta_o,N}(\kappa,P) \leqslant \rho^{MES}_{\Theta_o',N'}(\kappa',P')$ and $\rho^{ES}_{\Theta_o,N}(\kappa,P) \leqslant \rho^{ES}_{\Theta_o',N'}(\kappa',P')$.

(2) If $P \underset{c}{\leqslant} Q$, κ' is convex and Π is a monotonically increasing, convex strategy for $[A,O',N']$, then $E_P[\kappa(\Pi,\cdot)] \leqslant E_{P'}[\kappa'(\Pi,\cdot)]$, i.e. in particular $\rho^{ES}_{\Theta_o,N}(\kappa,P) \leqslant \rho^{ES}_{\Theta_o',N'}(\kappa',P')$.

We now aim at the harder cases, i.e. general or elementary or set strategies, where strategies are involved that are not monotonically increasing. For any such strategy, $P \leqslant Q$ will usually tell us nothing concerning the relation between the objective function values $\mathbb{E}_P[\kappa(\Pi,\cdot)]$ and $\mathbb{E}_Q[\kappa(\Pi,\cdot)]$. However w.r.t. the associated optimum value, our intuition might tell us - at least at first sight - that dealing with stochastically greater job durations should exclude a lower optimum value. This basic intuition turns in fact out to be wrong in this generality. There are two obstacles to deal with. The first has to do with stochastic dependences, i.e. with the degree of information about the future contained in the duration distribution. If this potentially available information has a "higher value" for the greater distribution, it may compensate for the greater durations. In fact that happens if we study in Example 4.5 the two distributions $P=\frac{1}{2}\varepsilon_{(2,2,2,4,2,2)}+\frac{1}{2}\varepsilon_{(2,2,2,2,4,2)}$ and $Q=\frac{1}{2}\varepsilon_{(2,2,2,4,2,2)}+\frac{1}{2}\varepsilon_{(3,2,2,2,4,2)}$, which obviously fulfill $P \leqslant Q$ but for which straightforwardly $\rho(\kappa,P) = 9 > 8,5 = \rho(\kappa,Q)$ is obtained, due to the fact that w.r.t. Q, we know the "future" by time 2, while w.r.t. P, we do not. So again, the information contained in the duration distribution makes things difficult, analoguously to the study of the stability behaviour.

Given the last remark, a general monotonicity behaviour may only be expected under assumptions concerning the contained information; these assumptions should cover the independence case. It turns out, that only for the really rich class of general strategies, this aim can be achieved. Assuming an appropriate SEPERATION CONDITION w.r.t. P and Q that reflects a "non-decreasing information degree" and that is always true if we are in the independence case, a quite involved argumentation [20] allows the statement that to each strategy Π there exists some strategy Π^* fullfilling $\mathbb{E}_P[\kappa(\Pi^*,\cdot)] \leq \mathbb{E}_Q[\kappa(\Pi,\cdot)]$, cf. Theorem 5.1.4 in [20]. Note however that Π^* may be completely different from Π and that the "availability" of Π^* is therefore not selfunderstood when dealing with procedurally restricted classes such as elementary or set strategies. Thus the basic result mentioned will on the one hand lead to the general monotonicity result, given next [20], but at the same time indicates what difficulties may occur in special subclasses of strategies.

THEOREM 4.8:

Let $[A,\mathcal{O}_0,N,P,\kappa]$ and $[A,\mathcal{O}_0',N',P',\kappa']$ be stochastic scheduling problems such that $\mathcal{O}_0 \subseteq \mathcal{O}_0', N \subseteq N', \kappa \leq \kappa'$ and $P \leq P'$, where $P = \bigotimes_{\alpha \in A} P_\alpha$ and $P' = \bigotimes_{\alpha \in A} P_\alpha'$. Then:

$$\rho_{\Theta_{o,N}}(\kappa,P) \leq \rho_{\Theta_{o,N'}'}(\kappa',P').$$

Theorem 4.8 can be viewed as the main generally available insight into the monotonicity behaviour of stochastic scheduling problems and shows that the intuition concerning these problems is basicly right. It should however be said again, that it is the "richness" of the class of general strategies that is essentially used at that point. If we consider instead restricted classes such as elementary or set strategies, things are different, as the greater distribution may allow a more diversified use of actions which in turn may compensate for the greater durations, cf. e.g. Example 4.9 for the case of set strategies. Consequently, Theorem 4.8 cannot be adapted to these cases which should - at second thoughts - really not be that surprising when taking into account the bad behaviour of priority-induced strategies as discussed in connection with Graham anomalies and Example 3.5.

EXAMPLE 4.9:

Let $[A,\mathcal{O}_0,N,\kappa]$ be given by $A = \{1,2,3,4,5,6\}$, $\mathcal{O}_0$ as given by the arrow diagramm in Figure 11, N be induced by 2 identical machines, i.e. $N = \{B \subseteq A \mid |B| = 3\}$ and $\kappa = \max$.

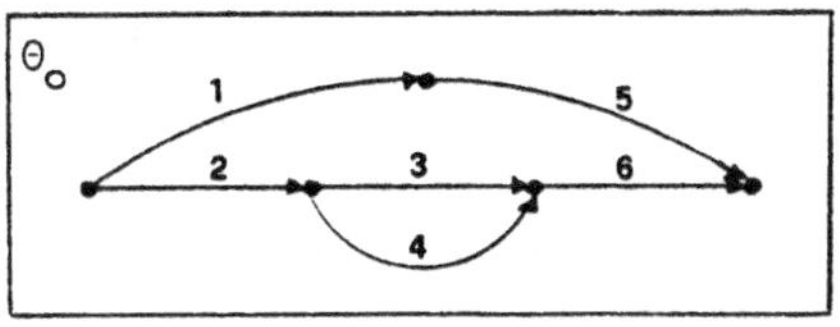

Figure 11

Let $P = \bigotimes_{i=1} P_i$ and $Q = \bigotimes_{i=1} Q_i$, where $P_1 = \frac{1}{2}\varepsilon_5 + \frac{1}{2}\varepsilon_9$, $Q_1 = \frac{1}{2}\varepsilon_5 + \frac{1}{2}\varepsilon_{11}$ and $P_i = Q_i$, $i = 2,\dots,6$ with $P_2 = \varepsilon_{10}$, $P_3 = P_4 = P_6 = \varepsilon_4$ and $P_5 = \varepsilon_5$. Obviously, we are in the independence case.

If we ask for the optimum value ρ^{SET} determined by the set strategies w.r.t. P, we have the difficulty that we must restrict ourselves to one action, independent of whether job 1 ends at time 5 or 9, since it always ends before job 2. The best thing to do under this restriction is to start job 5 immediately after the completion of job 1, yielding $\rho^{SET}(\kappa,P) = 20$.

Now w.r.t. Q, the situation is different, because we can vary our action in dependence on whether job 1 or job 2 ends first. The best set strategy Π for this case (in fact even the overall optimal strategy here) starts job 5 at time 5 if job 1 is completed at that time, and otherwise (i.e. if 2 ends first) puts jobs 3 and 4 on the machines at times 10 and 11, respectively. This procedure yields $\rho^{SET}(\kappa,Q) = 18.5$, and shows that we have no monotonicity w.r.t. the associated optimum values.

Note that because of the hints given above, there exists of course some strategy Π^* with $\mathbb{E}_P[\kappa(\Pi^*,\cdot)] \leq 18.5$. Such a strategy starts job 5 at time 5 if job 1 is completed at that time and starts jobs 3 and 4 at time 10 if job 1 is completed at time 9. Of course, this strategy is not a set strategy.

V. CONNECTIONS TO EXPONENTIAL MODELS

In the available literature on stochastic scheduling problems, cf. e.g. [3],[30], exponential models play a dominating role. The investigations made can usually be seen against a queuing-theoretical background [15], [31], and often aim at applications such as job scheduling in operating or switching systems, in which little is known concerning particular duration distributions. Also, the technical side-constraints not only allow but sometimes favour job preemptions. So the considered exponential models are often preemptive, do not include precedence constraints, and deal only with m-machine-type resource constraints, i.e. $\mathcal{N} = \{B \subseteq A \mid |B| = m+1\}$ with $1 \leq m < |A|$. The exponential nature of the problems lies in the fact that $P = \bigotimes_{\alpha \in A} P_\alpha$, where the P_α, $\alpha \in A$, are exponentially distributed with parameter $\lambda_\alpha > 0$, i.e. have the Lebesgue density $f_\alpha(y) = \lambda_\alpha \cdot e^{-\lambda_\alpha \cdot y}$ on $\mathbb{R}^1_>$. The cost functions κ may usually be interpreted via cost rates, i.e. they are additive in the sense that there exists some monotonically increasing set function g from the power set $P(A)$ of A into $\mathbb{R}^1_\geq$ with $g(\emptyset)=0$, such that, given ordered job completion times $t_{i_1} \leq t_{i_2} \leq \ldots \leq t_{i_n}$, κ can be written as $\kappa(t_1,\ldots,t_n) = t_{i_1} \cdot g(A) + (t_{i_2} - t_{i_1}) \cdot g(A_{i_1}) + \ldots + (t_{i_n} - t_{i_{n-1}}) g(A_{i_{n-1}})$, where $A_{i_o} = A$ and $A_{i_j} = A_{i_{j-1}} \setminus \{\alpha_{i_j}\}$, $j = 1,\ldots,n$, cf. [35]. Taking into account the memory-less property [29] of exponential distributions (i.e. the property $P(\{X>s+t \mid X>t\}) = P(\{X>s\})$ for all $s,t \in \mathbb{R}^n_>$ of exponentially distributed random variables X, which excludes "learning much about the future") and the strategical independence of the occurring cost from previous completion times and actual time (which enter into the project cost only via an additive term), these assupmtions lead into the nice framwork of semi-Markov decision processes. In particular, the states of the problem are comparatively simple and consist in the finitely many sets of yet uncompleted jobs, while possible actions at job completion times consist in starting (maximal) feasible sets of jobs. Furthermore, there is even a recursive formula available for the expexted cost assaciated with a particular strategy. In fact, if $\mathbb{E}$ denots this value, B is the set of jobs started at time 0 with associated parameters $\lambda_\beta, \beta \in B$, and if, for any $\beta \in B$, $\mathbb{E}_\beta$ is the (inductively obtained) expected cost for the subproblem occuring if β is the first completed job, then (with $\lambda := \sum_{\beta \in B} \lambda_\beta$):

$$\mathbb{E} = g(A) \cdot \frac{1}{\lambda} + \sum_{\beta \in B} \frac{\lambda_\beta}{\lambda} \mathbb{E}_\beta .$$

Note that this formula is based on the fact that the minimum of the durations of jobs in B is exponentially distributed with parameter λ and is stochastically independent of the future evolution of the process, where the different subcases occur with probability $\frac{\lambda_\beta}{\lambda}$, $\beta \in B$. Note also that actually performing the recursive computation will lead to an exponential time-complexity. Still, the representation is of great use in the really impressive deduction of some of the main results available in this context. The hard core of such results is contained in the following theorem, cf. [35].

THEOREM 5.1:

Let $[A,O_0,N,P,\kappa]$ be such that O_0 is trivial, N of m-machine type and P is a product of exponential distrubutions. Then

(1) For the additive cost function κ = max (project duration), and for related functions such as time to first idleness, the constant priority rule LEPT (longest expected processing time first) induces an overall optimal strategy.

(2) For the additive cost function Σ (flow time), and for related functions such as weighted flow time with agreeable weights, the constant priority rule SEPT (shortest expetcted processing time first) induces an overall optimal strategy.

Note that these results imply for quite common objectives completely different optimal strategies, which however, in both cases, can be determined in $\mathcal{O}(n \cdot \log n)$ time. Though this does not include the possibility of determining the associated optimum value in polynomially bounded time, the given results are extremely nice from a practical point of view. This is even more true as preemptions need really not be used, i.e. Theorem 5.1 remains valid in the non-preemptive case. Also, it is worthwhile to remember here the comments given w.r.t. GRAHAM ANOMALIES at the end of Section III. They imply for the m-machine models discussed here, that constant priority rules actually induce MES-strategies. Thus in the context of Theorem 5.1, the induced strategies behave really nicely, i.e. have all the desireable stability and monotonicity behaviour presented in Section IV.

There are at least two directions to proceed to from Theorem 5.1. One aims at generalizing the given result, cf. e.g. [34]. In this context, the weighted sum of completion times criteria seems for many reasons to be particularly promising. There is actually forthcoming a quite strong result [11] on that matter, which leads to an optimal list scheduling strategy if certain compatability conditions between weights and parameters are fulfilled. The nice feature about this result is that one is no longer restricted to the "extreme" cases of LEPT or SEPT but that instead, any priority ordering will turn out to be optimal for appropriately chosen weights and expected values.

A second direction consists in somehow closing the gap between the consideration of uncountably many strategies on one side and the determination of an optimal priority ordering in polynomial time on the other side. Actually, it is not hard to see, that already a result on the existence of an overall optimal priority ordering, that is agreeable with all subproblems, implies the possibility to find this ordering in polynomial time. In fact, this is the statement of the following theorem:

THEOREM 5.2:

Let $[A,O_o,N,P,\kappa]$ be such that O_o is trivial, N is of m-machine-type, P is a product of exponential distributions and κ is additive. If there is an overall optimal strategy induced by a constant priority rule, which is agreeable with all subproblems (i.e. the restricted versions of which induce overall optimal strategies for the subproblems), it can be determined in $\mathcal{O}(n^{m+1})$ time complexity.

To see, why Theorem 5.2 applies, take all sets of cardinality m+1 and use the recursive formula given above, to determine for any such set a job with the lowest priority, i.e. a job that has to wait when optimally scheduling the subproblem. This can be done in $\mathcal{O}((m+1)!)$ time. It is not hard to see that knowing all these relative priorities and having available the agreeability assumption leads to an optimal priority list for the problem under consideration in time bounded by $\mathcal{O}(n^{m+1})$.

With Theorem 5.2 in mind, an intermediate result should probably either deal with the existence of certain (dynamic) priority-induced strategies or even with something more general. In fact, a thorough investigation [21] showed that SET STRATEGIES are really the right class of strategies to aim at, particularly for general precedence and resource constraints; due to the nonpreemptiveness assumption that is basic in our model. It is then not hard to see that assuming P to be a product of exponential distributions allows us to eliminate from the set of all strategies any dependence of the durations of jobs already finished and of the current durations of jobs, presently being performed. Still, this does not yet mean a restriction to elementary strategies or set strategies, as Example 5.4 will demonstrate. However, if we also require a sort of strategical invariance of the cost function from the observed history, then things work out fine. The "greatest" class of such cost functions (in a particular sense), viz. cost functions with the SHIFT PROPERTY, are characterized in [21] and contain, as a particularly characterized subclass, the additive cost functions discussed above. The main theorem [21] then is as follows:

THEOREM 5.3:

Let $[A,O_o,N,P,\kappa]$ be such that P is a product of exponential distributions and κ has the shift property. Then there is an overall optimum set strategy, i.e. $\rho(\kappa,P) = \rho^{SET}(\kappa,P)$.

Note that this result can be obtained with standard arguments from semi-Markov decision theory and is quite general in the sense, that all additive cost functions such as project duration and weighted flow time are covered, and arbitrary precedence and resource constraints are allowed. With this result, one need only consider a finite set of strategies and obtains for the optimum value (in this particular case) the quasi-stability as formulated in Theorem 4.6, while notwithstanding Example 4.9, the nice monotonicity behaviour of Theorem 4.8 in this case also applies for ρ^{SET}.

As was mentioned above, Theorem 5.3 really needs some restrictive assumption concerning κ. Already costs of the tardiness type would necessitate to consider the whole variety of general strategies in order to obtain the overall optimum value. This is (partly) demonstrated by the following example.

EXAMPLE 5.4:

Let $[A,O_o,N,P,\kappa]$ be given by $A = \{1,2,3,4\}$, O_o by its arrow diagram in Figure 12, $N = \{B \subseteq A \mid |B| = 3\}$ (i.e. all jobs compete for two identical machines), $P = \bigotimes_{j=1}^{4} P_j$ where each P_j is an exponential distribution with (identical) parameter $\lambda_j = 1/2$, and κ is a weighted unit penalty cost function with (identical) due dates $d_j = 3$ for $j = 1,2,3,4$ and weights $w_1 = 0$, $w_2 = 2$, $w_3 = 10$ and $w_4 = 10$. This means that the project cost is the sum of individual cost terms for each job, which is zero if the job ends before its due date $d_j = 3$, and w_j otherwise.

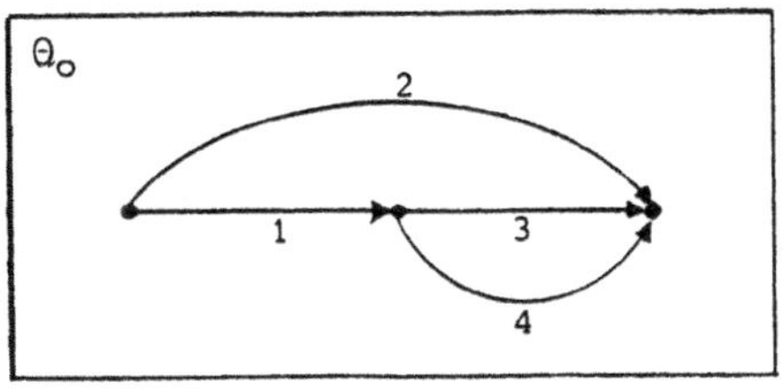

Figure 12

Certainly, job 1 should be started at time zero to allow job 3 and 4, which may cause the largest penalties w_j, to start early. For the same reason, one should not start job 2 immediately, but wait until a certain time t and put jobs 3 and 4 on the two machines if job 1 is completed before t. If, however, job 1 is not completed by time t, then for t sufficiently close to 3, it will become reasonable to start job 2, because then there is little hope for completing either job 3 or job 4 before its due date.

Altogether, one must consider a family of strategies Π^t, $t\in[0,3]$, with associated first decision ({1},t) which acts as described above. Each such strategy is λ^n-almost everywhere continuous. Moreover, the associated objective value $E_P[\kappa(\Pi^t,\cdot)]$ is a continuous function of t, as $t_j\to t$ implies $\Pi^{t_j}\to\Pi$ (pointwise for $x_1 \neq t$), and this in turn implies $E_P[\kappa(\Pi^{t_j},\cdot)]\to E_P[\Pi^t,\cdot)]$, analogously to the proof of Theorem 4.3 (3).

The values $E_P[\kappa(\Pi^t,\cdot)]$ were (simultaneously) determined for t = 0.0,0.1,0.2,...,2.8,2.9 and 3.0 by simulation. The resulting function of t is given in Figure 13. The approximated optimum value (obtained by numerical evaluation [10]) is 12.522 and was attained for t = 2.216, i.e. ({1},2.216) should be taken as first decision.

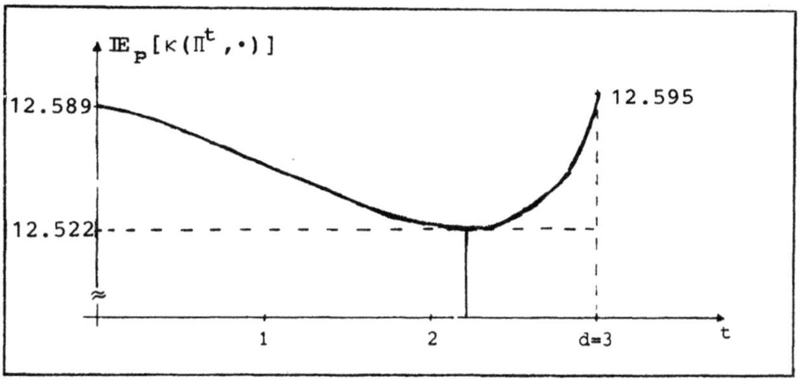

Figure 13

Theorem 5.3 is the only general intermediate result one can hope for. There is one particular further step one might try, viz. to be greedy, i.e. to avoid deliberate idleness of machines. Note that deliberate idleness (that is not using a machine, though some available job is waiting for it) is one of the most characteristic aspects of non preemptive scheduling problems as discussed in this paper (cf. e.g.Examples 4.4 and 5.4), for it reflects certain combinatorial effects on one side and the trade-off between information accumulation and immediate machine utilization on the other side. These effects are the deeper reason for the occurrence of GRAHAM ANOMALIES as discussed in Section IV, and it is hard to come up with reasonable general conditions under which these aspects can be neglected. In fact, as the following Example 5.5 shows, there is certainly little hope to avoid deliberate idleness, as soon as general precedence and resource constraints are considered. Of course, if we can somehow restrict to a greedy behaviour, things become easier, as we then are at least dealing with set-type priority-induced strategies. Still, as Example 5.6 demonstrates for the weighted sum of completion times, these priority orderings will generally not be constant, let alone be agreeable with restrictions to subproblems. Consequently, guaranteeing greedyness is still far from arriving at efficient ways of determination e.g. in the sense of Theorem 5.2.

EXAMPLE 5.5:

(1) Consider an exponential 2-machine model with $n>3$ jobs, in which job 1 precedes jobs 2 and 3 but where there are no other precedence relations. If jobs 2 and 3 have a dominating influence on the cost function, we will have to start with job 1 alone in order to allow for the earliest possible start of jobs 2 and 3. So at the beginning, we will have to leave a machine idle, though all jobs other then jobs 2 and 3 are available for scheduling.

(2) Consider an exponential 2-machine problem with 4 jobs $A = \{1,\ldots,4\}$ and without precedence constraints, where $\mathcal{N} = \{\{1,2\};\{1,3\};\{2,4\};\{3,4\}\}$. If job 1 has an overwhelming influence on the cost function, jobs 2 and 3 have a small cost impact and job 4 has no cost impact but has a comparatively high expected duration, then one will certainly have to start with job 1 but though job 4 would then still be available, one would postpone this job in order to allow for the earliest possible start of jobs 2 and 3.

EXAMPLE 5.6:

Consider an exponential 2-machine model with four jobs $A = \{1,2,3,4\}$, where $\lambda_1 = 10^6, \lambda_2 = 1, \lambda_3 = 10$ and $\lambda_4 = 1$, and the weighted flow time criteria with weights $w_1 = 10^6, w_2 = 10^6, w_3 = 2$ and $w_4 = 10$. It is easy to see that in exponential 2-machine models without precedence constraints, deliberate idleness can be avoided. We may therefore generally start with 2 jobs. Due to their great weights, jobs 1 and 2 are started at time 0, i.e. the associated priority ordering at time 0 may be chosen as $1>2>3>4$. Now it is not difficult to compute with the given recursive formula that, if job 1 ends first, 3 should go onto the free machine (the old priority list) while if job 2 ends first, the priority list has to be changed into 4>3. Consequently, the strategy is priority induced, but priorities are properly (set-type) dynamic.

With Example 5.5. in mind there is almost no hope for a further intermediate step via greedy strategies, if precedence and resource constraints are involved. Actually, current research concentrates at the rare cases such as strict interval orders and certain well-behaved systems of forbidden sets that from their very structure may be agreeable with an otherwise (i.e. for m-machine models without precedence constraints) optimal priority ordering, thus leaving it optimal. Certainly, the case of trivial precedence constraints and m-machine-type resource constraints, i.e. the framework of Theorem 5.1, is the common case among all such conditions. We will therefore close with some comments on the status of the deliberate idleness problem in that particular case. In fact, it seemed for some time to be a reasonable conjecture that there is an optimal greedy strategy in this context. But finally, necessitating a great deal of trials and a quite sophisticated computer program to handle such exponential models, the following counterexample was found:

EXAMPLE 5.7:

Let $[A,0_o,N,P,\kappa]$ denote a 3-machine problem with six independent, exponentially distributed jobs 1,...,6 with parameters $\lambda_1 = \lambda_2 = \lambda$ and $\lambda_3 = \lambda_4 = \lambda_5 = \lambda_6 = 1$. The additive cost function κ is given by its associated set function g, where

$$g(B) = \begin{cases} a >> 1 & \text{if } 1 \in B \text{ and } 2 \in B \\ 1 & \text{if } 1 \notin B \text{ and } \{2,5\} \subseteq B \text{ or } \{2,6\} \subseteq B \\ 1 & \text{if } 2 \notin B \text{ and } \{1,3\} \subseteq B \text{ or } \{1,4\} \subseteq B \\ 0 & \text{otherwise} \end{cases}$$

Due to symmetry reasons and the fact that $a >> 1$, only the following three strategies need to be considered:

Π_1: Start 1,2 at time $t = 0$ and leave the third machine idle. If 1 ends first, proceed with 2,5,6 according to priorities 5>6>3>4. If 2 ends first, proceed with 1,3,4 according to priorities 3>4 5>6.

Π_2: Start 1,2,3 at time $t = 0$. Proceed according to priorities
5 >6 >4 if 1 ends first
4 >5 >6 if 2 ends first
4 >5 >6 if 3 ends first

Π_3: Start 1,2,3 at time t = 0. Proceed according to priorities

$5 > 6 > 4$ if 1 ends first

$4 > 5 > 6$ if 2 ends first

$5 > 4 > 6$ if 3 ends first

The associated expected costs then are as follows:

$$\mathbb{E}[\kappa(\Pi_1,\cdot)] = \frac{a}{2\lambda} + \frac{1}{\lambda+2} + \frac{1}{(\lambda+2)(\lambda+1)}$$

$$\mathbb{E}[\kappa(\Pi_2,\cdot)] = \frac{a}{2\lambda} + \frac{\lambda}{2\lambda+1}\Big[\frac{2}{\lambda+2} + \frac{3}{(\lambda+2)(\lambda+1)} + \frac{1}{(\lambda+2)^2} + \frac{2}{(\lambda+2)^2(\lambda+1)}$$

$$+ \frac{1}{(2\lambda+1)(\lambda+1)} + \frac{1}{(2\lambda+1)(\lambda+2)} + \frac{1}{(2\lambda+1)(\lambda+2)^2} + \frac{1}{(2\lambda+1)(\lambda+2)^2(\lambda+1)}$$

$$+ \frac{1}{(2\lambda+1)(\lambda+2)(\lambda+1)} + \frac{1}{(2\lambda+1)^2(\lambda+2)} + \frac{1}{(2\lambda+1)^2(\lambda+2)(\lambda+1)}$$

$$+ \frac{1}{(2\lambda+1)(\lambda+1)}\Big]$$

Hence $\mathbb{E}[\kappa(\Pi_2,\cdot)] - \mathbb{E}[\kappa(\Pi_1,\cdot)] = \dfrac{2\lambda^4-8\lambda^3-23\lambda^2-19\lambda-6}{(\lambda+1)(\lambda+2)^2(2\lambda+1)^4}$

$$> 0 \Leftrightarrow \lambda > 6.1385$$

Similarly, $\mathbb{E}[\kappa(\Pi_3,\cdot)] - \mathbb{E}[\kappa(\Pi_2,\cdot)] = \dfrac{2\lambda^2+3\lambda^2+3\lambda+1}{(\lambda+1)(\lambda+2)^2(2\lambda+1)^4}$

$$> 0 \text{ for all } \lambda > 0.$$

Thus Π_1 is optimal for all $\lambda > 6.14$. Since Π_1 leaves a machine idle until the first job completion, Π_1 is not priority-induced.

Note that the deliberate idleness in Example 5.7 is closely related to the quite involved way, in which unfinished jobs may influence the project cost function. Thus, in particular, the defining set function g in the example is neither submodular nor supermodular, what is known to be equivalent to κ being neither convex nor concave. Both these properties constitute conjectures for conditions, under which deliberate idleness may be avoided in the above framework. The authors and others are working on this question, which seems to be one of the deep OPEN PROBLEMS in nonpreemptive models in the framework of stochastic scheduling problems. Probably, the weighted flow time criteria, which is both convex and concave, will play a key role in the research on settling this basic question.

SUMMARY:

This introductary text should have given some intuitive feeling concerning stochastic scheduling problems, the quite involved nature of the existing strategies, the knowledge concerning interesting subclasses of strategies, and the insights available into the optimality, stability and monotonicity behaviour. The whole theory relies considerably on the framework of stochastic dynamic optimization but also has its own features, which allowed some deep insights but also created some still open problems e.g. concerning Borel-measurability. Altogether, the general theoretical treatment is by now quite complete and it would be nice, if some of the techniques used could be adapted to other stochastic models such as inventory problems.

From an applicational point of view, the study of the "universe" of classes of strategies is probably quite useful, cf. e.g. the obtained insights concerning Graham anomalies. Employing many arguments from combinatorial, conceptual or analytical points of view together with aspects of the optimality, stability and monotonicity behaviour led to the three finite classes of ES, MES and set strategies, which seem particularly suited for applications. Here, ES strategies may be identified with feasible posets and convexity, the greater class of MES strategies with selections and with being the "greatest" class having a satisfactory analytical, stability and dominance behaviour, and finally, the greatest class of set strategies with incorporating list scheduling strategies and saving at least quasi-stability, while loosing a good monotonicity behaviour.

Finally, the covered connections with exponential models should have given at least some feeling for tractable cases and for the role a general theoretical background can play in this context. Certainly, the overall optimality of set strategies in this framework is a nice feature. The additional intermediate step to greedy strategies, at least for the special m-machine environment, is a similar challenging question and certainly constitutes at present one of the most interesting open problems in this field.

ACKNOWLEDGEMENT:

We would like to thank T.Kämpke (Passau), D.Kadelka (Karlsruhe) and S.M. Ross (Berkeley) for many stimulating discussions and significant suggestions that had an influence on the nature and exposition of this paper. We also like to thank the organizers of the Oberwolfach meeting on Operations Research for the opportunity to present this introductory text to stochastic scheduling problems.

This work was partly supported by the Minister für Wissenschaft und Forschung des Landes Nordrhein-Westfalen, West-Germany.

REFERENCES:

[1] BERTSEKAS, D.P., SHREVE, S.E.: Stochastic Optimal Control: The Discrete Time Case, Academic Press, New York, 1978

[2] BILLINGSLEY, P.: Convergence of Probability Measures, Wiley, New York, 1968

[3] DEMPSTER, M.A.H., LENSTRA, J.K., RINNOOY KAN, A.H.G. (eds.): Deterministic and Stochastic Scheduling, D. Reidel Publishing Company, Dordrecht, 1982

[4] ELMAGHRABY, S.E.: Activity Networks, Wiley, New York, 1977

[5] FISHER, M.L.: Worst-case analysis of heuristic algorithms for scheduling and packing, in: Dempster, M.A.H. et al. (eds.), Deterministic and stochastic Scheduling, D. Reidel Publishing Company, Dordrecht, 1982, p. 15 - 34

[6] GRAHAM, R.L.: Bounds on the performance of scheduling algorithms, in: Coffman, E.G. (ed.), Computer and Job-Shop Scheduling Theory, Wiley, New York, 1976, p. 165 - 227

[7] HINDERER, K.: Foundation of Non-stationary Dynamic Programming with Discrete Time Parameter, Springer Verlag, Berlin 1970

[8] IGELMUND, G., RADERMACHER, F.J.: Preselective strategies for the optimization of stochastic project networks under resource constraints, Networks 13 (1982) p. 1 - 29

[9] IGELMUND, G., RADERMACHER, F.J.: Algorithmic approaches to preselective strategies for stochastic scheduling problems, Networks 13 (1983) p. 29 - 48

[10] KADELKA, D.: personal communication

[11] KÄMPKE, T.: doctoral thesis (in preparation)

[12] KAERKES, R., MÖHRING, R.H., OBERSCHELP, W., RADERMACHER, F.J., RICHTER, M.M.: Netzplanoptimierung: Deterministische und stochastische Scheduling-Probleme über geordneten Strukturen, Springer Verlag, (to appear in 1984)

[13] KAMAE, T., KRENGEL, U., O'BRIEN, G.: Stochastic inequalities on partially ordered spaces, Ann. Probability 5 (1977) 899 - 912

[14] KEENEY, R.L., RAIFFA, H.: Decisions with multiple objectives John Wiley, New York, 1976

[15] KELLY, F.P.: Reversibility and stochastic networks, John Wiley, Toronto, 1979

[16] KLEINROCK, L.: Queuing Systems: Volume II-Computer Applications, Wiley, New York, 1976

[17] KOBAYASHI, H.: Modeling and analysis: an introduction to system performance evaluation methodology, Addison-Wesley, 1978

[18] MODER, J.J., PHILLIPS, C.R.: Project management with CPM and PERT, Reinhold, New York, 1964

[19] MÖHRING, R.H.: Minimizing Costs of Resource Requirements subject to a fixed Completion Time in Project Networks, Oper. Res. 32 (1984) p. 89 - 102

[20] MÖHRING, R.H., RADERMACHER, F.J. and WEISS, G.: Stochastic Scheduling problems I: general strategies (appears in ZOR)

[21] MÖHRING, R.H., RADERMACHER, F.J. and WEISS, G.: Stochastic Scheduling problems II: set strategies (appears in ZOR)

[22] NEUMANN, K.: Operations Research Verfahren, Band III, Carl Hanser Verlag, München, 1975

[23] RADERMACHER, F.J.: Kapazitätsoptimierung in Netzplänen, Math. System in Econ. 40, Anton Hain, Meisenheim, 1978

[24] RADERMACHER, F.J.: Cost-dependent essential systems of ES-strategies for stochastic scheduling problems, Methods of Oper. Res. 42 (1981) p. 17 - 31

[25] RADERMACHER, F.J.: Optimization of Resource Constraint Project Networks, preprint, RWTH Aachen, 1981

[26] RADERMACHER, F.J.: Optimale Strategien für stochastische Scheduling-Probleme, Habilitationsschrift 1981, erschienen in: Schriften zur Informatik und Angewandten Mathematik, Nr. 98, RWTH Aachen, 1984

[27] RINNOOY KAN, A.H.G.: Machine Scheduling Problems: Classification Complexity and Computation, Nijhoff, The Hague, 1976

[28] RIVAL, I.: Assembly lines have no timing anomalies, preprint 1984

[29] ROSS, S.M.: Applied Probability Models with Optimization Applications, Holden-Day, San Francisco, 1970

[30] ROSS, S.M.: Introduction to stochastic dynamic programming, Academic Press (1983)

[31] SCHASSBERGER, R.: Warteschlangen, Springer Verlag, Wien, 1973

[32] SCHNEEWEISS, H.: Entscheidungskriterien bei Risiko, Springer Verlag, Berlin, 1967

[33] STOYAN, D.: Qualitative Eigenschaften und Abschätzungen stochastischer Modelle, R. Oldenbourg Verlag, München, 1977

[34] WEBER, R.R., VARAIYA, P., WALRAND, J.: Scheduling jobs with stochastically ordered processing times on parallel machines to minimize expected flowtime, Memorandum No. UCB/ERL M 84/57, University of California, Berkeley, 1984

[35] WEISS, G., PINEDO, M.: Scheduling tasks with exponential service times on non-identical processors to minimize various cost functions, J. Appl. Probability 17 (1980) p. 187 - 202

[36] WHITTLE, P.: Optimization over time, Vol. I and II, John Wiley, New York, 1983

Aspects of Optimization in Automobile Insurance

M. Morlock

Universität Karlsruhe

Institut für Wirtschaftstheorie und

Operations Research

Abstract

In most of the countries experience rating is used in automobile insurance. On the basis of a simple model the resulting credibility premiums - optimal in the sense of Bayesian estimators - are compared with the bonus-malus-classes of motor insurance in the FRG of today. The critical point in this approach is the knowledge of the structure function; this is exemplified by the german automobile insurance and its actual problems. Results without using a structure function are presented. To derive an optimal bonus-system within the framework of the model an heuristic procedure is evaluated. The last aspect of optimization deals with optimal bounds for the "bonus-hunger" which can be computed by means of dynamic-programming. For the special case of an exponential distribution for the amount of claims, the solution of this optimization is given by the solution of some Bernoulli differential equations.

1. Introduction

Operations research methods are rarely applicated in insurance although the necessity is on hand and furthermore the economic importance of insurance is considerable with a total of about 92 milliards of premium income in 1982 for the FRG.

In automobile insurance, which has the second position of all the insurance branches with respect to premium income, a refined calculation of premiums is used, which makes it attractive for optimization considerations both from the viewpoint of the insured and the insurance company and, indeed, in the past a lot of changes in automobile insurance occurred not only concerning the lifting up of premiums implied by inflation, but also by modifications in the tariff structure.

In the sequel automobile liability insurance will be investigated and within especially the liability insurance of motor cars, which is the major part having a structure very similar to the others.

In the FRG in automobile liability insurance there are primary premium differences such as

- sort of the automobile (e.g. motor car, truck)
- region of the place of residence (e.g. city, country-side)
- horse-power of the engine (several classes)
- profession of the police holder (e.g. farmer, public-servant),

which are mainly of statistical interest and furthermore secondary premium differences according to

- bonus-malus-classes

where some optimization aspects are to be found.

The bonus-malus-classes summarize a lot of influences concerning the individual risk, often not quantitative, such as sense of responsibility, temperament or health of the driver(s) of the car. These classes are of essential importance for the premium and represent the claim experience of the company with the individual policy holder. The theoretical foundation is given by credibility theory (cf. e.g. BÜHLMANN (1970)), a cornerstone of acturial mathematics, which (according to JONG and ZEHNWIRTH (1983)) can be viewed as a set of Bayesian insurance models, the credibility estimators being linear Bayes rules which may be derived using a variety of arguments including minimum linear mean-square estimation theory and Markov theory.

2. Model

The underlieing model in this paper is given by:

- $1,\ldots, t,\ldots$; periods of insurance which are of equal lenght
- M_t^θ, poisson distributed i.i.d.r.v. ; number of claims in period t, $(t=1,2,\ldots\ldots)$ of a single risk, which is labelled with a characteristic quantity (risk parameter) θ, representing the accident proneness of the risk

  $$P(M_t^\theta=m)=\frac{\theta^m}{m!}e^{-\theta}, \qquad m=0,1,2,\ldots$$

- S_m, $m=1,\ldots,M_t$ i.i.d.r.v. ; amount of the m-th claim in period t mutually independent of M_t^θ.

- U(.), distribution function of r.v.Θ ; structure function with the meaning that the risk θ, connected with an insurance contract is the realisation of the r.v. Θ

3. Premium calculation

According to the equivalence principle, for known $\Theta=\theta$ the risk premium [1] is given by (conditional) expectation:

$$\pi_t^\theta = E\left(\sum_{m=1}^{M_t^\theta} S_m\right) = E\left(\sum_{m=1}^{M_t^\Theta} S_m \mid \Theta=\theta\right).$$

For unknown risk parameter in the framework of the model, the risk premium π_t^Θ (for period t) is a random variable and with respect to the history $(M_1=m_1,\dots, M_{t-1}=m_{t-1})$ of the policy holder, the so called credibility premium (cf. BÜHLMANN (1970) p. 93 ff.) can be defined by the conditional expectation $E(\pi_t^\Theta | M=m_1,\dots, M_{t-1}=m_{t-1})$.

For practical purposes however the variety of these premiums is too great, and therefore a rating basis, some function of the history,

$$Z_t = Z_t(M_1,\dots, M_{t-1}), \quad t=1,2,\dots$$

is introduced and consequently

$$\pi_t(Z_t) = E(\pi_t^\Theta | Z_t)$$

defines the credibility premium based on the rating basis Z_t in period t.

The most important example of a rating basis are the transition rules of bonus-malus-system, consisting of

- $\{1,\dots,K\}$; the bonus-malus-classes
- $T : \{1,\dots,K\} \times \mathbb{Z}_+ \to \{1,\dots,K\}$; the tansition rules
  $(k, m_{t-1}) \to T_{k,m_{t-1}}$; the bonus malus class in t, if in t-1 the insured had been in class k and m_{t-1} accidents occurred
- k_o ; the initial class.

---

1) For sake of simplicity surcharges are left out of consideration in the sequel

defining the rating bases:

$$Z_1 := k_0$$

$$\left.\begin{array}{llll} Z_t : & \mathbb{Z}_+^{t-1} & \to & \{1,\ldots,K\} \\ & (M_1,\ldots, M_{t-2}, M_{t-1}) & \to & T_{Z_{t-2}}, M_{t-1} \end{array}\right\} \quad t = 2,3,\ldots$$

In the following the rating basis will be supposed to be of this form and for period t the premium in class k is then given by

$$\pi_t(k) = E(\pi_t^{\Theta} | Z_t = k), \tag{1}$$

optimal with respect to the quadratic measure

$$\begin{aligned} Q_t(Z_t) &= E([\Theta - \pi_t(Z_t)]^2) \\ &= \min_{a_t(.)} \{E([\Theta - a_t(Z_t)]^2)\} \end{aligned} \tag{2}$$

of the efficiency of any premium formula $a_t(.)$.

This "best" premium $\pi_t(k)$ $(t=1,2,\ldots ; k=1,\ldots,K)$ has the disadvantage for tariffication in practice to be time dependent. From the fact that for any fixed θ of $\Theta, \{Z_t\}_{t=1,2,\ldots}$ is a Markovian chain with state space $\{1,\ldots,K\}$ which for all reasonable transition rules is ergodic, as easily can be shown, for all $k=1,\ldots,K$ the following asymptotic premiums exist:

$$\pi(k) = \lim_{t\to\infty} \pi_t(k) \tag{3}$$

and may be used (NORBERG (1976)) for a time independent bonus-malus-scale

To take into account for optimization not only the premiums to be payed after a "very long time" but the total of premiums during a driver's (policy holder's) lifetime BORGAN et al. (1981) suggested as a time independent bonus-malus-scale

$$\tilde{\pi}(k) = \sum_{t=1}^{\infty} \alpha_{tk} \, \pi_t(k) \tag{4}$$

with

$$\left.\begin{array}{l} \alpha_{tk} = w_t \, P(Z_t=k) \Big/ \sum_{t=1}^{\infty} w_t \, P(Z_t=k) \\ w_t \geqq 0 \quad , \sum_{t=1}^{\infty} w_t = 1 \end{array}\right\} \quad \begin{array}{l} k=1,\ldots,K \\ t=1,2,\ldots \end{array}$$

optimizing

$$\tilde{Q}(T) = \sum_{t=1}^{\infty} w_t \, Q_t(Z_t) \tag{5}$$

The bonus-malus-system of the FRG for motor cars for example has 18 classes, 16 of which are relevant (the two malus classes S_2 and S_3 are essentially identical and the initial class 0 exists only for the first period). For t=25 in criteria (2), contained as a special case in (5), the actual bonus-malus-scale is compared in table 1 with the optimal scale by (1) for exponentially distributed risk parameter Θ with parameter λ=0.11 which is about the observed average claim number in 1983.

k	name	actual % of the basis premium	optimal % of the basis premium	T_{km} m=0	m=1	m=2	m=3	m≧4
1	SF 13	40	25	1	5	10	12	16
2	SF 12	40	44	1	6	11	13	16
3	SF 11	40	47	2	7	11	13	16
4	SF 10	40	49	3	8	11	13	16
5	SF 9	40	52	4	10	12	13	16
6	SF 8	45	67	5	11	13	14	16
7	SF 7	50	72	6	11	13	14	16
8	SF 6	55	79	7	11	13	14	16
9	SF 5	60	86	8	11	13	14	16
10	SF 4	65	91	9	12	13	14	16
11	SF 3	70	101	10	13	14	15	16
12	SF 2	85	119	11	13	14	15	16
13	SF 1	100	132	12	14	15	16	16
14	SF 1/2	125	158	13	15	16	16	16
15	S1	175	185	13	16	16	16	16
16	S2, S3	200	213	13	16	16	16	16

table 1: bonus-malus-system of the FRG

The calculation within this simple model shows two effects which are also known from observation, namely that the best risks are charged with too high premiums whereas the worst risks should have to pay more. It must be noted at this point however that the crucial point in this investigation is, that there is little information about the structure function, although different calculations have shown that the results are not very sensitive to the shape of the structure function. Above all the use of such models consists in analysing the present state and the effects - especially long-time effects - of modifications, which can be done to a certain extend without knowledge of the structure function.

One modification in the bonus-malus-system of the FRG occurred in 1981 by adding three new bonus classes and changing some of the transition rules. The comparison of the two systems (cf. MORLOCK (1983)) with respect to the expectation and the variance of the asymptotic premiums show (see figure 1) that for $\Theta \varepsilon [0, 0.3]$, which is the majority of risks, the premium differentiation of the new system is worse, for rather good risks are charged with higher premiums (curves of the expectations). Furthermore the variances of the premiums there in general are greater for the new system indicating a diminished selecting power of the new system, and indeed new alterations both of premiums and transition rules are discussed at the moment.

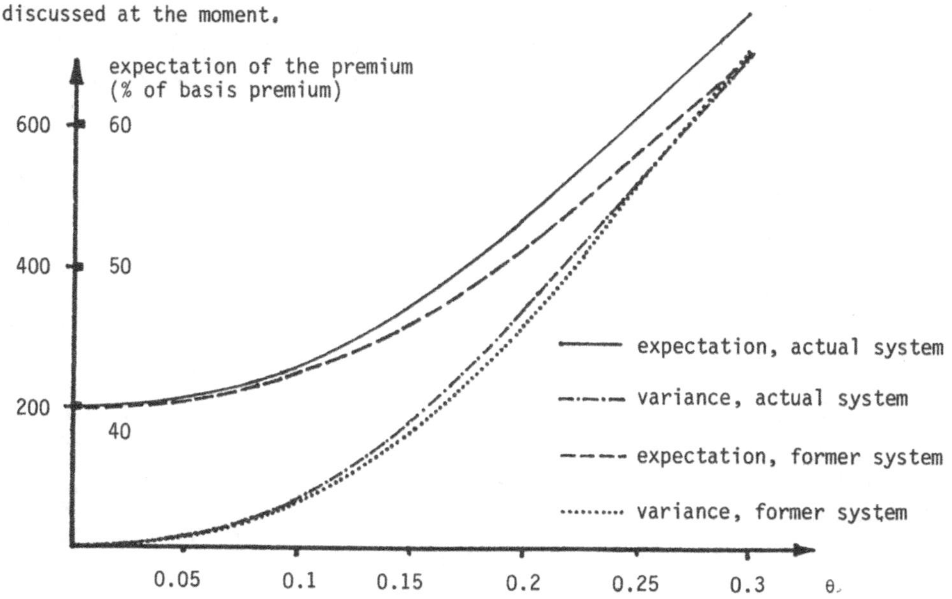

figure 1: Expectation and variance of asymptotic premiums for known risk parameter θ

Another comparison between the former and the actual bonus-malus-system without knowledg of the structure function, weakening the assumption of the time-independence of the risk variable θ, concerns the reaction of the systems on a sudden change of θ, which may take place for example when the policy holder's children start to drive with his car too. This situation is demonstrated in figure 2 (MORLOCK (1983)):

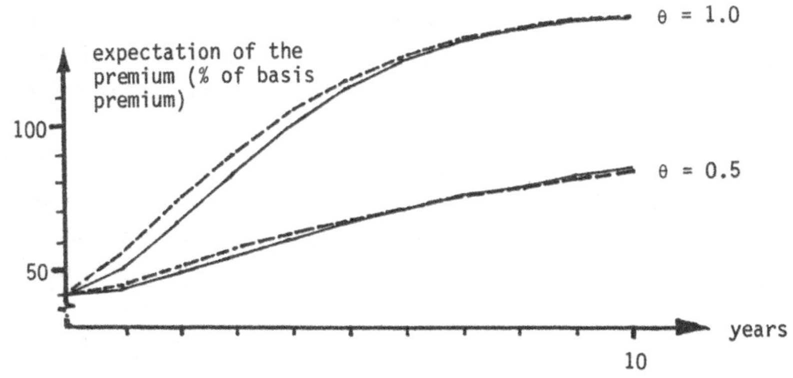

figure 2: Development of the expectation of premiums outgoing from the best bonus class

Starting in the best bonus-class the fair "descent" in both systems is shown, measured by the expectation of the payment of the premiums. The achievement of the fair premium (within the respective system) takes place more slowly in the present system which therefore is worse than the former one from this aspect too.

4. Optimal bonus-malus-system

Comparison of bonus-malus-systems can also be done by theoretical considerations (see e.g. NORBERG (1976), BORGAN et al. (1981)) minimizing $Q_t(Z_t)$ or $\bar{Q}(T)$ with respect to all possible transition rules. For sake of simplicity $Q_t(Z_t)$ with fixed t will be investigated further. In this case the minimization of $Q_t(Z_t)$ can be transformed by evaluation of the quadratic term $[\Theta-\pi_t\ (Z_t)]^2$ and the use of the theorem of iterated expectations to the following maximization problem:

$$e_t := \max_T \sum_{k=1}^{K} \pi_t(k)^2 p_t(k) \qquad (6)$$

with

$$\left.\begin{aligned} \pi_t(k) &= E(\pi_t^\Theta | Z_t=k) \\ p_t(k) &= E(P(Z_t=k|\Theta)) \end{aligned}\right\} \qquad k=1,\dots,K$$

both $\pi_t(.)$ and $p_t(.)$ depending on Z_t, defined by the transition rules T. The calculation of e_t is done easily for fixed T by considering the underlieing Markovian chain, but by a recursive formula for K=16 (present german system) the number of all (in a certain sense) reasonable transition rules T is above 10^{15}.

For the bonus-malus-system of the FRG with the structure function of exponential type, with parameter $\lambda=0.11$ as above, good experience was made by an heuristic procedure related to the approach of successive iteration used for concave maximization problems. In every step of that procedure successively the element $\bar{T}_{k\bar{m}} = T_{k\bar{m}}$ (k=1...,16; $\bar{m}$=0,1,...,3) of the matrix $\bar{T} = (\bar{T}_{k\bar{m}})_{16,4}$, representing the transition rules T, becomes a variable one by one with the boundary conditions

$$\bar{T}_{k,\bar{m}-1} \leqq \bar{T}_{k,\bar{m}} \leqq \bar{T}_{k,\bar{m}+1} \qquad (\bar{T}_{k,-1}:=1,\ \bar{T}_{k,4}:=16)$$

to maximize (6). Starting with k=1 and $\bar{m}$=0 and continueing row by row the procedure stops when no improvement was found in 64=K·4 successive steps. Numerical experiments with different starting transition rules turned out a relative quick convergence to always the same solution $T^*=(T^*_{k\bar{m}})_{16,4}$ given in table 2:

k	name	Improvement: $\bar{T}_{k\bar{m}} \rightarrow T^{*}_{k\bar{m}}$ $\bar{m}$=0	$\bar{m}$=1	$\bar{m}$=2	$\bar{m}$=3
1	SF 13	1→1	5→2	10→5	12→7
2	SF 12	1→1	6→5	11→7	13→9
3	SF 11	2→2	7→6	11→8	13→10
4	SF 10	3→3	8→7	11→9	13→10
5	SF 9	4→4	10→7	12→9	13→11
6	SF 8	5→5	11→8	13→10	14→12
7	SF 7	6→6	11→9	13→11	14→12
8	SF 6	7→7	11→10	13→12	14→13
9	SF 5	8→8	11→11	13→13	14→14
10	SF 4	9→9	12→12	13→13	14→15
11	SF 3	10→10	13→13	14→14	15→16
12	SF 2	11→11	13→14	14→15	15→16
13	SF 1	12→12	14→15	15→16	16→16
14	SF 1/2	13→13	15→16	16→16	16→16
15	S1	13→14	16→16	16→16	16→16
16	S2, S3	13→15	16→16	16→16	16→16

table 2: Improvement of the present transition rules (FRG)

The abstract of this table is, that within the comparison of the improved transition rules with the present ones policy holders in good bonus-classes (small k) are downgraded less whereas in the bad malus-classes they are downgraded more.

5. Optimal bounds for bonus hunger

The last aspect of optimization presented here concerns the possibility of the policy holder to make an optimal decision. In the case that he has caused an accident, he can pay the claim of his opponent, thus being treated by his insurance company with respect to the transition rules, as if this accident would not have been occurred. The reason of saving his bonus in this way, very lucidly is called "bonus hunger".

The question now is of the optimal bound for the amount of a claim up to which the insured has to pay the claim by himself. Clearly, the decision to file a claim for an accident when he is at fault depends on the insured's bonus-malus-class and the number of claims he has already filed in the current period (year). The criteria to minimize is the expected total sum of premiums and claims to be payed in the future. The following notations and assumptions (HAELING von LANZENAUER (1974)) will be used:

- $[0,T]$, time interval with time horizon T
- Δ , small time intervall in which the policy holder is assumed to cause at most one accident
- $P(M^\Delta=1)$, probability of one such accident with constant accident proneness $\theta=\lim_{\Delta\to 0} P(M^\Delta=1)/\Delta$
- S , r.v. representing the claim amount of one of the i.i.d. amounts of claims in the future
- $\hat{\pi}(k)$, premium in bonus-malus-class k
- $\phi_t^\Delta\binom{k}{m}$, minimum expected future costs of premiums and claims for the time interval $[t,T]$, if at time t the insured is in the bonus-malus-class k and has already filed m claims in the current year

By means of stochastic dynamic programming the optimal decision and the minimum expected future costs are calculated by exploiting the functional equation of BELLMAN:

$$\phi_{t-\Delta}^\Delta\binom{k}{m} = \begin{cases} \min\limits_{u\in\mathbb{R}_+} \{P(M^\Delta=1)[P(S\leq u)E(S|S\leq u) + \phi_t^\Delta\binom{k}{m} + P(S>u)\phi_t^\Delta\binom{k}{m+1}] \\ \quad + P(M^\Delta=0)\phi_t^\Delta\binom{k}{m}\}, & t\text{: not beginning of the year} \\ \min\limits_{u\in\mathbb{R}_+} \{P(M^\Delta=1)[P(S\leq u)E(S|S\leq u) + \phi_t^\Delta\binom{T_{km}}{0} + \hat{\pi}(T_{km}) \\ \quad + P(S>u)(\phi_t^\Delta\binom{T_{k,m+1}}{0} + \hat{\pi}(T_{k,m+1}))] \\ \quad + P(M^\Delta=0)(\phi_t^\Delta\binom{T_{km}}{0} + \hat{\pi}_t(T_{km})) & t\text{: beginning of the year} \end{cases} \tag{7}$$

An easy calculation shows (not depending on the density function of S) for the optimal decision $u_t^\Delta\binom{k}{m}$ in $t-\Delta$:

$$u_t^\Delta\binom{k}{m} = \begin{cases} \phi_t^\Delta\binom{k}{m+1} - \phi_t^\Delta\binom{k}{m}, & t\text{: not beginning of the year} \\ \phi_t^\Delta\binom{T_{k,m+1}}{0} + \hat{\pi}(T_{k,m+1}) - \phi_t^\Delta\binom{T_{km}}{0} - \hat{\pi}(T_{km}), & t\text{: beginning of the year} \end{cases}$$

For the case of exponentially distributed S substituting (8) in (7) and arranging the terms appropriately yields a differential equation of the BERNOULLI type for $\Delta\to 0$ which can be solved explicitly (MORLOCK (1981)).

To give an example some optimal bounds for the bonus hunger within the bonus-malus-system of the FRG are given by table 3 for accident proneness Θ=0.1 and exponential claim amount distribution of S with E(S) = 2700.

number of already filed claims in the year				bonus-malus-class		number of already filed claims in the year			
m=0	m=1	m=2	m=3	k	name	m=0	m=1	m=2	m=3
27	119	104	225	1	SF 13	18	121	95	143
43	145	128	158	2	SF 12	35	146	125	172
59	126	128	158	3	SF 11	53	126	125	172
76	104	128	158	4	SF 10	74	102	125	172
127	93	78	158	5	SF 9	130	95	71	172
160	123	93	70	6	SF 8	163	125	95	77
145	123	93	70	7	SF 7	146	125	95	77
126	123	93	70	8	SF 6	126	125	95	77
104	123	93	70	9	SF 5	102	125	95	77
125	73	93	70	10	SF 4	129	71	95	77
161	91	49	23	11	SF 3	166	95	52	25
123	91	49	23	12	SF 2	125	95	52	25
157	49	23	0	13	SF 1	166	52	25	0
137	23	0	0	14	SF 1/2	147	25	0	0
158	0	0	0	15,16	S1,S2,S3	172	0	0	0

table 3: Optimal bounds for a policy holder to file claims in % of his basis premium; Θ=0.1 and λ=2700

If more than 3 claims are already filed, the policy holder will be in the worst class for the next period and therefore will not pay claims on its own account.

References

BORGAN, O., J. HOEM and R. NORBERG: A Nonasymptotic Criterion for the Evaluation of Automobile Bonus Systems; Scan. Actuarial J.(1981), p. 165-178

BÜHLMANN, H.: Mathematical Methods in Risk Theory; Springer (1970)

HAELING von LANZENAUER, C.: Optimal Claim Decisions by Policy-holders in Automobile Insurance with Merit-Rating Structures; J. of the Op. Res. Soc. 11 (1974), p. 979-990

JONG, P. and B. ZEHNWIRTH: Credibility and Kalman filter; Insurance: Mathematics and Economics 2 (1983), p. 281-286

MORLOCK, M.: Zur Bestimmung optimaler Schranken für die Regulierung selbstverschuldeter Unfälle in der Kfz-Haftpflichtversicherung, in GÖPPL, H. und R. HENN: Geld, Banken und Versicherungen (II), Athenäum (1981), p. 824-833

MORLOCK, M.: Auswirkungen von Risikoänderungen beim Bonus-Malus-System in der Kfz-Haftpflichtversicherung; in GÖPPL, H. und R. HENN: Geld, Banken und Versicherungen (II); VVW Karlsruhe (1983) p. 1015-1028

NORBERG, R.: A Credibility Theory for Automobile Bonus Systems; Scand. Actuarial J. (1976), p. 92-107

GERT Networks with Tree Structure: Properties, Temporal Analysis, Cost Minimization, and Scheduling

Klaus Neumann, Karlsruhe [1)]

Abstract

GERT networks all of whose nodes have OR entrance and deterministic or stochastic exit and which are called OR networks are considered. The assumption that, figuratively speaking, different walks emanating from a deterministic node do not meet anywhere in an OR network results in a certain tree structure: If we shrink all strong components of the network to one node each, then any partial network whose activities are carried out during a single project execution represents an outtree. The above assumption also permits an OR network with "deterministic degree" d to be covered by d+1 STEOR networks (that is, GERT networks all of whose nodes have exclusive-or entrance and stochastic exit).

Each STEOR network is associated with a Markov renewal process whose renewal functions provide the "temporal analysis" of the STEOR network. The determination of optimal time-cost trade-offs for STEOR networks leads to a stochastic dynamic programming problem or an optimal control problem. Owing to the above "covering property", temporal analysis and cost minimization of OR networks can be reduced to the same problems for STEOR networks.

If one resource of capacity 1 is required to execute each activity of a project described by an OR network, we obtain a stochastic single-machine scheduling problem with precedence constraints given by the OR network. The tree structure of the network permits this scheduling problem with expected weighted sum of the activity completion times as objective function to be solved by a generalization of Smith's ratio rule in polynomial time.

1. Introduction and Basic Concepts

GERT networks, sometimes also called stochastic project networks, aid in the planning, scheduling and controlling of projects with stochastic evolution structure and feedback. To this end, GERT networks have different node types, stochastic arc weights and cycles. We use the well-known activity-on-arc representation, that is, the activities of the project correspond to arcs and the project events to nodes of the network. For basic concepts, time-oriented evaluation and applications of GERT networks we refer to Neumann/Steinhardt [9]. Some recent results can be found in Neumann [7].

1) Prof. Dr. Klaus Neumann, Institut für Wirtschaftstheorie und Operations Research, Universität Karlsruhe, Kaiserstraße 12, D-7500 Karlsruhe 1

This paper gives an overview of GERT networks that have some kind of tree structure. We discuss some properties of those networks and deal with temporal analysis and optimal time-cost trade-offs for those networks as well as sequencing and scheduling with those networks as precedence constraints.

For simplicity, we assume that the network has exactly one source, which is supposed to be activated (that is, the corresponding beginning event of the project occurs) at time 0. GERT networks with several sources are discussed in Neumann [6], [8]. Moreover, the network in question is assumed to have at least one sink (corresponding to a terminal event of the project). It is typical of a project network that each node of the network is reachable from the source and from each node at least one sink is reachable.

We assume without loss of generality that the network does not have parallel arcs. The arc with initial node i and final node j is designated by <i,j>. Each arc <i,j> of a GERT network is assigned a weight vector $\begin{pmatrix} p_{ij} \\ F_{ij} \end{pmatrix}$, where p_{ij} is the conditional probability that the corresponding activity <i,j> is executed given that its initial event i has occurred, and F_{ij} is the conditional distribution function of the duration D_{ij} of activity <i,j> given that activity <i,j> is carried out.

Each node of a GERT network consists of an entrance side and an exit side. A node i has *deterministic exit* if the execution of all activities emanating from node i can be begun as soon as the corresponding project event i has occurred during a project execution. Node i has *stochastic exit* if the execution of exactly one of the activities emanating from node i can be begun as soon as event i has occurred. A node with at most one successor is, by convention, assigned the stochastic exit.

As regards the entrance side of a node i, we only consider the case that node i has *OR entrance*, that is, the corresponding project event i occurs as soon as an activity leading into node i is terminated. Nodes with *AND entrance*, where the respective project event occurs as soon as all activities leading into the node are terminated, would destroy any tree structure of the network.

GERT networks without nodes having AND entrance we are going to study in what follows are also called *OR networks*. An OR network contains two types of nodes: nodes with OR entrance and deterministic exit (called *deterministic nodes*) and nodes with OR entrance and stochastic exit (called *stochastic nodes*).

2. Properties of an OR Network

In the sequel, some assumptions are supposed to be satisfied. The first assumption expresses some kind of Markov property and independence property and reads, figuratively speaking, as follows:

Assumption A1. The project evolution beginning at any time t is independent of the past history provided that the "present state" of the project at time t is given. Moreover, executions of different activities that do not follow one another are independent of one another.

Assumption A1 implies in particular that the durations D_{ij} of the individual activities <i,j> are independent random variables. The next assumption is essential to the tree structure of the OR network. Let $\mathcal{R}(j)$ be the set of the nodes reachable from node j. Then we require

Assumption A2. For each deterministic node i and for every two distinct successors j,k of i it holds that $\mathcal{R}(j)\cap\mathcal{R}(k)=\emptyset$.

Assumption A2 says, figuratively speaking, that different walks emanating from a deterministic node do not meet anywhere in the network. It can be tested in $O(|V|^2)$ time, where V is the node set of the network, whether assumption A2 is satisfied in a given OR network (cf. Rubach [12]).

Fig. 1 shows an OR network (without arc weights) satisfying assumption A2. The meaning of the darker partial network will be explained later on.

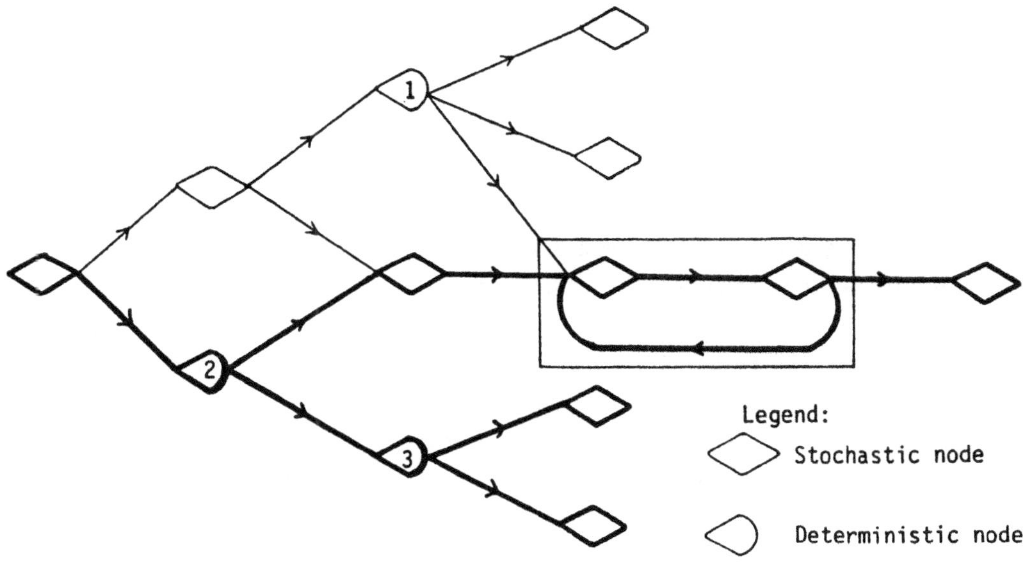

Figure 1

It can be shown that owing to assumption A2 an OR network has some interesting properties. To formulate these properties we need the concept of a cycle structure. A *cycle structure* is a strong component of a network different from a single node, in other words, a cycle structure represents a maximal set of connected cycles. An *entrance arc* of a cycle structure C is an arc whose final node belongs to C but which does not belong itself to C. Then we have

Property P1. Every node in a cycle is stochastic.

Property P2. For each node i outside any cycle at most one arc leading into i is executed during a single project execution with probability 1.

Property P3. For each cycle structure C at most one of the entrance arcs of C is executed during a single project execution with probability 1.

Property P4. If we shrink all cycle structures of an OR network N to one (stochastic) node each, then any partial network of N whose activities are carried out during a single project execution represents an outtree, whose root is the source of N.

A proof of properties P1, P2, P3 can be found in Neumann [8]. Property P4, which is a simple consequence of the definition of stochastic and deterministic nodes, says that an OR network has a certain *tree structure*. Note that even if all cycle structures are shrunk to single nodes, an OR network itself does not form a tree; only a partial network that corresponds to a single project execution represents, after the "cycle reduction", a tree. In Fig. 1 the darker partial network forms an outtree after shrinking the cycle inside the frame to a stochastic node.

Properties P2 and P3 say that each node of an OR network behaves like a node with so-called exclusive-or entrance, that is, the corresponding project event occurs every time when exactly one activity leading into the node is terminated (recall that "OR" means "at least one"). Such a node is also called an *EOR node*, and a GERT network all of whose nodes have exclusive-or entrance is referred to as an *EOR network*. A GERT network all of whose nodes have exclusive-or entrance and stochastic exit is called a *STEOR network*.

Next, we show that each OR network can be "covered" by a several STEOR networks. As we shall see later, a Markov renewal process can be assigned to each STEOR network, and this correspondence can be exploited for the temporal analysis and cost minimization of STEOR networks and hence of OR networks, too.

Let $i_1,\dots,i_r$ be the "foremost" deterministic nodes of the OR network in question, that is, the deterministic nodes with the property that all nodes "before" them are stochastic. In Fig. 1 nodes 1 and 2 are the foremost deterministic nodes. Node 3 is not a foremost deterministic node because node 2 is a predecessor of node 3. Let M_ρ be the set of the deterministic nodes reachable from i_ρ $(\rho=1,\dots,r)$ and let $S(j)$ be the set of the successors of node j. Then

$$d := \max_{\rho=1,\dots,r} \sum_{j\in M_\rho} (|S(j)|-1)$$

is called the *deterministic degree* of the OR network. We have $d>0$ if the network contains at least one deterministic node. The OR network of Fig. 1 has deterministic degree 2. For a STEOR network we put $d:=0$.

A set of k different partial networks N_κ of an OR network N with node sets V_κ is called a *covering* of N of *size* k if

(i) each partial network N_κ contains the source of N

(ii) $i \in V_\kappa$ deterministic implies that exactly one arc emanating from i belongs to N_κ, $i \in V_\kappa$ stochastic implies that all arcs emanating from i belong to N_κ

(iii) each walk from the source to a sink of N belongs to at least one partial network N_κ.

In Neumann [8] the following result is proved

Property P5. The minimum size of a covering of an OR network with deterministic degree d is d+1.

The OR network in Fig. 1 has deterministic degree 2 and hence there is a covering of size 3. The arcs of the 3 partial networks of such a covering are illustrated by normal, dark and broken arrows in Fig. 2.

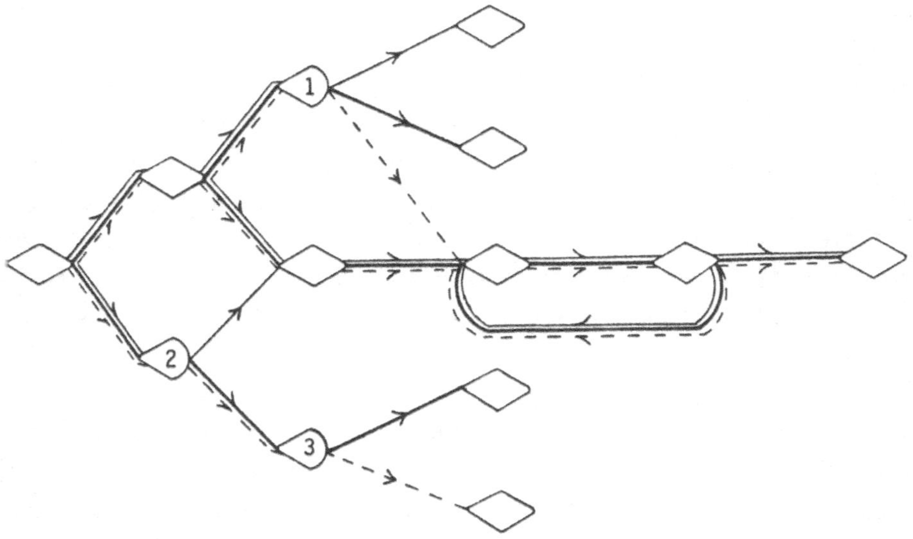

Figure 2

If any partial network N_κ from a covering of an OR network is taken on its own, every deterministic node in N_κ has only one successor and, as agreed upon, has to be replaced by a stochastic node, that is, N_κ represents a STEOR network. In other words, each OR network with deterministic degree d can be covered by d+1 STEOR networks. From this we obtain another property of an OR network. We state the additional

Assumption A3. For each node k of a cycle structure C there is a path from k to a node outside C such that $p_{ij}>0$ for every arc $<i,j>$ of this path.

Assumption A3 says, figuratively speaking,that each cycle structure is "left" with positive probability. It is well-known that owing to assumption A3 at most one and with probability 1 exactly one terminal event occurs during each execution of a project corresponding to a STEOR network (cf. Neumann/Steinhardt [9]). As a consequence, we have

Property P6. At most d+1 terminal events and with probability 1 at least one terminal event occur during each execution of a project corresponding to an OR network with deterministic degree d.

3. Temporal Analysis of OR Networks

We wish to complete the project in question as early as possible, that is, all times of occurrence of project events are supposed to be the earliest times for the respective events. In other words, we stipulate that as soon as a project event i has occurred all outcoming activities, if i corresponds to a deterministic node, or respectively exactly one outcoming activity, if i corresponds to a stochastic node, are begun (recall that in Section 1 we said "can be begun" instead).

First we deal with STEOR networks. Temporal analysis of STEOR networks is a well-known field and hence we only list the most important results in what follows. For details and proofs of the results presented we refer to Neumann/Steinhardt [9] and Nicolai [10].

Let $V=\{1,\dots,n\}$ be the node set of the network in question where node 1 is supposed to be the source. Let $K_j(t)$ be the number of activations of node j in the time interval $[0,t]$ (recall that the source is activated at time 0).

Then the mapping $Y_j : \mathbb{R}_+ \to \mathbb{R}_+$ given by

$$Y_j(t) := E[K_j(t)] \quad \text{for } t \in \mathbb{R}_+,$$

where E[K] is the expected value of random variable K, is called the *activation function of node* j.

Now let j be a node outside any cycle. Since node j is activated at most once during a single project execution, we can define T_j to be the (earliest) time of occurrence of the corresponding project event j. Moreover, let q_j be the probability that project event j occurs. Then it holds that

$$(1) \quad \begin{cases} P(T_j \leqq t) = Y_j(t) & \text{for } t \geqq 0 \\ q_j = \lim\limits_{t \to \infty} Y_j(t). \end{cases}$$

Formula (1) holds in particular for each terminal event j of the project. Furthermore, for $q_j > 0$ $\frac{Y_j}{q_j}$ is the conditional distribution function of the (shortest) project duration given that terminal event j has occurred. Since the latter quantities, which are important to time planning of projects, can easily be determined from the activation functions, we mean by *temporal analysis* the computation of the activation functions Y_j $(j=1,\ldots,n)$.

By definition the nodes of a STEOR network activated during a single project execution are activated one after another, where nodes within cycles may be activated several times. Let the index $\nu \geqq 0$ count the successive activations of nodes, and let X_ν be that node whose activation is the νth node activation in turn and Θ_ν be the time of this activation. Then by assumption A1 the sequence $(X_\nu, \Theta_\nu)_{\nu \in \mathbb{N}_0}$ represents a homogeneous Markov renewal process with state space $V \times \mathbb{R}_+$ and transition functions $Q_{ij}(\cdot) = p_{ij} F_{ij}(\cdot)$.

The activation functions Y_j we seek to determine coincide with special renewal functions of the Markov renewal process associated with the STEOR network. It is well-known that the renewal functions satisfy a system of integral equations. Hence, the activation functions also satisfy a system of integral equations, which has the form

$$(2) \quad \left.\begin{aligned} & Y_j(t) = Q_{1j}(t) + \sum_{k=2}^{n} \int_{[0,t]} Q_{kj}(t-s) Y_k(ds), \quad j=2,\ldots,n \\ & Y_1(t) = 1 \end{aligned}\right\} (t \geqq 0),$$

where $Q_{kj}(t):=0$ for $t\geq 0$ if there is no arc <k,j>. To solve this system of integral equations approximately, we replace it by a system of linear equations for the values of the activation functions at certain points in time.

Next, we turn to OR networks. The definition of the activation functions and formula (1) remain valid for OR networks. Consider an OR network N with deterministic degree d and let $\{N_\kappa|\kappa=1,\ldots,d+1\}$ be a covering of N. The activation function Y_j of any node j in N coincides with the activation function Y_j^κ of node j in each STEOR network N_κ that contains node j. As a consequence, the activation functions of an OR network, which again provide the temporal analysis, also satisfy the system of integral equations (2).

For $\emptyset\neq U\subseteq V$ let t_U be the vector with the components $t_j, j\in U$. The mapping $Y_U: \mathbb{R}_+^{|U|}\to\mathbb{R}_+$ defined by

$$Y_U(t_U) := E[\prod_{j\in U} K_j(t_j)] \quad \text{for } t_j\in\mathbb{R}_+, j\in U$$

is called the *activation function of set* U.

Let S' be a nonvoid subset of the sink set S of the OR network. Then the probability $q_{S'}$ that all terminal events $j\in S'$ occur during a project execution is

$$q_{S'} = \lim_{t_{S'}\to\infty} Y_{S'}(t_{S'}),$$

and for $q_{S'}>0$ $\frac{Y_{S'}}{q_{S'}}$ is the conditional distribution function of the project duration given that all terminal events $j\in S'$ have occurred. The determination of the set of functions

$$Y(S) := \{Y_{S'}|\emptyset\neq S'\subseteq S\}$$

is sometimes called the *complete evaluation* of the network in question (cf. Neumann [7]).

Since for a STEOR network exactly one sink is activated with probability 1 during a single project execution, we have

(3) $$Y_{S'} = 0 \quad \text{for all } S'\subseteq S \text{ with } |S'|>1.$$

For an OR network with deterministic degree $d \geq 1$, (3) does not apply, in other words, the computation of the activation functions Y_j, $j \varepsilon V$, is not sufficient for the complete evaluation of the network. A method for completely evaluating such a network can be found in Neumann [8].

4. Cost Minimization for OR Networks

First we again consider STEOR networks. To deal with cost optimization, we stipulate that the execution probability p_{ij} and the distribution function F_{ij} of the duration of each activity <i,j> depend on the time of occurrence of the initial event i of that activity. The preceding results remain valid for STEOR networks with those time-dependent arc weights. In particular, a Markov renewal process can again be assigned to such a STEOR network (cf. Nicolai [10]).

Now assume that when a project event i occurs at time s, an action from a nonvoid action set $\Delta(i,s) \subseteq \mathbb{R}$ can be executed. The weight vectors of the arcs emanating from node i are assumed to be specified only after the selection of such an action. A measurable mapping $\delta: V \times \mathbb{R}_+ \to \mathbb{R}_+$ with $\delta(i,s) \varepsilon \Delta(i,s)$ for all $(i,s) \varepsilon V \times \mathbb{R}_+$ is called a *policy*. The set of all policies is denoted by Δ. The selection of a policy $\delta \varepsilon \Delta$ implies the specification of the weights of all activities and thus of a Markov renewal process $(X_\nu, \Theta_\nu)^\delta_{\nu \varepsilon \mathbb{N}_0}$ corresponding to the STEOR network.

Next, we consider several types of cost associated with the project:

(a) The *event cost* $c_i^e(s)$, which results from the occurrence of project event i at time s

(b) The *activity cost* $c_{ij}(s,t)$, which arises when the execution of activity <i,j> is begun at time s and is terminated at time t

(c) The *action cost* $c_i(\delta(i,s),s)$ is incurred when event i occurs at time s and action $\delta(i,s)$ is taken.

The expected values of these three costs depend only on the activation functions Y_i of node i (see Delivorias/Neumann/Steinhardt [3] and Nicolai [11]), where we again stipulate that the times of occurrence of project events are the earliest possible times. The expected total cost of the project results from summing up the expected costs of types (a), (b), (c) over all nodes and arcs, respectively, of the network.

Let $G^{\delta}(i,s)$ be the expected total cost of the "partial project" starting at state (i,s) if policy $\delta\varepsilon\Delta$ is selected. $G^{\delta}(i,s)$ can be expressed in terms of the above three cost functions and the transition functions of the Markov renewal process $(X_{\nu},\Theta_{\nu})^{\delta}_{\nu\varepsilon\mathbb{N}_0}$. Since we want to minimize the expected total cost of the project, we wish to compute the function G^* given by

$$G^*(i,s) := \inf_{\delta\varepsilon\Delta} G^{\delta}(i,s), \quad (i,s)\varepsilon V\times\mathbb{R}_+$$

and, if existing, a corresponding *optimal policy* δ^*, that is, a policy $\delta^*\varepsilon\Delta$ with $G^{\delta^*}=G^*$. The project starts at state $(1,0)$. Hence, $G^*(1,0)$ is the infimum of the expected total cost of the project.

The problem of determining G^* represents an infinite-stage stochastic dynamic programming problem. A stage corresponds to a transition from a state (i,s) to another state. To compute G^* approximately, well-known methods of dynamic programming such as the method of successive approximations and the policy-improvement routine can be used (cf. Nicolai [11]).

Without going into details we only want to mention that the cost minimization problem can also be solved by an optimal control approach (for details we refer to Delivorias/Neumann/Steinhardt [3]). The control variables are the time-dependent execution probabilities of certain activities, and the state variables are the so-called activation densities of the nodes of the network. Here we have to assume that the distributions of the durations of all activities, except for the dummy activities, are continuous with bounded distribution densities. The system of integral equations for the activation densities, which is analog to the system (2) for the activation functions, acts the part of a constraint of the control problem. An optimal solution to the control problem can be found by means of a gradient-projection method if the range of the controllers is a closed convex set or again by a policy-improvement technique if the range of the controllers is a finite set.

As mentioned above, the expected total cost of the project depends only on the activation functions Y_j of the individual nodes j of the underlying network.[4] Since the activation function of any node j in an OR network N coincides with the activation function of node j in each STEOR network from a covering of N that contains node j, the cost minimization problem for OR networks can be solved in the same manner as for STEOR networks.

5. Scheduling with OR Networks as Precedence Constraints

Suppose there is one resource required to execute each activity of a project described by an OR network. We seek to determine a sequence of activities that minimizes a certain objective function subject to limited capacity of resource and precedence constraints (as well as execution probabilities and durations of activitites) given by the OR network. We assume that the resource has capacity 1 and think of the resource as a machine, and we identify the activities with jobs processed on that machine. Then we get a stochastic single-machine scheduling problem with precedence constraints given by the OR network.

Let $w_{ij} \geqq 0$ be a weighting factor describing the importance of activity <i,j> and $C_{ij}^{(\mu)}$ be the completion time of the μth execution of activity <i,j> $(\mu \in \mathbb{N})$, where $C_{ij}^{(\mu)} := 0$ if activity <i,j> is carried out less than μ times. Then we take the expected weighted sum of the completion times of all activity executions as objective function:

$$E(\sum w_{ij} C_{ij}^{(\mu)}) := E[\sum_{<i,j> \in A} \sum_{\mu=1}^{\infty} w_{ij} C_{ij}^{(\mu)}]. \tag{4}$$

In (4) A is the set of the activities or arcs, respectively.

We restrict ourselves to the case where the activities are carried out without preemption and without idle times between them. The latter assumption is automatically satisfied owing to the monotonicity of the objective function (4). In analogy to the three-field classification of deterministic scheduling problems (cf. Lawler/Lenstra/Rinnooy Kan [5]), our stochastic scheduling problem is designated by the symbol $1|OR, D_{ij} \sim G_{ij}|E(\sum w_{ij} C_{ij}^{(\mu)})$, where "1" is the number of machines, "OR" describes the precedence constraints, $D_{ij} \sim G_{ij}$ refers to general distribution of activity durations, and the last field contains the objective function.

It is well-known that the deterministic scheduling problem $1||\sum w_\nu C_\nu$ can be solved by the following ratio rule of Smith (cf. Smith [13]). Let $\rho_\nu := \frac{D_\nu}{w_\nu}$, where D_ν is the processing time of job ν. Then any sequence of jobs is optimal that puts the jobs in order of nondecreasing ratios ρ_ν.

It is also well-known that Smith's rule can be generalized to the case $1|tree|\sum w_\nu C_\nu$, where we have precedence constraints given by a rooted tree, as follows (cf. Adolphson/Hu [1], Horn [4]). Consider, for example, an outtree.

Find a job l different from the source such that $\rho_l=\min_{\nu} \rho_\nu$. Let job k be the (unique) predecessor of job l. Then the subsequence (k,l) appears in at least one optimal job sequence and can be treated as one job with processing time D_k+D_l and weight w_k+w_l. By successive application of this device we eventually obtain an optimal schedule.

A stochastic single-machine scheduling problem with tree precedence constraints has been studied by Bruno [2]. A set of jobs without precedence constraints is to be processed on a single machine. Each job is considered a decision tree whose nodes correspond to tasks. The execution time of a task k and the decision as to the next task, if any, to be executed following k are stochastic. The execution of a job consists of the execution of some chain of tasks in the tree, where job executions may be interrupted only at task terminations in order to assign the processor to another job. The objective function is the expected weighted sum of the task completion times.

Bruno's scheduling problem can be viewed as a problem of type $1|OR,D_{ij}\sim G_{ij}|E(\sum w_{ij}C_{ij}^{(\mu)})$ for a special OR network whose arcs correspond to the tasks. The respective problem for general OR networks permits precedence constraints for the jobs and feedback to be taken into account. Exploiting the tree structure property P4, Rubach [12] has proposed a polynomial algorithm for the general problem $1|OR,D_{ij}\sim G_{ij}|E(\sum w_{ij}C_{ij}^{(\mu)})$, which represents some kind of generalization of Smith's ratio rule and will be sketched in what follows.

Recall that when a stochastic node i is activated, exactly one outcoming activity is carried out. We have a resource of capacity 1 or one machine, respectively, on which that single activity can be executed. Hence, the set of all arcs emanating from a stochastic node i can be considered one *stochastic operation* O with *beginning event* i. The *terminal events* of stochastic operation O are the final nodes of the arcs from O.

If a deterministic node i is activated, each outcoming activity is carried out. Thus, each individual arc <i,j> emanating from node i or the corresponding one-element set {<i,j>}, respectively, is considered a *deterministic operation* with *beginning event* i and *terminal event* j.

The set of all operations of the OR network in question is denoted by $\mathbb{O}$. An operation O_k is said to be a *predecessor* of an operation O_l if one of the terminal events of O_k coincides with the beginning event of O_l. Observe that an operation may have more than one predecessor.

Now we construct an optimal sequence of operations which is implemented as a queue Q. Let

$$\tau_\nu := \sum_{\langle i,j\rangle \in O_\nu} p_{ij} E(D_{ij})$$

be the expected duration and

$$\omega_\nu := \sum_{\langle i,j\rangle \in O_\nu} p_{ij} w_{ij}$$

be the expected weight of operation O_ν and let

$$\rho_\nu := \frac{\tau_\nu}{\omega_\nu},$$

where we put $\rho_\nu := \infty$ for $\omega_\nu = 0$. Then the algorithm runs as follows.

At the beginning Q is empty and $\mathbb{O}$ is the set of all operations. Determine an operation O_l such that

$$\rho_l = \min_{O_\nu \in \mathbb{O}} \rho_\nu$$

and insert O_l at the rear of Q. Let O_k be any predecessor of O_l and let i and j be the beginning events and S_k and S_l be the sets of the terminal events of O_k and O_l, respectively. Then replace the two operations O_k, O_l by one "composite" operation and delete O_l from $\mathbb{O}$. The composite operation, which is again designated by O_k, has expected duration

$$\frac{\tau_k + p_{ij}\tau_l}{1 - p_{ij}p_{ji}},$$

expected weight

$$\frac{\omega_k + p_{ij}\omega_l}{1 - p_{ij}p_{ji}},$$

and the set of terminal events $S_k \cup S_l \setminus \{i,j\}$. The execution probability of an activity or arc, respectively, whose initial node is the beginning event i and whose final node s is a terminal event of the composite operation, becomes

$$\frac{p_{is}+p_{ij}p_{js}}{1-p_{ij}p_{ji}} .$$

In the above formulas, we put $p_{\alpha\beta}:=0$ if there is no arc $<\alpha,\beta>$. If O_l has more than one predecessor, each pair (O_k, O_l) where O_k is a predecessor of O_l has to be replaced by one composite operation. If O_l is the source of the network, we only insert O_l into Q and replace $\mathbb{O}$ by $\mathbb{O}\setminus\{O_l\}$.

Repeat this process until $\mathbb{O}$ is empty. The algorithm can be implemented to run in $O(|A|^2|V|)$ time.

Finally we show how to obtain an optimal sequence of activities carried out during a given project execution. To this end we need another list of operations L, which contains the so-called *performable operations*, that is, those operations whose beginning events have occurred. L is viewed as a priority queue, where in L operation O_μ is of higher priority than operation O_ν if in Q the position of O_μ is before the position of O_ν. Then the operation performed next is the operation of highest priority in L.

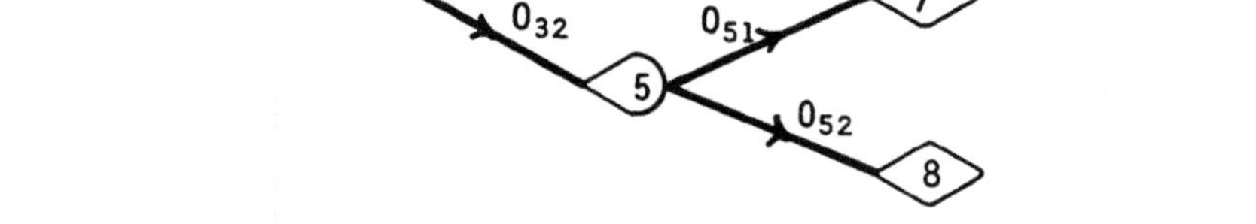

Figure 3

As an example consider the OR network shown in Fig. 3. The subscript of a stochastic operation coincides with the number of its beginning event. For a deterministic operation, the first subscript is the number of its beginning event. The activities carried out during the project execution in question are illustrated by darker arrows. Assume that if node 6 is activated for the first time, activity <6,4> is executed, if node 6 is activated for the second time, activity <6,9> is carried out. Suppose the optimal sequence of operations Q found by the above algorithm is $Q=(O_{32},O_2,O_6,O_1,O_{52},O_4,O_{31},O_{51})$. The following table shows the list L and the sequences of events occurred, operations performed, and activities executed.

Event occurred	L	Operation performed	Activity executed
1	(O_1)	O_1	<1,3>
3	(O_{32},O_{31})	O_{32}	<3,5>
5	(O_{52},O_{31},O_{51})	O_{52}	<5,8>
8	(O_{31},O_{51})	O_{31}	<3,4>
4	(O_4,O_{51})	O_4	<4,6>
6	(O_6,O_{51})	O_6	<6,4>
4	(O_4,O_{51})	O_4	<4,6>
6	(O_6,O_{51})	O_6	<6,9>
9	(O_{51})	O_{51}	<5,7>

References

[1] Adolphson, D., Hu, T.C., "Optimal Linear Ordering" *SIAM J. Appl. Math.* 25(1973), 403-423

[2] Bruno, J.L., "Scheduling Algorithms for Minimizing the Mean Weighted Flow-Time Criterion," in Coffman, E.G., Jr. (Ed.), *Computer and Job-Shop Scheduling Theory*. John Wiley & Sons, New York, 1976

[3] Delivorias, P.N., Neumann, K., Steinhardt, U., "Gradient-Projection and Policy-Iteration Methods for Solving Optimization Problems in STEOR Networks," *ZOR* 28(1984)

[4] Horn, W.A., "Single-Machine Job Sequencing with Treelike Precedence Ordering and Linear Delay Penalties," *SIAM J. Appl. Math.* 23(1972), 189-202

[5] Lawler, E.L., Lenstra, J.K., Rinnooy Kan, A.H.G., "Recent Developments in Deterministic Sequencing and Scheduling: A Survey," in Dempster, M.A.H., Lenstra, J.K., Rinnooy Kan, A.H.G. (Eds.), *Deterministic and Stochasting Scheduling.* D. Reidel Publ. Comp., Dordrecht, 1982

[6] Neumann, K., "GERT Networks with Several Sources," Report WIOR-164, Inst. für Wirtschaftstheorie und Opns. Res., University of Karlsruhe, 1983

[7] Neumann, K., "Recent Developments in Stochastic Activity Networks," *INFOR* 22(1984), 70-99

[8] Neumann, K., "EOR Project Networks," to appear in *Computing*

[9] Neumann, K., Steinhardt, U., *GERT Networks.* Lecture Notes in Economics and Math. Systems, Vol. 172, Springer Verlag, Berlin, 1979

[10] Nicolai, W., "On the Temporal Analysis of Special GERT Networks Using a Modified Markov Renewal Process," *ZOR* 24(1980), 263-272

[11] Nicolai, W., "Optimization of STEOR Networks via Markov Renewal Programming," *ZOR* 26(1982), 7-19

[12] Rubach, T., "Stochastische Reihenfolgeplanung mit Hilfe von GERT-Netzplänen," Ph. D. Thesis, University of Karlsruhe, 1984

[13] Smith, W.E., "Various Optimizers for Single-Stage Production," *Naval Res. Logist. Quart.* 3(1956), 59-66

ON STABILITY OF LINEAR TIME-VARYING INFINITE DIMENSIONAL SYSTEMS

K.Maciej Przyłuski and Stefan Rolewicz

Institute of Mathematics
Polish Academy of Sciences
Śniadeckich 8, P.O.Box 137
00-950 Warszawa, Poland

Abstract. An overview of recent results on the problem of stability of linear time-varying discrete-time and continuous-time systems is given. Particular attention is devoted to the relations between stability of a continuous-time system and its (appropriately defined) discretization.

0. Introduction

Most methods used in the analysis of linear control systems require that the system be well described by a model that is time-invariant. It is also true for infinite dimensional systems, sometimes called distributed parameter systems.

This paper deals primarily with systems that are not necessarily time-invariant. Thus attention is focused on the class of systems which are linear, infinite dimensional, and time-varying. The equations characterizing linear infinite dimensional time-varying systems are similar to those characterizing linear time-invariant systems with the exception that the (operator-valued) coefficients can be functions of time. Thus linear infinite dimensional time-varying discrete-time systems are characterized by difference equations and linear infinite dimensional continuous-time systems are described by linear differential equations, and the coefficients of these equations are linear "time-varying" operators.

This paper presents an exposition of the concepts and of the results on the problem of stability of linear time-varying infinite dimensional discrete -time and continuous-time systems. For linear time-invariant systems the problem is widely considered in the existing literature. The discrete-time case is desrcribed in [20],[22],[24],[28], [29],[30] and [34], whereas the continuous-time case in presented in [7],[8],[26],[27],[29] and [30]. The problem of stability of linear time-varying systems is studied, for discrete-time systems, in [31], and, for continuous-time systems, in[9],[25] and [32]. Some aspects of stability theory are also treated in [1],[4],[5],[11],[13],[14], [15] and [18]. All of the mentioned above works are devoted to infinite dimensional systems. The finite dimensional case is described in numerous text-books, monographs and papers. We list here only [3], [6],[16],[17] and [19].

The aim of this paper is to describe some of the main theoretical results on stability theory of linear infinite dimensional time-varying discrete--time and continuous-time systems. Our intention is to give an introduction to this area. We will give a number of the most important results but we do not give proofs. The paper is based entirely on our works [31] and [32]. The last paper is a "time-varying" extension of [30] and, in consequence, of [29]. Thus, our treatment of continuous-time systems will be based on the "discrete-time" theory. In the sense, the present paper (and also [32]) generalizes the approach to continuous-time systems taken previously in [30] and [29].

The contents of the present paper are as follows. In this section we introduce some notations which will be used throughout the paper. Section 1 describes the class of discrete-time systems we will consider. In Section 2 the class of continuous-time systems to be studied in the paper is defined. Section 3 develops a discretization method for linear continuous-time systems. In Section 4 the concept of power equistability of a discrete-time system is studied. Sections 5 and 6 describe the notions of l^p-equistable and $l^{p(x)}$-equistable discrete-time systems, respectively. In Section 7 we define the concept of exponentially equistable continuous-time system and develop a "discrete-time" method to study the concept. Section 8 gives a relation between $L^{p(x)}$- equistability of a continuous-time system and $l^{p(x)}$-equistability of its discretization. In Section 9 we study the notion of L^p-equistability of a continuous-time system.

Now, we describe some notations and terminology to be used in the paper. $\mathbb{Z}^+$ will denote the set of all positive integers; $\mathbb{R}^+$ will denote the set of all positive real numbers. If $i \in \mathbb{Z}$, we shall write $\mathbb{Z}_i^+$ for the set of all integers not less than i; in other words, $\mathbb{Z}_i^+ := \{i, i+1, i+2, \ldots\}$. If $t \in \mathbb{R}$, we shall write $\mathbb{R}^+(t)$ to denote the set of all real numbers not less than t, i.e., $\mathbb{R}^+(t) := [t, \infty)$. For any $i_o \in \mathbb{Z}$, let

$$\Delta_{i_o} := \{(j,i) \in \mathbb{Z}_{i_o}^+ \times \mathbb{Z}_{i_o}^+ \mid j \geq i\}$$

and, for any $t_o \in \mathbb{R}$, let

$$\Delta(t_o) := \{(t,s) \in \mathbb{R}^+(t_o) \times \mathbb{R}^+(t_o) \mid t \geq s\}.$$

Throughout the paper $\underline{\underline{X}}$ will denote a Banach space and $\underline{\underline{L}}(\underline{\underline{X}})$ will stand for the (Banach) algebra of all linear and bounded operators $\underline{\underline{X}} \to \underline{\underline{X}}$. The norm on $\underline{\underline{X}}$ will be denoted by $\|\cdot\|$; the same notation will be used for the corresponding norm on $\underline{\underline{L}}(\underline{\underline{X}})$.

Let $\{A_k\}_{k=i_o}^{\infty}$, $A_k \in \underline{\underline{L}}(\underline{\underline{X}})$, be a given sequence. For $(k,i) \in \Delta_{i_o}$, we define $\prod_{t=i}^{k-1} A_t := A_{k-1}A_{k-2}\ldots A_{i+1}A_i$, for $k > i$, and $\prod_{t=i}^{k-1} A_i := I$ (= the identity operator on $\underline{\underline{X}}$), if $k = i$.

We shall deal also with linear operators that are neither bounded nor everywhere defined. Let T be any such operator. We shall assume that T is defined on a linear subspace of $\underline{\underline{X}}$ and takes its values in $\underline{\underline{X}}$, i.e., $T:\mathrm{dom}(T) \to \underline{\underline{X}}$ and $\mathrm{dom}\,(T) \subset \underline{\underline{X}}$. Let T be closed and dom (T) be dense in $\underline{\underline{X}}$. Then, under certain additional conditions which are given by the Hille-Yosida-Phillips theorem (see e.g.[10, Theorem VIII.1.13] or[23, Theorem 2.3.1]),T is the infinitesimal generator of a strongly continuous semigroup of linear and bounded operators on $\underline{\underline{X}}$. The class of all closed and densely-defined linear operators, which are infinitesimal generators of some strongly continuous semigroups in $\underline{\underline{L}}(\underline{\underline{X}})$, is denoted by $\underline{\underline{G}}(\underline{\underline{X}})$.

1. Discrete - Time Systems. Basic Definitions

Let $i_o \in \mathbb{Z}$ and $\{A_k\}_{k=i_o}^{\infty}$, $A_k \in \underline{\underline{L}}(\underline{\underline{X}})$, be given. Suppose $k_o \in \mathbb{Z}$ is a given integer not less than i_o and $\{x_k\}_{k=k_o}^{\infty}$ is a sequence with $x_k \in \underline{\underline{X}}$. We say that the relation

$$(*) \qquad x_{k+1} = A_k x_k,$$

$k \in \mathbb{Z}_{k_o}^+$, is a <u>linear difference equation</u>. A sequence $X := \{x_k\}_{k=k_o}^{\infty}$ is said to be a <u>solution of the linear difference equation</u> (*) <u>with initial value</u> x <u>at</u> i or simply a <u>solution through</u> (i,x) iff $k_o = i$, $x_{k_o} = x$ and the relation (*) holds for all $k \in \mathbb{Z}_{k_o}^+$.

The set of all solutions of the difference equation (*) is called a <u>linear time-varying discrete-time system</u> (or shortly a <u>linear discrete-time system</u>) and is denoted by $\$_d(\{A_k\}_{k=i_o}^{\infty})$.

Here and elsewhere we shall assume that the sequence $\{A_k\}_{k=i_o}^{\infty}$ (which defines $\$_d(\{A_k\}_{k=i_o}^{\infty})$) is bounded, i.e., the number $\sup\{\|A_k\| \mid k \in \mathbb{Z}_{i_o}^+\}$ is finite.

Clearly, for every $(i,x) \in \mathbb{Z}_{i_o}^+ \times \underline{\underline{X}}$ there exists a unique solution of the equation (*) with initial value x at i. The solution is given by the formumla $x_k = (\prod_{t=1}^{k-1} A_t)x$, where $k \in \mathbb{Z}_i^+$. If a sequence $X := \{x_k\}_{k=k_o}^{\infty}$ belongs to $\$_d(\{A_k\}_{k=i_o}^{\infty})$ the sequence is called a trajectory of the system considered; if $k_o = i$ and $x_{k_o} = x$, we say that X is the trajectory (of $\$_d(\{A_k\}_{k=i_o}^{\infty})$) with initial value x at i.

We recall that $\$_d(\{A_k\}_{k=i_o}^{\infty})$ is said to be a linear time-invariant discrete-time system iff there exists an operator $A \in \underline{\underline{L}}(\underline{\underline{X}})$ such that $A = A_k$ for all $k \in \mathbb{Z}_{i_o}^+$. In that case we shall write $\$_d(A)$ instead of $\$_d(\{A_k\}_{k=i_o}^{\infty})$.

2. Continuous-Time Systems. Basic Definitions

Let $t_o \in \mathbb{R}$ and $A(.) : \mathbb{R}^+(t_o) \to \underline{\underline{G}}(\underline{\underline{X}})$ be given. Suppose s_o is a given real number not less than t_o and $x(.) : \mathbb{R}^+(s_o) \to \underline{\underline{X}}$ is a function. We say that the relation

$$(*) \qquad dx(t)/dt = A(t)x(t),$$

$t \in \mathbb{R}^+(s_o)$ is a linear differential equation. A function $x(.) : \mathbb{R}^+(s_o) \to \underline{\underline{X}}$ is said to be a solution of the linear differential equation (*) with initial value x at s or simply a solution through (s,x) iff $s_o = s$, $x(s_o) = x$, the function $x(.)$ is continuously differentiable for $t \in \mathbb{R}^+(s_o)$ and the relation (*) holds for all $t \in \mathbb{R}^+(s_o)$.

The above defined concept of solution is rather restrictive. In particular, if $x(.)$ is a solution of (*) through (s,x), it is required that $x \in \mathrm{dom}(A(s))$. In the paper we shall consider a more general concept of solution which will allow that $x \in \underline{\underline{X}}$ is arbitrary. To define the more general concept of solution we assume that there exists a function $U(.,.) : \Delta(t_o) \to \underline{\underline{L}}(\underline{\underline{X}})$ with the following properties:

(a) $U(t,t) = I$, for all $t \in \mathbb{R}^+(t_o)$;

(b) $U(t,r)U(r,s) = U(t,s)$, for all $(t,r,s) \in \mathbb{R}^+(t_o) \times \mathbb{R}^+(t_o) \times \mathbb{R}^+(t_o)$

such that $t \geq r \geq s$;

(c) $U(.,s)x$ is a continuous function $\mathbb{R}^+(s) \to \underline{\underline{X}}$, for all $(s,x) \in \mathbb{R}^+(t_o) \times \underline{\underline{X}}$;

(d) $\| U(t,s) \| \leq M_\beta \exp(\beta(t-s))$, for some $M_\beta \geq 1$, $\beta \in \mathbb{R}$, and all $(t,s) \in \Delta(t_o)$.

Any function $U(.,.):\Delta(t_o) \to \underline{\underline{L}}(\underline{\underline{X}})$ which satisfies the above defined conditions (a) - (d) is called a <u>continuous-time evolutionary process on $\underline{\underline{X}}$</u>.

Let a continuous-time evolutionary process $U(.,.):\Delta(t_o) \to \underline{\underline{L}}(\underline{\underline{X}})$ satisfy the following condition:

(e) $U(.,s)x$ is a solution of the linear differential equation (*) with initial value x at s, for all $s \in \mathbb{R}^+(t_o)$ and all $x \in \underline{\underline{D}}(s)$, where $\underline{\underline{D}}(s) \subset \mathrm{dom}(A(s))$ is a linear subspace of $\underline{\underline{X}}$ which is dense in $\underline{\underline{X}}$ (for all $s \in \mathbb{R}^+(t_o)$.

Then, we say that $U(.,.):\Delta(t_o) \to \underline{\underline{L}}(\underline{\underline{X}})$ is a <u>fundamental solution of the linear differential equation</u> (*). If, for every $(s,x) \in \mathbb{R}^+(t_o) \times \underline{\underline{D}}(s)$, the solution of (*) through (s,x) is unique, the fundamental solution of (*) (if it exists) is also uniquely defined. <u>Throughout the paper it will be assumed that there exists a unique fundamental solution of the considered equation</u> (*). Various versions of the above definition of a fundamental solution are considered in the existing literature, see e.g. [4],[5],[12],[21],[23] and [33]. A construction of the fundamental solution is also described in the mentioned references. In particular, some conditions are given in the literature for the equation (*) to have a fundamental solution. These conditions allow to develop some methods of solving a broad class of time-dependent partial differential equations and apply them to the initial and mixed problems of hyperbolic and parabolic equations.

Let $(s,x) \in \mathbb{R}^+(t_o) \times \underline{\underline{X}}$ be arbitrary. Suppose $x(.):\mathbb{R}^+(s) \to \underline{\underline{X}}$ is given, for all $t \in \mathbb{R}^+(s)$, by

$$x(t):=U(t,s)x,$$

where $U(.,.):\Delta(t_o) \to \underline{\underline{L}}(\underline{\underline{X}})$ is the fundamental solution of (*).

The defined above function $x(.)$ is called a generalized solution of the linear differential equation (*) with initial value x at s or simply a generalized solution through (s,x). Clearly, $x(.)$ is a continuous function, $x(s) = x$ and, for x's belonging to a dense subspace of $\underline{\underline{X}}$, $x(.)$ is a solution of (*).

The set of all generalized solutions of the differential equation (*) is called a linear time-varying continuous-time system (or shortly a linear continuous-time system) and is denoted by $\$_c(\{A(t);\ t \in \mathbb{R}^+(t_o)\})$. Clearly,

$$\$_c(\{A(t);t \in \mathbb{R}^+(t_o)\}) = \bigcup_{(s,x) \in \mathbb{R}^+(t_o) \times \underline{\underline{X}}} U(.,s)x.$$

and $U(.,s)x$ is also called a trajectory of $\$_c(\{A(t);t \in \mathbb{R}^+(t_o)\})$ with initial value x at s.

We recall that if $A(t) = A$, for all $t \in \mathbb{R}^+(t_o)$ and some $A \in \underline{\underline{G}}(\underline{\underline{X}})$, the corresponding linear continuous-time system is said to be time-invariant and the system is denoted by $\$_c(A)$.

3. Discretization of Linear Continuous-Time Systems

Let a linear continuous-time system $\$_c(\{A(t);t \in \mathbb{R}^+(t_o)\})$ be given and $U(.,.):\Delta(t_o) \to \underline{\underline{L}}(\underline{\underline{X}})$ be the fundamental solution of the differential equation $dx(t)/dt = A(t)x(t)$. Let $(i_o,\tau) \in \mathbb{Z} \times \mathbb{R}^+$ be fixed. Then, for all $k \in \mathbb{Z}^+_{i_o}$, $(t_o + (k+1-i_o)\tau,\ t_o + (k-i_o)\tau) \in \Delta(t_o)$. Let, for $k \in \mathbb{Z}^+_{i_o}$,

$$A_k := U(t_o + (k+1-i_o)\tau,\ t_o + (k-i_o)\tau).$$

Clearly, for all $k \in \mathbb{Z}^+_{t_o}$, the inequality

$$||A_k|| \leq \max\{M_\beta \exp(\beta\tau), M_\beta\}$$

holds.

Let us consider the difference equation $x_{k+1} = A_k x_k$. The difference equation defines a linear discrete-time system, namely, $\$_d(\{A_k\}_{k=i_o}^{\infty})$, which is called the (i_o,τ)-discretization of the linear continuous-time system $\$_c(\{A(t);t \in \mathbb{R}^+(t_o)\})$. In order to study more closely connections between trajectories of a linear continuous-time system and its discretization, we introduce the following notations:

$$j(t) := \sup\{j \in \mathbf{Z}^+_{i_o} \mid t_o + (j-i_o)\tau \leq t\},$$

$$i(s) := \inf\{i \in \mathbf{Z}^+_{i_o} \mid t_o + (i-i_o)\tau \geq s\}.$$

It is important to note that, for all $(t,s) \in \Delta(t_o)$, $(t, t_o + (j(t)-i_o)\tau)$ and $(t_o + (i(s)-i_o)\tau, s)$ belong also to $\Delta(t_o)$. If $(t,s) \in \Delta(t_o)$ and $(t-s)$ is not less than τ, $(j(t), i(s)) \in \Delta_{i_o}$.

We have the following

Theorem. <u>Let</u> $\$_c(\{A(t); t \in \mathbb{R}^+(t_o)\})$ <u>be a given linear continuous--time system and</u> $U(.,.): \Delta(t_o) \to \underline{\underline{L}}(\underline{\underline{X}})$ <u>be the fundamental solution of the differential equation</u> $dx(t)/dt = A(t)x(t)$. <u>Let</u> $(i_o, \tau) \in \mathbf{Z} \times \mathbb{R}^+$ <u>be fixed and</u> $\$_d(\{A_k\}^{\infty}_{k=i_o})$ <u>be the</u> (i_o, τ)<u>-discretization of</u> $\$_c(\{A(t); t \in \mathbb{R}^+(t_o)\})$.

(a) <u>Suppose</u> $\{x_k\}^{\infty}_{k=i}$ <u>is the trajectory of</u> $\$_d(\{A_k\}^{\infty}_{k=i_o})$ <u>with initial value</u> x <u>at</u> i (<u>where</u> $(i,x) \in \mathbf{Z}^+_{i_o} \times \underline{\underline{X}}$) <u>and</u> $x(.)$ <u>is the trajectory of</u> $\$_c(\{A(t); t \in \mathbb{R}^+\})$ <u>with initial value</u> x <u>at</u> $(t_o + (i-i_o)\tau)$.

<u>Then, for all</u> $j \in \mathbf{Z}^+_i$, $x(t_o + (j-i_o)\tau) = x_j$.

(b) <u>Suppose</u> $x(.)$ <u>is the trajectory of</u> $\$_c(\{A(t); t \in \mathbb{R}^+(t_o)\})$ <u>with initial value</u> x <u>at</u> s (<u>where</u> $(s,x) \in \mathbb{R}^+(t_o) \times \underline{\underline{X}}$) <u>and</u> $\{x_k\}^{\infty}_{k=i(s)}$ <u>is the trajectory of</u> $\$_d(\{A_k\}^{\infty}_{k=i_o})$ <u>with initial value</u> $U(t_o + (i(s)-i_o)\tau, s)x$ <u>at</u> $i(s)$. <u>Then, for all</u> $t \in \mathbb{R}^+(t_o)$ <u>satisfying</u> $t-s \geq \tau$, <u>the equality</u> $x(t) = U(t, t_o + (j(t)-i_o)\tau)x_{j(t)}$ <u>holds</u>.

4. Power stability

Let $\$_d(\{A_k\})^{\infty}_{k=i_o}$ be a linear discrete-time system. It is said that the system is <u>power equistable</u> iff for every $x \in \underline{\underline{X}}$ there exist $M \in \mathbb{R}$ and r, $0 \leq r < 1$, such that for every $i \in \mathbf{Z}^+_{i_o}$ and, for every trajectory $\{x_k\}^{\infty}_{k=i}$ (of $\$_d(\{A_k\}^{\infty}_{k=i_o})$) with initial value x at i, the inequality

$$\|x_k\| \leq M r^{k-i}$$

is satisfied for all $k \in \mathbf{Z}^+_i$.

The above inequality can be rewritten as follows

$$\|(\prod_{t=i}^{k-1} A_t)x\| \leq Mr^{k-i}.$$

The numbers M and r are dependent on x. The fact motivates our next definition.

It is said that a linear discrete-time system $\$_d(\{A_k\}_{k=i_o}^{\infty})$ is <u>uniformly power equistable</u> iff there exist $M_u \in \mathbb{R}$ and r_u, $0 \leq r_u \leq 1$, such that the inequality

$$\|(\prod_{t=i}^{k-1} A_t)\| \leq M_u r_u^{k-i}$$

holds for all $(k,i) \in \Delta_{i_o}$.

Using the Baire category theorem we can prove the following

Theorem. <u>Let</u> $\$_d(\{A_k\}_{k=i_o}^{\infty})$ <u>be any linear discrete-time system. The system is power equistable if and only if it is uniformly power equistable</u>.

It is well known (see e.g. [30, Thm.21]) that any linear time--invariant discrete-time system $\$_d(A)$ is power equistable if and only if the spectral radius of A is less than one. A similar result can be formulated for time-varying systems.

Let $\{A_k\}_{k=i_o}^{\infty}$, $A_k \in \underline{\underline{L}}(\underline{\underline{X}})$, be any bounded sequence. The number

$$g(\{A_k\}_{k=i_o}^{\infty}):=\limsup_{j\to\infty}(\sup\{\|\prod_{t=i}^{i+j-1} A_t\|^{1/j} \mid i \in \mathbf{Z}_{i_o}^{+}\}$$

is called the <u>generalized spectral radius</u> of $\{A_k\}_{k=i_o}^{\infty}$. If $A_k = A$, for some $A \in \underline{\underline{L}}(\underline{\underline{X}})$ and all $k \in \mathbf{Z}_{i_o}^{+}$,

$$g(\{A_k\}_{k=i_o}^{\infty}) = \limsup_{j\to\infty}(\|A^j\|^{1/j}).$$

In consequence, the generalized spectral radius and the spectral radius coincide for constant sequences of operators, as it follows the Bourling-Gelfand formula for spectral radius (see e.g. [2, Chap. I, § 2, No 3]).

We have the following

Theorem. <u>Let</u> $\$_d(\{A_k\}_{k=i_o}^{\infty})$ <u>be any linear discrete-time system. The system is power equistable if and only if the generalized spectral</u>

<u>radius of the sequence</u> $\{A_k\}_{k=i_o}^{\infty}$ <u>is less than one</u>.

5. <u>l^p-Stability</u>

Let $\$_d(\{A_k\}_{k=i_o}^{\infty})$ be a linear discrete-time system and p, $1 \leq p < \infty$, be fixed. It is said that the system is <u>l^p-equistable</u> iff for every $x \in \underline{X}$ there exists a number c such that for every $i \in \mathbf{Z}_{i_o}^{+}$ and for every trajectory $\{x_k\}_{k=i}^{\infty}$ (of $\$_d(\{A_k\}_{k=i_o}^{\infty})$), with initial value x at i, the inequality

$$\left(\sum_{k=i}^{\infty} \|x_k\|^p\right)^{1/p} \leq c$$

is satisfied.

We can rewrite the above inequality in the following way:

$$\left(\sum_{k=i}^{\infty} \|\left(\prod_{t=i}^{k-1} A_t\right)x\|^p\right)^{1/p} \leq c.$$

The constant c may happen to be dependent on x, even if we consider only the x's which belong to the unit sphere of $\underline{X}$. Thus, it is reasonable to introduce the following definition.

A linear discrete-time system $\$_d(\{A_k\}_{k=i_o}^{\infty})$ is said to be <u>uniformly</u> <u>l^p-equistable</u> iff there exists a number c_u such that for every $(i,x) \in \mathbf{Z}_{i_o}^{+} \times \underline{X}$ and for every trajectory $\{x_k\}_{k=i}^{\infty}$ (of $\$_d(\{A_k\}_{k=i_o}^{\infty})$), with initial value x at i, the inequality

$$\left(\sum_{k=i}^{\infty} \|x_k\|^p\right)^{1/p} \leq c_u\|x\|$$

holds.

The Baire category theorem allows us to prove

Theorem. <u>Let</u> $\$_d(\{A_k\}_{k=i_o}^{\infty})$ <u>be any linear discrete-time system. The system is</u> <u>l^p-equistable if and only if it uniformly</u> <u>l^p-equistable</u>.

The most important result in stability theory of linear discrete-time systems seems to be the following

Theorem. <u>Let</u> $\$_d(\{A_k\}_{k=i_o}^{\infty})$ <u>be a linear discrete-time system. The system is power equistable if and only of it is</u> <u>l^p-equistable</u>.

We have also the following immediate

Corollary. If a linear discrete-time system is l^p-equistable for some p, $1 \leq p < \infty$, the system is l^p-equistable for all p, $1 \leq p < \infty$.

6. $l^{p(x)}$-Stability

A modification of the (given in Section 5) definition of l^p-equistability obtained by allowing the number p to be dependent on (the initial value) x is the following concept of $l^{p(x)}$-equistability.

Let $\$_d(\{A_k\}_{k=i_o}^{\infty})$ be any linear discrete-time system. The system is said to be $l^{p(x)}$-equistable iff for every $x \in \underline{X}$ there exist numbers c and p such that $1 \leq p < \infty$ and for all $i \in \mathbf{Z}_{i_o}^+$ and every trajectory $\{x_k\}_{k=i}^{\infty}$ (of $\$_d(\{A_k\}_{k=i_o}^{\infty})$), with initial value x at i, the inequality

$$\left(\sum_{k=i}^{\infty} ||x_k||^p\right)^{1/p} \leq c$$

holds.

Let us note that the number p may happen to be dependent on x. If a system is l^p-equistable for some $1 \leq p < \infty$, the system is $l^{p(x)}$-equistable. The converse of the result (which can be proven using the Baire category theorem) is also true. In fact, we have the following

Theorem. Let $\$_d(\{A_k\}_{k=i_o}^{\infty})$ be a linear discrete-time system. The system is $l^{p(x)}$-equistable if and only if it is l^p-equistable for some (for every) p, $1 \leq p < \infty$.

7. Exponential Stability

In this section we begin our study of continuous-time systems.

Let $\$_c(\{A(t); t \in \mathbb{R}^+(t_o)\})$ be any linear continuous-time system. It is said that the system is exponentially equistable iff for every $x \in \underline{X}$ there exist $C \in \mathbb{R}$ and α, $\alpha < 0$, such that for every $s \in \mathbb{R}^+(t_o)$ and, for every trajectory $x(.)$ (of $\$_c(\{A(t); t \in \mathbb{R}^+(t_o)\})$) with initial value x at s, the inequality

$$||x(t)|| \leq C \exp(\alpha(t-s))$$

is satisfied for all $t \in \mathbb{R}_s^+$.

If $U(.,.):\Delta(t_o) \to \underline{\underline{L}}(\underline{\underline{X}})$ is the fundamental solution of the differential equation $dx(t)/dt = A(t)x(t)$, the above inequality can be rewritten as follows:

$$\| U(t,s)x \| \leq C \exp(\alpha(t-s)).$$

The fact that the numbers C and α may happen to be dependent on x, even if we consider the x's which belong to the unit sphere of $\underline{\underline{X}}$, motivates the following definition.

It is said that a linear continuous-time system $\$_c(\{A(t); t \in \mathbb{R}^+(t_o)\})$ is <u>uniformly exponentially equistable</u> iff there exist $C_u \in \mathbb{R}$ and α_u, $\alpha_u < 0$, such that the inequality

$$\| U(t,s) \| \leq C_u \exp(\alpha_u(t-s))$$

holds for all $(t,s) \in \Delta(t_o)$.

It is possible to prove the following

Theorem. <u>Let</u> $\$_c(\{A(t); t \in \mathbb{R}^+(t_o)\})$ <u>be a given linear continuous -time system and</u> $(i_o,\tau) \in \mathbf{Z} \times \mathbb{R}^+$ <u>be fixed</u>. <u>Let</u> $\$_d(\{A_k\}_{k=i_o}^{\infty})$ <u>be the</u> (i_o,τ) <u>- discretization of</u> $\$_c(\{A(t); t \in \mathbb{R}^+(t_o)\})$. <u>Then</u>, $\$_c(\{A(t); t \in \mathbb{R}^+(t_o)\})$ <u>is (uniformly) exponentially equistable if and only if</u> $\$_d(\{A_k\}_{k=i_o}^{\infty})$ <u>is (uniformly) power equistable</u>.

A proof of the above theorem can be based on the results of Section 3 and on the obvious inequality

$$\sup\{\| U(t,s) \| \mid (t,s) \in \Delta(t_o),\ t-s \leq \tau\} < \infty .$$

Let us note that we also have

Theorem. <u>Let</u> $\$_c(\{A(t); t \in \mathbb{R}^+(t_o)\})$ <u>be a linear continuous-time system. The system is exponentially equistable if and only if it is uniformly exponentially equistable</u>.

8. $L^{p(x)}$ - <u>Stability</u>

Let $\$_c(\{A(t); t \in \mathbb{R}^+(t_o)\}$ be any linear continuous-time system. It is said that the system is $L^{p(x)}$-equistable iff for every $x \in \underline{\underline{X}}$ there exist numbers c and p such that $1 \leq p < \infty$ and for all $s \in \mathbb{R}^+(t_o)$ and every trajectory $x(.)$ (of $\$_c(\{A(t); t \in \mathbb{R}^+(t_o)\})$),with initial value x at s, the inequality

$$(\int_s^\infty ||x(t)||^p dt)^{1/p} \leq c$$

is satisfied.

We have the following remarkable

Theorem. Let $\$_c(\{A(t);t\in \mathbb{R}^+(t_o)\})$ be a given linear continuous--time system and $(i_o,\tau)\in \mathbf{Z}\times\mathbb{R}^+$ be fixed. Let $\$_d(\{A_k\}_{k=i_o}^\infty)$ be the (i_o,τ)-discretization of $\$_c(\{A(t);t\in \mathbb{R}^+(t_o)\})$. Then $\$_d(\{A_k\}_{k=i_o}^\infty)$ is $l^{p(x)}$-equistable if $\$_c(\{A(t);t\in \mathbb{R}^+(t_o)\})$ is $L^{p(x)}$-equistable.

It is possible to give a rather simple proof of the above theorem.

9. L^p - Stability

Let $\$_c(\{A(t);t\in \mathbb{R}^+(t_o)\})$ be a linear continuous-time system and p, $1\leq p<\infty$ be a fixed number. It is said that the system is L^p-equistable iff for every $x\in \underline{\underline{X}}$ there exists a number c such that for every $s\in\mathbb{R}^+(t_o)$ and for every trajectory $x(\cdot)$ (of $\$_c(\{A(t);t\in \mathbb{R}^+(t_o)\})$), with initial value x at s, the inequality

$$(\int_s^\infty ||x(t)||^p dt)^{1/p} \leq c$$

holds.

Let $U(.,.):\Delta(t_o)\to \underline{\underline{L}}(\underline{\underline{X}})$ be the fundamental solution of the differential equation $dx(t)/dt = A(t)x(t)$. Our last definition is as follows.

A linear continuous-time system $\$_c(\{A(t);t\in \mathbb{R}^+(t_o)\})$ is said to be uniformly L^p-equistable iff there exists c_u such that for every $(s,x)\in\mathbb{R}^+(t_o)\times \underline{\underline{X}}$ and for every trajectory $x(.)$ (of $\$_c(\{A(t);t\in \mathbb{R}^+(t_o)\})$), with inital value x at s, the inequality

$$(\int_s^\infty ||x(t)||^p dt)^{1/p} \leq c_u||x||$$

is satisfied.

Let us note that every L^p-equistable system is $L^{p(x)}$-equistable. In consequence, every discretization of an L^p-equistable linear continuous-time system is $l^{p(x)}$-equistable, as it follows from the previous section. From Section 6, we see that this discretization is l^p-equistable. Now, using the results of Sections 4,5 and 7 we have the following two theorems.

Theorem. Let $\$_c(\{A(t);t\in\mathbb{R}^+(t_o)\})$ be a given continuous-time system and $(i_o,\tau)\in\mathbb{Z}\times\mathbb{R}^+$ be fixed. Let $\$_d(\{A_k\}_{k=i_o}^{\infty})$ be its (i_o,τ)-discretization. Then, $\$_c(\{A(t);t\in\mathbb{R}^+(t_o)\})$ is (uniformly) L^p-equistable if and only if $\$_d(\{A_k\}_{k=i_o}^{\infty})$ is (uniformly) l^p-equistable.

Theorem. Let $\$_c(\{A(t);t\in\mathbb{R}^+(t_o)\})$ be a linear continuous-time system. The system is exponentially equistable if and only if it is L^p-equistable.

References

[1] A.Bensoussan, M.C.Delfour and S.K.Mitter, Representation and Control of Infinite Dimensional Systems. Forthcoming Monograph, M.I.T.Press.

[2] N.Bourbaki, Théorie Spectrales, Chapters 1-2. Hermann: Paris, 1967

[3] R.W.Brockett, Finite Dimensional Linear Systems. Wiley: New York, 1970

[4] R.F.Curtain and A.J.Pritchard. Infinite Dimensional Linear Systems Theory. Springer-Verlag: Berlin 1978.

[5] Ju.L.Daleckiĭ and M.G.Kreĭn, Stability of Solutions of Differential Equations in Banach Space. (Russian) Izdat. "Nauka": Moscow 1970. English translation: Amer.Math. Soc.:Providence, 1974.

[6] H.D'Angelo, Linear Time-Varying Systems: Analysis and Synthesis. Allyn and Bacon: Boston 1970

[7] R.Datko, "An extension of a theorem of A.M.Lyapunov to semi--groups of operators", J.Math.Anal.Appl., vol.24,pp. 290-295, 1968.

[8] R.Datko, "Extending a theorem of A.M.Lyapunov to Hilbert space", J.Math.Anal.Appl., vol.32, pp.610-616, 1970.

[9] R.Datko, "Uniform asymptotic stability of evolutionary processes in a Banach space", SIAM J.Math.Anal., vol.3, pp.428-445, 1972.

[10] N. Dunford and J.T.Schwartz, Linear Operators, Part I. Wiley--Insterscience: New York, 1966.

[11] L.E.El'sgol'tz, Introduction to the Theory of Differential Equations with Deviating Arguments. (Russian) Izdat. "Nauka": Moscow, 1964 English translation: Holden-Day, 1966.

[12] H.O.Fattorini, The Cauchy Problem. Addison-Wesley: Reading, 1983.

[13] P.A.Fuhrmann, "On weak and strong reachability and controllability of infinite dimensional linear systems", JOTA, vol. 9, pp. 77-89, 1972 .

[14] P.A.Fuhrmann, "On observability and stability in infinite dimensional linear systems", JOTA, vol.12, pp.173-181, 1973

[15] W.W.Hager and L.L.Horowitz, "Convergence and stability properties of the discrete Riccati operator equation and the associated optimal control and filtering problems", SIAM J.Contr. and Optim. vol.14, pp.295-312, 1976.

[16] W.Hahn, Theory and Application of Liapunov's Direct Method. Prentice Hall: Englewood Cliffs, 1963.

[17] A.Halanay and D.Wexler, Teoria Calitativă a Sistemelor cu Impulsuri. Editura Academiei R.S.R.:Bucareşti, 1968.

[18] J.K.Hale, Theory of Functional Differential Equations. Springer--Verlag: New York, 1977.

[19] R.E.Kalman and J.E.Bertram, "Control system analysis and design via the "second method" of Lyapunov", Trans. ASME, J.Basic Eng. Ser. D., vol. 82, pp.371-400, 1960.

[20] E.W.Kamen and W.L.Green, "Asymptotic stability of linear difference equations defined over a commutativa Banach algebra " J.Math. Anal.Appl., vol.75, pp.584-601, 1980

[21] S.G.Kreĭn, Linear Differential Equations in Banach Spaces. (Russian) Izdat."Nauka":Moscow, 1967. English translation: Amer.Math.Soc.: Providence, 1971.

[22] C.S.Kubrusly, "Mean square stability for discrete bounded linear systems in Hilbert space", Report, Laboratório de Computação Científica: Rio de Janerio, 1983.

[23] G.E.Ladas and V.Lakshmikantham, Differential Equations in Abstract Spaces. Academic Press: New York, 1972.

[24] K.Y.Lee, S.N.Chow and R.O.Barr, "On the control of discrete-time distributed parameter systems", SIAM J.Contr., vol.10, pp.361-376, 1972.

[25] L.Pandolfi. "Stabilization of control processes in Hilbert spaces", Proc.Royal Soc.Edinburgh.Ser.A., vol.81, pp.247-258, 1978.

[26] A.Pazy, "On the applicability of Lyapunov's theorem in Hilbert space", SIAM J.Math.Anal., vol.3, pp.291-294, 1972

[27] A.J.Pritchard and J.Zabczyk, "Stability and stabilizability of infinite dimensional systems", SIAM Review, vol.30, pp. 25-52, 1981

[28] K.M.Przyluski, "Infinite dimensional discrete-time equations as models for linear systems with time delay", Preprints of the 2nd IFAC Symp. on Distributed Parameter Systems,Warwick (England) 1977.

[29] K.M.Przyluski, "The Lyapunov equation and the problem of stability for linear bounded discrete-time systems in Hilbert space", Appl.Math.Optim., vol.6.,pp.97-112, 1980.

[30] K.M.Przyluski, "Stability of linear infinite dimensional systems revisited", Memorandum 1982-17, Eindhoven Univ. of Technology, Dept. of Math., Eindhoven:1982.

[31] K.M.Przyluski and S.Rolewicz, "On stability of linear time-varying infinite dimensional discrete-time systems", Syst.Control Lett. vol.4., 1984.

[32] K.M.Przyluski and S.Rolewicz, "Stability of linear continuous--time evolutionary processes on a Banach space. The discrete--time approach", to appear.

[33] H.Tanabe, Equations of Evolution. Pitman: London, 1979.

[34] J.Zabczyk, "Remarks on the control of discrete-time distributed parameter systems", SIAM J.Contr., vol.12, pp.721-735, 1974.

OPTIMAL STOPPING AND LEAVABLE GAMBLING MODELS WITH THE AVERAGE RETURN CRITERION.

Manfred Schäl, Univ. Bonn, Inst. Angew. Math.

Dedicated to Professor Dr. P.H. Müller on the occasion of his sixtieth birthday.

Summary. It is well-known that for the problem of stopping a Markov chain with finite state space there exists an optimal a.s. finite stopping time which is the entrance time into the set where the value function coincides with the utility function. In this paper, this result is extended to the case where more than one continue action is available. The result of the paper also yields a sufficient condition for the existence of a stationary optimal policy in a leavable gambling house with a compact action space.

Key words and phrases: Dynamic programming, gambling, optimal stopping, average return, limit supremum payoff, stationary policy, finite stopping times

Research supported by 'Deutsche Forschungsgemeinschaft, Sonderforschungsbereich 72'.

§1 The decision model with the average utility criterion.

We consider a system with a finite number of states $i \in S$. Periodically we observe the current state of the system, and then choose an action a from a set A of possible actions. As a result of the current state i and the chosen action a, the system moves to a new state j with the probability $p_{ij}(a)$. Our desires are summarized, in a certain sense, by a function u from S to real numbers, called the utility function. The worth of the state i is $u(i)$. If $h = (i_o, i_1, i_2, \ldots)$ is a possible history of the system which stagnates at time n, i.e., $i_n = i_{n+1} = i_{n+2} = \ldots$, then the history is valued according to the utility $u(i_n)$ of its terminal state i_n. If the history does not stagnate at some finite epoch n, then it is no longer obvious how to value the history. In the framework of gambling models (cp. Dubins & Savage (1965), Sudderth (1971)) and optimal stopping models (Chow, Robbins & Siegmund (1971)), the history is valued according to the real number $\overline{\lim}_{n\to\infty} u(i_n)$. In the present paper, the utility of the history h will be defined as $\lim_{n\to\infty} \frac{1}{n} \{u(i_o) + \ldots + u(i_n)\}$. This definition enables us to build on methods and results from dynamic programming with the average return criterion. In the case of a leavable model it will be shown in the last section that the value function, that is the maximal expected utility, does not depend on what definition for the utility of histories is used.

The underlying model is given by a tupel (S,A,p,u).

(i) S stands for the <u>state space</u> and is assumed to be finite.

(ii) A is the <u>action space</u> and is assumed to be a compact metric space.

(iii) $p_{ij}(a)$ are the <u>transition probabilities</u>. We assume that $\Sigma_j p_{ij}(a) = 1$ for all i and a and that $a \to p_{ij}(a)$ is continuous.

(iv) $u: S \to A$ is the <u>utility function</u>.

Denote by $\mathbb{F}$ the (compact) set of functions f from S to A. Any $f \in \mathbb{F}$ is considered as a stationary policy. Using policy f means that, if we find the system in state i at time n, the action chosen that epoch is $f(i)$. In the first part we can restrict attention to such stationary policies $f \in \mathbb{F}$. More general policies are considered only in the last section.

Under each $f \in \mathbb{F}$, the sequence of states form a Markov chain. We write $\mathbb{P}_f = (p_{ij}(f(i)))$ for the transition matrix and $\mathbb{P}_f^*$ for the matrix of the Cesaro limits $\lim_{n\to\infty} \frac{1}{n} (\mathbb{P}_f + \ldots + \mathbb{P}_f^n)$. Further, let R_f and T_f denote the sets of recurrent and transient states, resp., and n_f the number of recurrent classes. We agree to identify real-valued functions

on S with the corresponding column vector.
With each $f \in \mathbb{F}$ we associate the <u>average utility</u> g_f and define the <u>value function</u> g according to

$$g_f = \mathbb{P}_f^* u \quad , \quad g = \sup_{f \in \mathbb{F}} g_f$$

where the supremum is to be taken pointwise. The average utility $g_f(i)$ coincides with the expected value of the utility $\lim_{n\to\infty} \frac{1}{n} \{u(i_o) + \ldots + u(i_n)\}$ of the histories $(i_o, i_1, \ldots)$ given the initial state $i_o = i$ according to the following Lemma.

<u>Lemma</u>. For any Markov chain (x_n) with finite state space S and any initial distribution,

$$\lim \frac{1}{n} \{u(x_o) + \ldots + u(x_n)\}$$

exists almost surely and

$$E\,[\lim \frac{1}{n} \{u(x_o) + \ldots + u(x_n)\}] = \lim \frac{1}{n} \{Eu(x_o) + \ldots + Eu(x_n)\}$$

for any real-valued function u on S.

The Lemma is probably well-known. We will not use it in the following analysis but only for the motivation of our objective function g_f. Therefore, the proof is omitted. It can be carried through as in the case with only one recurrent class and possibly transient states by considering the conditional probabilities given that the chain enters a certain recurrent class.

The continuity and compactness properties of the model as defined above do not guarantee the existence of an optimal policy, because they do not guarantee the continuity of the mapping $f \to \mathbb{P}_f^*$. The continuity of $f \to \mathbb{P}_f^*$ again is equivalent with the continuity of the mapping $f \to n_f$ according to a result by Schweitzer (1968). Of course, the continuity of $f \to n_f$ means that $f_n \to f_o$ implies $n_{f_n} = n_{f_o}$ for almost all n .

<u>Proposition</u>. If $f \to n_f$ is continuous, then there exists some f^* such that $g_{f^*} = g$, and $g \geq \mathbb{P}_f g$ for all $f \in \mathbb{F}$.

The proposition follows from results on Markov decision processes with a more general state space by Wijngaard (1977), Deppe (1981), Hordijk & Dekker (1982), Mann (1983), Zijm (1982). Since the proof is much simpler for the present situation with a finite state space and follows directly from results by Blackwell (1962) we indicate the proof here.

Proof. We start from the identity

$$(1-\beta)\Sigma_{n=0}^{\infty} \beta^n \mathbb{P}_f^n u = \beta \mathbb{P}_f^* u + (1-\beta)(I-\beta(\mathbb{P}_f-\mathbb{P}_f^*))^{-1} u \ , \ 0 \le \beta < 1 \ .$$

The latter expression also exists for $\beta = 1$ and equals $\mathbb{P}_f^* u$. Since matrix inversion is a continuous operation, we conclude that $\psi(f,\beta)$, defined as one the expressions in the above identity for $\beta < 1$ and equal to $\mathbb{P}_f^* u$ for $\beta = 1$, is continuous on $\mathbb{F} \times [0,1]$. From discounted dynamic programming, we know that there exists for all $\beta < 1$ some $f_\beta \in \mathbb{F}$ such that

$$\psi(f_\beta,\beta) \ge \psi(f,\beta) \quad , \quad f \in \mathbb{F} \ .$$

Now for any accumulation point f^* of $\{f_{n/(n+1)} \ n \in \mathbb{N}\}$ one has

$$\psi(f^*,1) \ge \psi(f,1) \quad , \quad f \in \mathbb{F} \ .$$

The second statement of the Proposition follows from the fact that g_{f^*} cannot be improved by the Howard algorithm.

□

§2 Leavable models with the average utility criterion.

In this section, we will consider a leavable model. The model is called leavable if A can be written as

$$A = A_o + \{e\} \quad \text{where} \quad p_{ij}(e) = \delta_{ij} \ .$$

As Dubins & Savage (1965) we interpret stopping at time n by continuation such that, with probability 1 , the state remains i_n time after time. In the case where A_o is a singleton set, one has an ordinary stopping model. We assume that A_o is a compact metric space and e is an isolated point. Moreover $a \to p_{ij}(a)$ is assumed to be continuous on A_o . Then the continuity and compactness assumptions of the model of section 1 are obviously satisfied.
The continuity of $f \to n_f$ is more delicate. We introduce the following condition.

Condition (C): $\{a \in A_o \ , \ p_{ij}(a) > 0\}$ is closed for all $i,j \in S$.

Condition C is satisfied in the two important cases where A_o is finite or where signum of $p_{ij}(a)$ is independent of a for all $i,j \in S$.

Lemma. Under Condition (C), $f \to n_f$ is continuous in the present leavable model.

Proof. Let $f_n \to f_o$. Then Condition (C) implies that sign $(p_{ij}(f_n(i)))$ = sign $(p_{ij}(f_o(i)))$, $n \geq n_o$, for some n_o . Hence the class structure (and in particular the number of recurrent classes) of $\mathbb{P}_{f_n}$ agrees with that of $\mathbb{P}_{f_o}$ for $n \geq n_o$.

□

Proposition. Assume (C).

(a) $g \geq u$;

(b) $g \geq \mathbb{P}_f g \geq \mathbb{P}^*_f g \geq \mathbb{P}^*_f u = g_f$ for all $f \in \mathbb{F}$;

(c) The following statements are equivalent:

(i) $g_f = g$,

(ii) $g = \mathbb{P}^*_f g$ and $\mathbb{P}^*_f g = \mathbb{P}^*_f u$.

(iii) $g = \mathbb{P}_f g$ and $\{i, g(i) \neq u(i)\} \subset T_f$.

Proof. a) Define $f(i) = e$, $i \in S$; then $\mathbb{P}_f u = u$ and hence $g_f = u$.

b) From the Proposition in §1 , it follows that $g \geq \mathbb{P}_f g$. It can easily be shown that $g \geq \mathbb{P}_f g$ implies that the sequence $\{\frac{1}{n} (\mathbb{P}_f g + \ldots + \mathbb{P}^n_f g),\ n = 1,2,\ldots\}$ is decreasing. The rest is obvious.

c) The equivalence of (i) and (ii) directly follows from part b). The equivalence of "$g = \mathbb{P}^*_f g$" and "$g = \mathbb{P}_f g$" is also clear. The condition "$\mathbb{P}^*_f g = \mathbb{P}^*_f u$" means that "$\mathbb{P}^*_f (g-u) = 0$" where $(g-u) \geq 0$.

□

Theorem. Assume (C).

There exists an optimal policy f^* (that means $g_{f^*} = g$) such that

$$f^*(i) = e \quad \text{if} \quad g(i) = u(i),$$
$$f^*(i) \in A_o \quad \text{if} \quad g(i) \neq u(i).$$

Proof. According to the Proposition of §1 there exists an optimal policy f . Now define f^* through

$$f^*(i) = f(i) \quad \text{if} \quad g(i) \neq u(i),$$
$$f^*(i) = e \quad \text{if} \quad g(i) = u(i).$$

Under f^* all states on the set $[g = u]$ are absorbing and hence recurrent. From the Proposition we know that $g = \mathbb{P}_f g$ and $[g \neq u] \subset T_f$. Passing from f to f^* means that we made the states in $[g = u]$ absorbing, but then the states, which were transient under f and were not made absorbing, obviously remain transient under f^*. Hence

$$[g \neq u] = T_{f^*} .$$

To see that f^* is optimal we note that

$$\Sigma_j p_{ij}(f^*(i))g(j) = \Sigma_j p_{ij}(f(i))g(j) = g(i) \quad \text{if} \quad g(i) \neq u(i)$$

$$\Sigma_j p_{ij}(f^*(i))g(j) = \Sigma_j p_{ij}(e)g(j) = g(i) \quad \text{if} \quad g(i) = u(i).$$

Now the Proposition applies.

□

Corollary. Assume (C). The optimal policy f^* of the Theorem let the process stagnate after some a.s. finite stopping time τ^* which is the entrance time into the set $[g = u]$.

Proof. It is sufficient to remind that $[g \neq u] = T_{f^*}$.

□

§3 The leavable gambling model.

In this section we will consider a model which essentially coincides with a leavable gambling model in the sense of Dubins & Savage. Now, non-Markovian policies are admitted, i.e. the choice of the action a_t at time t may depend on the history $h_t = (i_o,\ldots,i_t) \in H_t = S \times \ldots \times S$ ($t+1$ factors) through a decision function $\delta_t: H_t \to A$. A sequence $\delta = (\delta_t)$ of such decision functions is a policy. Let Δ denote the set of all policies. For each $\delta \in \Delta$ and each initial state $i \in S$, there are defined a probability measure $P_{i\delta}$ on H_∞ and a stochastic process $\{X_t, t = 0,1,\ldots\}$, where X_t denotes the state of the system at time t . With each $\delta \in \Delta$ we now associate the Dubins & Savage utility v_δ and define the corresponding value function v according to

$$v_\delta(i) = E_{i\delta}\, \overline{\lim}\, u(X_n) \;, \; \delta \in \Delta \;, \quad v(i) = \sup_{\delta\in\Delta} v_\delta(i) \;, \; i \in S .$$

Obviously,

$g_f \leq \nu_f$, $f \in \mathbb{F}$, and $g \leq \nu$.

We essentially use the following result (cp. Dubins & Savage §3.3).

Proposition. The value function ν is the smallest of all those functions w for which $w \geq \mathbb{P}_f w$ for all $f \in \mathbb{F}$ and $w \geq u$.

Theorem. Assume (C). Then the value functions of sections 2 and 3 coincide and the stationary optimal policy f^* of the Theorem of section 2 is also optimal for the model of section 3 within the class Δ of all (possibly non-stationary) policies, i.e.,

$$g = \nu \quad \text{and} \quad \nu_{f^*} = \nu \ .$$

Proof. From the Propositions of sections 1, 2 and 3 we conclude that $\nu \leq g$, hence $\nu = g$. Further, $g = g_{f^*} \leq \nu_{f^*} \leq \nu$, hence $\nu_{f^*} = \nu$.

□

References

1. Blackwell, D.: Discrete dynamic programming. Ann. Math. Statist. 33, 719 - 726 (1962).

2. Chow, Y.S., Robbins, H., Siegmund, D.: Great Expectations: The theory of optimal stopping. Boston: Houghton Mifflin Company (1971).

3. Deppe, H.: On the existence of average optimal policies in semi-regenerative decision models. Univ. Bonn, Inst. Angew. Math., SFB 72 preprint No. 476 (1981).

4. Dubins, L.E., Savage, L.J.: How to gamble if you must. New York: Mc Graw-Hill 1965.

5. Hordijk, A.; Dekker, R.: Denumerable Markov chains: sensitive optimality criteria. Operations Research Proc. 1982, Springer-Verlag Berlin Heidelberg (1983).

6. Mann, E.: Optimality equations and bias-optimality in bounded Markov decision processes. Univ. Bonn, Inst. Angew. Math., SFB 72 preprint No. 574 (1983).

7. Schweitzer, P.J.: Perturbation theory and finite Markov chains. J. Appl. Prob. 5 , 401 - 413 (1968).

8. Sudderth, W.D.: On measurable gambling problems. Ann. Math. Statist. 42, 260 - 269 (1971).

9. Wijngaard, J.: Sensitive optimality in stationary Markov decision problems on a general state space. Math. Centre Tracts 93, 85 - 93 , Amsterdam (1977).

10. Zijm, W.H.M.: The optimality equations in multichain denumerable state Markov decision processes with the average cost criterion: the bounded cost case. A & E Report 2182, Univ. of Amsterdam (1982).

A CLOSED NETWORK MODEL FOR I/O SUBSYSTEMS*

R. Wijbrands and J. Wessels
Eindhoven University of Technology
Department of Mathematics and Computing Science
5600 MB Eindhoven, P.O. Box 513 / The Netherlands

Abstract

In this paper we look at the problem of modelling and analyzing an I/O subsystem. There are two conventional ways to look at this problem. The first is to model the I/O subsystem as an $M|G|1$ queue, thus neglecting the CPU influence on the arrival stream. The second way is to use the central server model, treating the nonexponentially distributed I/O service times as exponentially distributed.
Here we try to combine the benefits of both methods. We use a closed network model and analyze this by using an adjusted mean-value scheme. In this scheme service times depend on the number of clients in system. We make use of the residual lifetime distribution of the client in disk service. Some experiments show that the model yields accurate results.

1. Introduction

In this paper we look at the problem of modelling and analyzing I/O subsystems. The modelling of these systems has been extensively dealt with in literature ([4]). Many of the models proposed there, try to compare the alternative configurations by looking at them as $M|G|1$ queues. Then the Pollaczek-Khintchine formula for response time, gives a comparison measure for the different alternatives. A major disadvantage of these methods is that they cannot tell you the system throughput, but in fact need this information as input for the model. Further the input stream cannot be expected to be a Poisson stream. In Section 3 we will show that this may lead to a considerable overestimation of the I/O response times.

*) The investigations were supported in part by the Foundation for Computer Science in The Netherlands SION with financial aid from The Netherlands Organisation for the Advancement of Pure Research (ZWO).

A second way to look at the problem is to model the CPU-disk system as a central server model. In this case the disk units are treated as exponential servers. This model does give you a system throughput, but it is obvious that this throughput cannot be very accurate.

In this paper we try to combine the two methods. We look at a closed network and analyze it by using a mean-value scheme, which is adjusted in a Pollaczek-Khintchine way. This method proofs to be very accurate.

In Section 2 we will look at the system configuration underlying our models. In Section 3 we will discuss an example and give some results for the $M|G|1$ model. In Section 4 we will discuss our approximation using the same example. Finally in Section 5 we will make some concluding remarks.

2. The CPU-disk system

In this section we describe the basic components of the system under consideration and their interconnections.
The system consists of a CPU and several strings of disk units interconnected by paths. These paths are made up by a channel, a control unit (CU) and a head of string controller (HSC). Each channel may be connected to several HSC's and vice versa, and each HSC may be connected to several disk units. Each disk unit however, can be connected to only one HSC. This configuration encloses the possibility that the CPU and a selected disk unit are interconnected through more than one path (multipathing).
An example (a slight modification of an example used by Brandwajn [2]) of the system is represented in Figure 1.

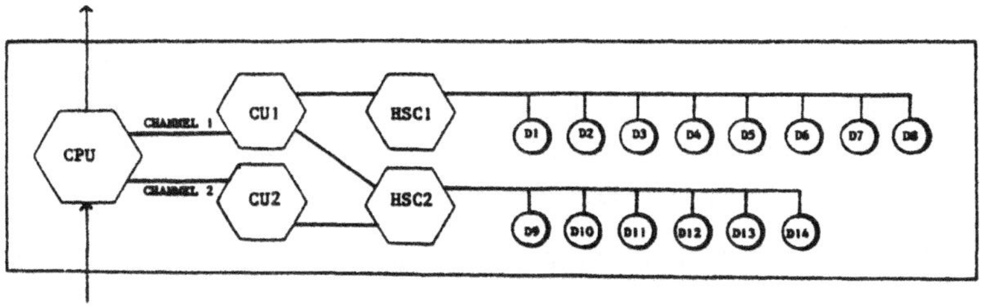

Figure 1. An example of the system configuration

A job enters the system at the CPU. After being processed for a while, the job either leaves the system (ready), or it proposes an I/O request. Whenever a job leaves the system, it is immediately replaced by a new job; we assume that the number of jobs in the system is constant and equals the multiprogramming level.

The processing in the CPU is assumed to follow a PS discipline. The CPU service time distribution may take any form. In the example of Sections 3 and 4 it is taken to be exponential.

The process controlling the I/O requests is less straight (see e.g. [6] or [7]). In this paper we only consider disk units that have the RPS feature (rotational position sensing). For these disk units the disk access process can be described as follows. When the CPU has an I/O request, it has to submit a Start I/O command. It therefore needs a free path to the disk, causing a possible delay. The transfertime for the SIO can and will be neglected. Now the disk unit, which is not considered in the path, can be busy, causing a second possible delay for the request. After this possible wait, the disk service will start. The disk service time can be split up in several phases (we assume them to be independent), here described for a read operation:

- The seek; The read/write head has to move to the proper cylinder. We assume that the time being considered with this seek, is uniformly distributed between 0 and $T_{seekmax}$. Note that this assumption is only needed for expository reasons and is, like all distribution assumptions in this section, unessential to the methods described in Sections 3 and 4.
- The latency; The read/write head has to wait until the rotating disk has brought the proper sector in the right position to be read. Assuming the latency to be uniformly distributed, this causes an expected latency of half a disk revolution: $0.5 \cdot T_{ROT}$.
- The extra latency; Now the disk is ready for transfer of the requested information, but, as with the SIO command, the path has to be free. When the disk finds the path to be busy, this causes a delay of one full revolution before a second reconnect attempt can be made. When p is the probability that a disk unit finds the path busy (note that p is to be estimated), the number of misses thus caused can be approximated by a geometric distribution with parameter p. Here implicitly the assumption is made that the probability of a reconnect miss is independent of the past, which is obviously not true. Some adjustments on the geometric approach are proposed by e.g. Bard [1] and Brandwajn [3], who take the probability of a second miss to be somewhat higher than the probability of the first miss.
- Data transfer; When the disk is ready for transfer and it finds the path to be free, the information is read and transferred immediately. We assume the message length to be exponentially distributed with mean $1/\mu_{TR}$.

The write operations do not differ essentially from the read operation. For the sake of simplicity of representation we will consider all I/O requests to be read operations.

In the multipathing case, we have to distinguish between two types of I/O systems with a different level of intelligence. In the first system a disk has to use that path for the data transfer that intially was used for the corresponding SIO command. In the second system there is some more intelligence; the disk can choose any free path for data transfer. In the next we will only consider the first of these systems, but the methods are easily extended to the second case.

In some cases the disk units cannot store the SIO commands; a job has to wait at the CPU for the disk to become free. In such a case the channel wait has to be included in the disk service time. The methods described in the next two sections are easily modified to this case.

3. The open network solution

When we replace the CPU in the Section 2 network by a source, submitting a Poisson stream of I/O requests, the system can rather easily be analyzed. However, this method may lead to a considerable overestimation of the response time, as we will show in an example in this section.

Suppose we know the size of the input stream. Then, given the routing of the jobs, the utilization of the channels, CU's and HSC's are known and thus the path utilization. The probability of a disk finding the path busy is then easily estimated by taking the conditional probability on a disk being ready for data transfer (e.g. [2], [3]). Then, using the detailed description of the disk service time distribution, one can estimate the variation coefficient of this distribution. With the Pollaczek-Khintchine formula for $M|G|1$ waitinglines, one has the response time of the disk unit. In this way we can compare different I/O configurations.

A disadvantage of the method, however, is that the throughput has to be known in advance. When we compare two I/O configurations using this method we can tell whether the one performs much better than the other or not, given a certain throughput. But the question whether the alternative configuration indeed greatly improves the total system throughput, or not, remains unanswered.

Now let us examine the results of this method, by comparing it with a discrete event simulation of the original system (containing a CPU with exponential distributed service times). We will look at the response time as a function of the throughput and CPU utilization. To get a certain combination of throughput and utilization we estimate the number of clients in system and the CPU service time in the simulation experiment by means of trial and error.

Let us use the example represented in Figure 1 due to Brandwajn [2]. In this example the two channels (and CU's) are used equally. A job passing CU1 on its way to a disk unit, contains with probability 1/3 a SIO command for a string 1 disk unit and with probability 2/3 a SIO command for one of the other disk units. For all disk units the average transfertime is 8 ms, a revolution period equals 16.7 ms, and the average seektimes are set to 25 ms. When we use these data combined with Brandwajn's approximation for extra latency [3], we will get the following picture.

When the CPU is in full utilization, causing a Poisson stream of I/O requests, the open network solution gives a fairly good approximation of disk unit response time. Lowering the CPU utilization to 85% or 50%, as shown in Figure 2 and 3, leads to a considerable overestimation of the response time by the open network approximation, especially for the highly utilized string 2 disk units. Apparently the M|G|1 method overestimates the variance of the inter-arrivaltime distribution.

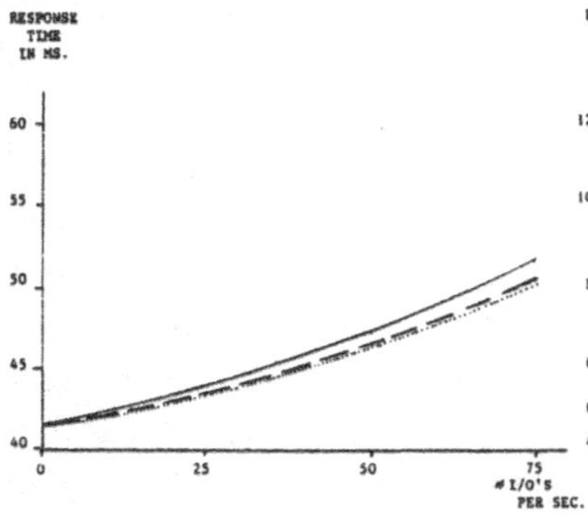

Figure 2. Response time for string 1 disk units

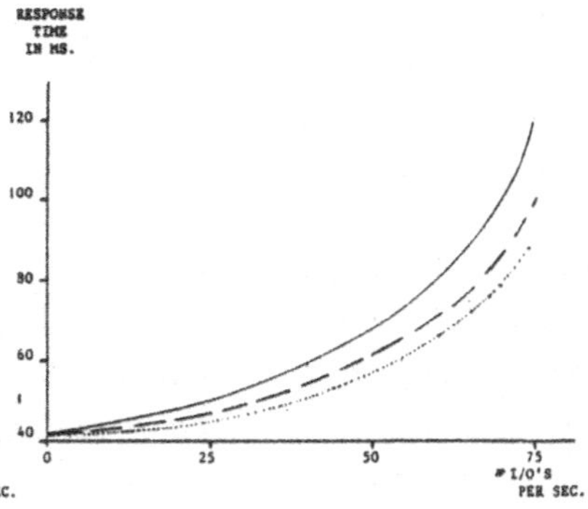

Figure 3. Response time for string 2 disk units

———— M|G|1 result ≃ simulation with a 100% CPU utilization,

-------- simulation with a 85% CPU utilization,

.... simulation with a 50% CPU utilization.

4. The closed network solution

From the example in Section 3 one can conclude that the CPU utilization has a certain influence on the response time which cannot be neglected. It is therefore that we propose in this section a solution including this CPU influence.

We use the closed network model as represented in Figure 4.

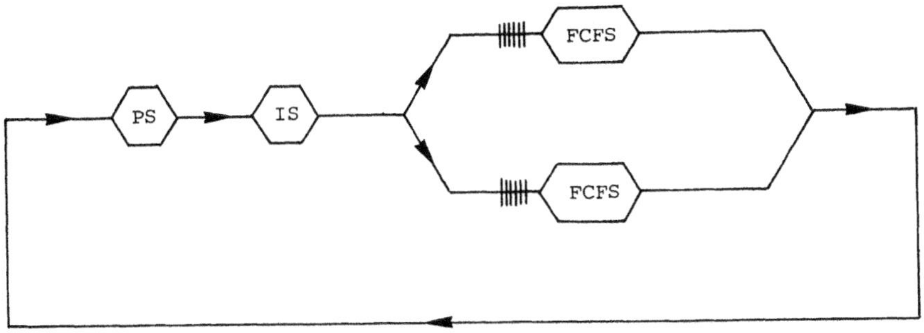

Figure 4. The closed network.

A job is served with Processor Sharing (PS) by the CPU. Then it has to wait until a path becomes free to be used for the SIO command. Given the zero service time assumption for SIO transfer, the only time to consider here is waiting time. We model this as an Infinite Server station (IS) with an estimation of the waiting time as its service time. Next the job will arrive at the disk, working with a First Come First Served discipline (FCFS). Finally, the job returns to the CPU, where the story starts again.

When the FCFS stations had exponentially distributed service times, the performance characteristics could be solved exactly by using e.g. the mean value algorithm (MVA). Unfortunately this is not true. But let us assume that the basic idea of the MVA, a client finding the system in equilibrium, still holds. Then we can solve an adjusted mean-value scheme.
Let us denote the response time of the CPU, the channels i and the disks j as a function of the number of clients K in system by $R_{CPU}[K]$, $R_{CH_i}[K]$ and $R_{D_j}[K]$. Following the same convention let Q denote the length of the waitingline, Λ denote the station's throughput (in the case of the channel we only count the throughput caused by the data transfer), and let ρ denote the utilization. The expected disk-i-service time depending on the number of clients K in system (because of the path blocking included) we denote by $1/\mu_{D_i}[K]$. With $\sigma^2_{D_i}[K]$ we denote the variance of the service time. Further, let $1/\nu_{D_i}[K]$ be the average residual service time of the client in service at desk i upon arrival of a new client, in the situation of K clients in system. Let e_{CH_i} denote the probability channel i is used for an I/O request and let e_{D_j} denote the probability disk j is used for an I/O request. Finally, let us denote the probability of disk i finding its path busy, K clients in system, by $\rho_{P_i}[K]$.
Now we can estimate the system performance characteristics by initiating K = 1 and $Q_{\bullet}[0] = \rho_{\bullet}[0] = 0$ and solving the following recursive scheme:

$$1/\mu_{D_i}[K] = 0.5\ T_{seekmax} + 0.5\ T_{ROT} + \frac{\rho_{P_i}[K-1]}{1 - \rho_{P_i}[K-1]}\ T_{ROT} + 1/\mu_{TR}$$

$$1/\nu_{D_i}[K] = \frac{\mu_{D_i}[K-1] \cdot (\sigma^2_{D_i}[K-1] + 1/\mu^2_{D_i}[K-1])}{2}$$

$$R_{CPU}[K] = (1 + Q_{CPU}[K-1]) \cdot \frac{1}{\mu_{CPU}}$$

$$R_{CH_i}[K] = \rho_{CH_i}[K-1] \cdot \frac{1}{\mu_{TR}}$$

$$R_{D_j}[K] = \rho_{D_j}[K-1] \cdot \frac{1}{\nu_{D_j}[K]} + (1 + Q_{D_j}[K-1] - \rho_{D_j}[K-1]) \cdot \frac{1}{\mu_{D_j}[K]}$$

$$sum = R_{CPU}[K] + \sum_i e_{CH_i} R_{CH_i}[K] + \sum_j e_{D_j} R_{D_j}[K]$$

$$\Lambda_{CPU}[K] = K/sum$$

$$\Lambda_{CH_i}[K] = e_{CH_i}\ K/sum$$

$$\Lambda_{D_j}[K] = e_{D_j}\ K/sum$$

$$\rho_{CPU}[K] = \Lambda_{CPU}[K]/\mu_{CPU}$$

$$\rho_{CH_i}[K] = \Lambda_{CH_i}[K]/\mu_{TR}$$

$$\rho_{D_j}[K] = \Lambda_{D_j}[K]/\mu_{D_j}[K]\ .$$

The residual service time approximation needs some further explanation. Because we know that there are at least two clients at the disk, we use the formula for the average residual service time ([5]) for the equivalent system with one job less.

The way in which to calculate $\rho_{P_i}[K]$ varies with the I/O configuration. Again let us use Brandwajn's example to demonstrate this way of modelling. Here the string 1 disks have one path to the CPU, which is to be shared with the second string. We can estimate the probability of a path busy for a string 1 disk unit by:

$$\rho_{P_{D_i}}[K] = \rho_{CH_1}[K]\ , \qquad D_i \in \text{string } 1\ .$$

A string 2 disk has two paths. With probability 0.4 the disk has chosen for channel 1, with probability 0.6 for channel 2. This leads to the following expression for the path 2 busy probability

$$\rho_{P_{D_i}}[K] = 0.4 \left\{\rho_{CH_2}[K] + 2/3\rho_{CH_1}[K] + (1 - \rho_{CH_2}[K] - 2/3\rho_{CH_1}[K]) \cdot \right.$$

$$\left. \cdot\ 1/3\rho_{CH_1}[K]\right\} + 0.6 \left\{\rho_{CH_2}[K] + 2/3\rho_{CH_1}[K]\right\} ,$$

$$D_i \in \text{string } 2 .$$

The results of this method fit very well the results of the simulation experiments we ran for this example. In Table 1 we give the system throughput of Brandwajn's example under varying conditions.

		SIMULATION RESULTS				ADJUSTED MVA RESULTS			
# clients	$1/\mu_{CPU}$	ρ_{CPU}	Λ_{CPU}	$R_{string\ 1}$	$R_{string\ 2}$	ρ_{CPU}	Λ_{CPU}	$R_{string\ 1}$	$R_{string\ 2}$
1	17	0.50	29.7	42.8	45.8	0.51	30.2	42.6	43.7
6	7	0.49	69.6	48.9	78.5	0.49	69.3	48.9	76.2
3	30	0.85	28.1	43.3	48.1	0.83	27.8	43.6	48.0
10	11	0.85	76.4	50.7	100.4	0.82	74.8	50.4	98.9
~	33.3	1.00	30.0	44.9	51.9	1.00	30.0	44.4	52.3
~	13.3	1.00	75.0	51.2	119.5	1.00	75.0	50.9	120.6

Table 1. Some experiments.

5. Conclusions

Although the solution method presented in the preceding section is based on an assumption about the behaviour in equilibrium, which is clearly not met, the method seems to yield very accurate results. The method is easy to apply and can be extended to solve more complicated situations. The method seems to be an appropriate tool to use in the comparison of the performance characteristics of alternative I/O configurations.

References

[1] Bard, Y.: "A model of Shared DASD and Multipathing", Comm. ACM 23 (1980), 564-572.

[2] Brandwajn, A.: "DASD Subsystem Modelling", Computer Performance 3 (1982), 40-44.

[3] Brandwajn, A.: "A Capacity Planning Model of a DASD Subsystem", Kylstra, F.J. (editor), "Performance 81", 401-413, North-Holland Publishing Company, Amsterdam, 1981.

[4] Hunter, D.: "Modelling Real DASD Configurations", Disney, R.L. and Ott, J.O.: "Applied Probability-Computer Science", 451-468, Birkhäuser, Boston, 1982.

[5] Kleinrock, L.: "Queueing Systems Vol. 1", J. Wiley & Sons, New York, 1975.

[6] Paans, R.: "An Accurate Model for MVS Disk I/O", ECOMA-10, Conference Proceedings (1982), 225-234.

[7] Wilhelm, N.C.: "A General Model for the Performance of Disk Systems", J. ACM 24 (1977), 14-31.

Vol. 157: Optimization and Operations Research. Proceedings 1977. Edited by R. Henn, B. Korte, and W. Oettli. VI, 270 pages. 1978.

Vol. 158: L. J. Cherene, Set Valued Dynamical Systems and Economic Flow. VIII, 83 pages. 1978.

Vol. 159: Some Aspects of the Foundations of General Equilibrium Theory: The Posthumous Papers of Peter J. Kalman. Edited by J. Green. VI, 167 pages. 1978.

Vol. 160: Integer Programming and Related Areas. A Classified Bibliography. Edited by D. Hausmann. XIV, 314 pages. 1978.

Vol. 161: M. J. Beckmann, Rank in Organizations. VIII, 164 pages. 1978.

Vol. 162: Recent Developments in Variable Structure Systems, Economics and Biology. Proceedings 1977. Edited by R. R. Mohler and A. Ruberti. VI, 326 pages. 1978.

Vol. 163: G. Fandel, Optimale Entscheidungen in Organisationen. VI, 143 Seiten. 1979.

Vol. 164: C. L. Hwang and A. S. M. Masud, Multiple Objective Decision Making – Methods and Applications. A State-of-the-Art Survey. XII, 351 pages. 1979.

Vol. 165: A. Maravall, Identification in Dynamic Shock-Error Models. VIII, 158 pages. 1979.

Vol. 166: R. Cuninghame-Green, Minimax Algebra. XI, 258 pages. 1979.

Vol. 167: M. Faber, Introduction to Modern Austrian Capital Theory. X, 196 pages. 1979.

Vol. 168: Convex Analysis and Mathematical Economics. Proceedings 1978. Edited by J. Kriens. V, 136 pages. 1979.

Vol. 169: A. Rapoport et al., Coalition Formation by Sophisticated Players. VII, 170 pages. 1979.

Vol. 170: A. E. Roth, Axiomatic Models of Bargaining. V, 121 pages. 1979.

Vol. 171: G. F. Newell, Approximate Behavior of Tandem Queues. XI, 410 pages. 1979.

Vol. 172: K. Neumann and U. Steinhardt, GERT Networks and the Time-Oriented Evaluation of Projects. 268 pages. 1979.

Vol. 173: S. Erlander, Optimal Spatial Interaction and the Gravity Model. VII, 107 pages. 1980.

Vol. 174: Extremal Methods and Systems Analysis. Edited by A. V. Fiacco and K. O. Kortanek. XI, 545 pages. 1980.

Vol. 175: S. K. Srinivasan and R. Subramanian, Probabilistic Analysis of Redundant Systems. VII, 356 pages. 1980.

Vol. 176: R. Färe, Laws of Diminishing Returns. VIII, 97 pages. 1980.

Vol. 177: Multiple Criteria Decision Making-Theory and Application. Proceedings, 1979. Edited by G. Fandel and T. Gal. XVI, 570 pages. 1980.

Vol. 178: M. N. Bhattacharyya, Comparison of Box-Jenkins and Bonn Monetary Model Prediction Performance. VII, 146 pages. 1980.

Vol. 179: Recent Results in Stochastic Programming. Proceedings, 1979. Edited by P. Kall and A. Prékopa. IX, 237 pages. 1980.

Vol. 180: J. F. Brotchie, J. W. Dickey and R. Sharpe, TOPAZ – General Planning Technique and its Applications at the Regional, Urban, and Facility Planning Levels. VII, 356 pages. 1980.

Vol. 181: H. D. Sherali and C. M. Shetty, Optimization with Disjunctive Constraints. VIII, 156 pages. 1980.

Vol. 182: J. Wolters, Stochastic Dynamic Properties of Linear Econometric Models. VIII, 154 pages. 1980.

Vol. 183: K. Schittkowski, Nonlinear Programming Codes. VIII, 242 pages. 1980.

Vol. 184: R. E. Burkard and U. Derigs, Assignment and Matching Problems: Solution Methods with FORTRAN-Programs. VIII, 148 pages. 1980.

Vol. 185: C. C. von Weizsäcker, Barriers to Entry. VI, 220 pages. 1980.

Vol. 186: Ch.-L. Hwang and K. Yoon, Multiple Attribute Decision Making – Methods and Applications. A State-of-the-Art-Survey. XI, 259 pages. 1981.

Vol. 187: W. Hock, K. Schittkowski, Test Examples for Nonlinear Programming Codes. V. 178 pages. 1981.

Vol. 188: D. Bös, Economic Theory of Public Enterprise. VII, 142 pages. 1981.

Vol. 189: A. P. Lüthi, Messung wirtschaftlicher Ungleichheit. IX, 287 pages. 1981.

Vol. 190: J. N. Morse, Organizations: Multiple Agents with Multiple Criteria. Proceedings, 1980. VI, 509 pages. 1981.

Vol. 191: H. R. Sneessens, Theory and Estimation of Macroeconomic Rationing Models. VII, 138 pages. 1981.

Vol. 192: H. J. Bierens: Robust Methods and Asymptotic Theory in Nonlinear Econometrics. IX, 198 pages. 1981.

Vol. 193: J. K. Sengupta, Optimal Decisions under Uncertainty. VII, 156 pages. 1981.

Vol. 194: R. W. Shephard, Cost and Production Functions. XI, 104 pages. 1981.

Vol. 195: H. W. Ursprung, Die elementare Katastrophentheorie. Eine Darstellung aus der Sicht der Ökonomie. VII, 332 pages. 1982.

Vol. 196: M. Nermuth, Information Structures in Economics. VIII, 236 pages. 1982.

Vol. 197: Integer Programming and Related Areas. A Classified Bibliography. 1978 – 1981. Edited by R. von Randow. XIV, 338 pages. 1982.

Vol. 198: P. Zweifel, Ein ökonomisches Modell des Arztverhaltens. XIX, 392 Seiten. 1982.

Vol. 199: Evaluating Mathematical Programming Techniques. Proceedings, 1981. Edited by J.M. Mulvey. XI, 379 pages. 1982.

Vol. 200: The Resource Sector in an Open Economy. Edited by H. Siebert. IX, 161 pages. 1984.

Vol. 201: P. M. C. de Boer, Price Effects in Input-Output-Relations: A Theoretical and Empirical Study for the Netherlands 1949–1967. X, 140 pages. 1982.

Vol. 202: U. Witt, J. Perske, SMS – A Program Package for Simulation and Gaming of Stochastic Market Processes and Learning Behavior. VII, 266 pages. 1982.

Vol. 203: Compilation of Input-Output Tables. Proceedings, 1981. Edited by J. V. Skolka. VII, 307 pages. 1982.

Vol. 204: K. C. Mosler, Entscheidungsregeln bei Risiko: Multivariate stochastische Dominanz. VII, 172 Seiten. 1982.

Vol. 205: R. Ramanathan, Introduction to the Theory of Economic Growth. IX, 347 pages. 1982.

Vol. 206: M. H. Karwan, V. Lotfi, J. Telgen, and S. Zionts, Redundancy in Mathematical Programming. VII, 286 pages. 1983.

Vol. 207: Y. Fujimori, Modern Analysis of Value Theory. X, 165 pages. 1982.

Vol. 208: Econometric Decision Models. Proceedings, 1981. Edited by J. Gruber. VI, 364 pages. 1983.

Vol. 209: Essays and Surveys on Multiple Criteria Decision Making. Proceedings, 1982. Edited by P. Hansen. VII, 441 pages. 1983.

Vol. 210: Technology, Organization and Economic Structure. Edited by R. Sato and M. J. Beckmann. VIII, 195 pages. 1983.

Vol. 211: P. van den Heuvel, The Stability of a Macroeconomic System with Quantity Constraints. VII, 169 pages. 1983.

Vol. 212: R. Sato and T. Nôno, Invariance Principles and the Structure of Technology. V, 94 pages. 1983.

Vol. 213: Aspiration Levels in Bargaining and Economic Decision Making. Proceedings, 1982. Edited by R. Tietz. VIII, 406 pages. 1983.

Vol. 214: M. Faber, H. Niemes und G. Stephan, Entropie, Umweltschutz und Rohstoffverbrauch. IX, 181 Seiten. 1983.

Vol. 215: Semi-Infinite Programming and Applications. Proceedings, 1981. Edited by A. V. Fiacco and K. O. Kortanek. XI, 322 pages. 1983.

Vol. 216: H. H. Müller, Fiscal Policies in a General Equilibrium Model with Persistent Unemployment. VI, 92 pages. 1983.

Vol. 217: Ch. Grootaert, The Relation Between Final Demand and Income Distribution. XIV, 105 pages. 1983.

Vol. 218: P. van Loon, A Dynamic Theory of the Firm: Production, Finance and Investment. VII, 191 pages. 1983.

Vol. 219: E. van Damme, Refinements of the Nash Equilibrium Concept. VI, 151 pages. 1983.

Vol. 220: M. Aoki, Notes on Economic Time Series Analysis: System Theoretic Perspectives. IX, 249 pages. 1983.

Vol. 221: S. Nakamura, An Inter-Industry Translog Model of Prices and Technical Change for the West German Economy. XIV, 290 pages. 1984.

Vol. 222: P. Meier, Energy Systems Analysis for Developing Countries. VI, 344 pages. 1984.

Vol. 223: W. Trockel, Market Demand. VIII, 205 pages. 1984.

Vol. 224: M. Kiy, Ein disaggregiertes Prognosesystem für die Bundesrepublik Deutschland. XVIII, 276 Seiten. 1984.

Vol. 225: T. R. von Ungern-Sternberg, Zur Analyse von Märkten mit unvollständiger Nachfragerinformation. IX, 125 Seiten. 1984

Vol. 226: Selected Topics in Operations Research and Mathematical Economics. Proceedings, 1983. Edited by G. Hammer and D. Pallaschke. IX, 478 pages. 1984.

Vol. 227: Risk and Capital. Proceedings, 1983. Edited by G. Bamberg and K. Spremann. VII, 306 pages. 1984.

Vol. 228: Nonlinear Models of Fluctuating Growth. Proceedings, 1983. Edited by R. M. Goodwin, M. Krüger and A. Vercelli. XVII, 277 pages. 1984.

Vol. 229: Interactive Decision Analysis. Proceedings, 1983. Edited by M. Grauer and A. P. Wierzbicki. VIII, 269 pages. 1984.

Vol. 230: Macro-Economic Planning with Conflicting Goals. Proceedings, 1982. Edited by M. Despontin, P. Nijkamp and J. Spronk. VI, 297 pages. 1984.

Vol. 231: G. F. Newell, The $M/M/\infty$ Service System with Ranked Servers in Heavy Traffic. XI, 126 pages. 1984.

Vol. 232: L. Bauwens, Bayesian Full Information Analysis of Simultaneous Equation Models Using Integration by Monte Carlo. VI, 114 pages. 1984.

Vol. 233: G. Wagenhals, The World Copper Market. XI, 190 pages. 1984.

Vol. 234: B. C. Eaves, A Course in Triangulations for Solving Equations with Deformations. III, 302 pages. 1984.

Vol. 235: Stochastic Models in Reliability Theory. Proceedings, 1984. Edited by S. Osaki and Y. Hatoyama. VII, 212 pages. 1984.

Vol. 236: G. Gandolfo, P. C. Padoan, A Disequilibrium Model of Real and Financial Accumulation in an Open Economy. VI, 172 pages. 1984.

Vol. 237: Misspecification Analysis. Proceedings, 1983. Edited by T. K. Dijkstra. V, 129 pages. 1984.

Vol. 238: W. Domschke, A. Drexl, Location and Layout Planning. IV, 134 pages. 1985.

Vol. 239: Microeconomic Models of Housing Markets. Edited by K. Stahl. VII, 197 pages. 1985.

Vol. 240: Contributions to Operations Research. Proceedings, 1984. Edited by K. Neumann and D. Pallaschke. V, 190 pages. 1985.

GPSR Compliance

The European Union's (EU) General Product Safety Regulation (GPSR) is a set of rules that requires consumer products to be safe and our obligations to ensure this.

If you have any concerns about our products, you can contact us on ProductSafety@springernature.com

In case Publisher is established outside the EU, the EU authorized representative is:

Springer Nature Customer Service Center GmbH
Europaplatz 3
69115 Heidelberg, Germany

Batch number: 10838292

Printed by Printforce, the Netherlands